First World War
and Army of Occupation
War Diary
France, Belgium and Germany

25 DIVISION
7 Infantry Brigade
Duke of Edinburgh's (Wiltshire Regiment)
1st Battalion
4 November 1915 - 30 June 1918

WO95/2243/3

The Naval & Military Press Ltd
www.nmarchive.com
Published in association with The National Archives

Published by

The Naval & Military Press Ltd

Unit 10 Ridgewood Industrial Park,

Uckfield, East Sussex,

TN22 5QE England

Tel: +44 (0) 1825 749494

www.naval-military-press.com

www.nmarchive.com

This diary has been reprinted in facsimile from the original. Any imperfections are inevitably reproduced and the quality may fall short of modern type and cartographic standards.

© Crown Copyright
Images reproduced by permission of The National Archives, London, England, 2015.

Contents

Document type	Place/Title	Date From	Date To
Heading	WO95/2243/3		
Heading	1st Bn Wilts Regt Nov 1915-Jun 1918		
Miscellaneous			
Heading	3rd Division 1/Wiltshire Nov 1915 Vol XVI		
War Diary	Ploegsteert Wood	04/11/1915	07/11/1915
War Diary	The Piggeries Ploegsteert	07/11/1915	12/11/1915
War Diary	Ploegsteert	13/11/1915	18/11/1915
War Diary	Papot	19/11/1915	23/11/1915
War Diary	Ploegsteert Wood Trenches	24/11/1915	28/11/1915
War Diary	Piggerries	29/11/1915	30/11/1915
Heading	1st Bn Wiltshire Regt Dec Vol XVII		
War Diary	Piggerries	01/12/1915	03/12/1915
War Diary	Ploegsteert Wood	04/12/1915	08/12/1915
War Diary	Papot	09/12/1915	13/12/1915
War Diary	Ploegsteert Wood	16/12/1915	19/12/1915
War Diary	Piggeries	20/12/1915	24/12/1915
War Diary	Ploegsteert Wood	25/12/1915	29/12/1915
War Diary	Papot	30/12/1915	31/12/1915
Heading	1st Battn. Wiltshire Regiment January 1916		
Miscellaneous			
Heading	1st Wilts Regt Jan Vol XVIII		
War Diary	Papot	01/01/1916	02/01/1916
War Diary	Ploegsteert Wood	03/01/1916	07/01/1916
War Diary	Piggerries	08/01/1916	12/01/1916
War Diary	Ploegsteert Wood	13/01/1916	19/01/1916
War Diary	Papot	20/01/1916	23/01/1916
War Diary	Outter Steene	24/01/1916	31/01/1916
Heading	1st Battn. Wiltshire Regiment February 1916		
Miscellaneous			
War Diary	Outter Stene	01/02/1916	29/02/1916
Heading	1st. Battn. Wiltshire Regiment March 1916		
Miscellaneous			
War Diary	Outterstene	01/03/1916	10/03/1916
War Diary	Robecq	10/03/1916	11/03/1916
War Diary	Valhuon	12/03/1916	16/03/1916
War Diary	Ternas	17/03/1916	31/03/1916
Heading	1st Battn. Wiltshire Regiment April 1916		
Miscellaneous			
War Diary	Ternas	01/04/1916	09/04/1916
War Diary	Ternas Savy	09/04/1916	11/04/1916
War Diary	La Targette	12/04/1916	19/04/1916
War Diary	Mont St Eloy	20/04/1916	23/04/1916
War Diary	Trenches La Targette	24/04/1916	26/04/1916
War Diary	Acq	27/04/1916	30/04/1916
Heading	1st Battn. Wiltshire Regiment. May, 1916		
Miscellaneous			
War Diary	Acq	01/05/1916	02/05/1916
War Diary	Trenches La Targette	03/05/1916	03/05/1916
War Diary	Trenches	03/05/1916	04/05/1916
War Diary	Trenches La Targette	04/05/1916	06/05/1916

War Diary	Trenches	07/05/1916	09/05/1916
War Diary	Pylones and Bethune Arras Rd		
War Diary	Support Trenches	13/05/1916	16/05/1916
War Diary	Trenches	17/05/1916	31/05/1916
Heading Miscellaneous	1st Battn. Wiltshire Regiment. June, 1916		
War Diary	Acq	01/06/1916	01/06/1916
War Diary	Chelers	02/06/1917	13/06/1917
War Diary	Penin	14/06/1916	14/06/1916
War Diary	Barly	15/06/1916	17/06/1916
War Diary	Gezaincourt	18/06/1916	18/06/1916
War Diary	Pernois	19/06/1916	28/06/1916
War Diary	Puchevillers	29/06/1916	30/06/1916
Heading Miscellaneous	1st Battalion The Wiltshire Regiment July 1916		
War Diary	Varennes	01/07/1916	03/07/1916
War Diary	Trenches in Front of Leipzig Salient	04/07/1916	04/07/1916
War Diary	Imp Leipzig Salient	05/07/1916	05/07/1916
War Diary	Leipzig Salieut	05/07/1916	07/07/1916
War Diary	Aveluy Wood	08/07/1916	08/07/1916
War Diary	Usna Hill	09/07/1916	13/07/1916
War Diary	La Buisselle	14/07/1916	14/07/1916
War Diary	Albert	15/07/1916	15/07/1916
War Diary	Forceville	16/07/1916	18/07/1916
War Diary	Beaual	19/07/1916	20/07/1916
War Diary	Bois-de-Warnimont	21/07/1916	22/07/1916
War Diary	Trenches (Hamel)	23/07/1916	28/07/1916
Heading Miscellaneous	1st Battalion Wiltshire Regiment August 1916		
War Diary	Mailly Wood	29/07/1916	06/08/1916
War Diary	Bus-Les Artois	07/08/1916	11/08/1916
War Diary	Sarton	12/08/1916	15/08/1916
War Diary	Puchevillers	16/08/1917	17/08/1917
War Diary	Hedauville	18/07/1916	18/07/1916
War Diary	Trenches Leipzig Salient	19/08/1916	22/08/1916
War Diary	Leipzig Salient	22/08/1916	26/08/1916
War Diary	Hedauville	27/08/1916	28/08/1916
War Diary	Bouzincourt	29/08/1916	30/08/1916
Miscellaneous	Report On Operations Under From By 1st Bn The Wiltshire Rgt	22/08/1916	22/08/1916
Miscellaneous	1st Wilts Report on Operation 24/25	26/08/1916	26/08/1916
Miscellaneous Heading Miscellaneous	1st. Wiltshire Regt. September 1916		
War Diary	Bouzincourt	31/08/1916	02/09/1916
War Diary	Trenches Leipzig Salient	03/09/1916	03/09/1916
War Diary	Bouzincourt	04/09/1916	05/09/1916
War Diary	Lealvillers	06/09/1916	06/09/1916
War Diary	Lealvillers & Raincheval	07/09/1916	07/09/1916
War Diary	Raincheval	08/09/1916	10/09/1916
War Diary	Hardinval	10/09/1916	11/09/1916
War Diary	Beaumetz	12/09/1916	12/09/1916
War Diary	Coulonvillers	13/09/1916	24/09/1916
War Diary	Coullon-Villers & Hardinval	25/09/1916	25/09/1916
War Diary	Hardinval & Raincheval	26/09/1916	26/09/1916
War Diary	Raincheval	27/09/1916	27/09/1916

Heading	1st Battn. Wiltshire Regiment October 1916		
Miscellaneous			
War Diary	Raincheval Hedauville	29/09/1916	29/09/1916
War Diary	Hedauville	30/09/1916	30/09/1916
War Diary	Trenches Nr Thiepval	01/10/1916	02/10/1916
War Diary	Trenches Stuff Ledoubt	02/10/1916	07/10/1916
War Diary	Support Trenches South of Thiepval	07/10/1916	14/10/1916
War Diary	Trenches left of Stuff Redoubt	14/10/1916	17/10/1916
War Diary	Donnets Post	17/10/1916	17/10/1916
War Diary	Trenches N of Mouquey Farm	18/10/1916	22/10/1916
War Diary	Bouzincourt	23/10/1916	23/10/1916
War Diary	Bouzincourt & Rubempre	23/10/1916	23/10/1916
War Diary	Rubempre & Gezaincourt	24/10/1916	24/10/1916
War Diary	Gezaincourt	25/10/1916	30/10/1916
War Diary	Papot	31/10/1916	31/10/1916
Operation(al) Order(s)	7th Infantry Brigade Operation Order No. 158	07/10/1916	07/10/1916
Miscellaneous	Addenda And Corrections To 7th Infantry Brigade Operation Order No. 158	07/10/1916	07/10/1916
Miscellaneous	3rd Worcestershire Regt.	15/10/1916	15/10/1916
Operation(al) Order(s)	74th Infantry Brigade Operation Order No. 83	17/10/1916	17/10/1916
Heading	1st Battn. Wiltshire Regiment November 1916		
Miscellaneous			
War Diary	Ploegsteert Wood	01/11/1916	03/11/1916
War Diary	Pont De Nieppe	01/11/1916	06/11/1916
War Diary	Trenches	07/11/1916	12/11/1916
War Diary	Le Bizet	13/11/1916	18/11/1916
War Diary	Trenches	19/11/1916	24/11/1916
War Diary	Pont De Nieppe	25/11/1916	30/11/1916
Heading	1st Battn. Wiltshire Regiment. December 1916		
Miscellaneous			
War Diary	Trenches Le Touquet	01/12/1916	07/12/1916
War Diary	Le Bizet	08/12/1916	12/12/1916
War Diary	Trenches	13/12/1916	24/12/1916
War Diary	Pont De Nieppe	25/12/1916	25/12/1916
War Diary	Trenches (Le Touquet)	26/12/1916	30/12/1916
War Diary	Trenches	30/12/1916	31/12/1916
War Diary	Le Bizet	01/01/1917	06/01/1917
War Diary	Trenches	07/01/1917	13/01/1917
War Diary	Pont De Nieppe	14/01/1917	16/01/1917
War Diary	De Seule	17/01/1917	01/02/1917
War Diary	Ploegsteert Wood	02/02/1917	06/02/1917
War Diary	Trenches	06/02/1917	10/02/1917
War Diary	Romarin	11/02/1917	17/02/1917
War Diary	Trenches	18/02/1917	18/02/1917
War Diary	Ploegsteert Wood	19/02/1917	22/02/1917
War Diary	Mont Des Cats	23/02/1917	10/03/1917
War Diary	Sercus	12/03/1917	18/03/1917
War Diary	Pradelles	19/03/1917	20/03/1917
War Diary	Outtersteene	21/03/1917	22/03/1917
War Diary	Noote Boom	23/03/1917	31/03/1917
War Diary	Steentje	01/04/1917	06/04/1917
War Diary	Trenches Le Touquet	05/04/1917	10/04/1917
War Diary	Pont De Nieppe	11/04/1917	18/04/1917
War Diary	Neuve Eglise	19/04/1917	29/04/1917
War Diary	Strazeele	30/04/1917	03/05/1917
War Diary	Sercus	04/05/1917	04/05/1917

War Diary	Esquerdes	05/05/1917	17/05/1917
War Diary	Sercus	18/05/1917	18/05/1917
War Diary	Strazeele	19/05/1917	19/05/1917
War Diary	Ravelsberg	20/05/1917	24/05/1917
War Diary	Wulverghem	25/05/1917	25/05/1917
War Diary	Trenches	25/05/1917	31/05/1917
War Diary		01/06/1917	02/06/1917
War Diary	Ravelsberg Hill	03/06/1917	06/06/1917
War Diary	Wulverghem Trenches	07/06/1917	20/06/1917
War Diary	Neuve Eglise	21/06/1917	21/06/1917
War Diary	Ravelsberg Hill	22/06/1917	24/06/1917
War Diary	Le Parc	24/06/1917	25/06/1917
War Diary	St Venant	25/06/1917	26/06/1917
War Diary	Nedunchelles	26/06/1917	27/06/1917
War Diary	Delette	27/06/1917	24/07/1917
War Diary	Reninghelst	22/07/1917	31/07/1917
War Diary	Sheet Hooge	01/08/1917	14/08/1917
War Diary	Rweld near Steenvorde	15/07/1917	19/07/1917
War Diary	Dominion Camp Area	20/07/1917	22/07/1917
War Diary	Steenvorde	23/07/1917	31/07/1917
War Diary	Trenches E of Ypres	01/09/1917	11/09/1917
War Diary	Lozinghem	13/09/1917	03/10/1917
War Diary	Bethune	04/10/1917	04/10/1917
War Diary	Givenchy Sector	05/10/1917	16/10/1917
War Diary	Gorre	17/10/1917	22/10/1917
War Diary	Trenches	23/10/1917	31/10/1917
War Diary	Ref Sheet La Bassee 36c N. W. (1/10000)	01/11/1917	10/11/1917
War Diary	Gorre	11/11/1917	16/11/1917
War Diary	Trenches	16/11/1917	30/11/1917
War Diary	Delette (Ref Sheets Hazebrouck 5A Lens II)	01/12/1917	03/12/1917
War Diary	Lisbourg	04/12/1917	04/12/1917
War Diary	Barastre	05/12/1917	09/12/1917
War Diary	Trenches East of Lagnicourt	10/12/1917	15/12/1917
War Diary	Vaulx	16/12/1917	21/12/1917
War Diary	Faureuil	22/12/1917	31/12/1917
War Diary	Lagnicourt Sector	02/01/1918	02/01/1918
War Diary	Pronville Sector Scale 1/10000	08/01/1918	08/01/1918
War Diary	Add & Favreuil	01/01/1918	01/01/1918
War Diary	Lagnicourt Sector (Ref Sheet Pronville Scale 1/10000)	08/01/1918	14/01/1918
War Diary	Favreuil	15/01/1918	26/01/1918
War Diary	Lagnicourt Trenches	26/01/1918	31/01/1918
War Diary	Trenches in Lagnicourt Sector	27/01/1918	31/01/1918
War Diary	Lagnicourt Sector	01/02/1918	01/02/1918
War Diary	Vaulx	02/02/1918	03/02/1918
War Diary	Lagnicourt Sector (Ref Sheet 57 C N.W. Scale 1/20000 and Pronville Special Sheets Scale 1/10000)	04/02/1918	07/02/1918
War Diary	Faureuil	08/02/1918	10/02/1918
War Diary	Achiet Le Grand	11/02/1918	28/02/1918
Heading Miscellaneous	1st Battalion Wiltshire Regiment March 1918		
War Diary	Achiet Le Grand	01/03/1918	31/03/1918
Heading Miscellaneous	1st Battalion The Wiltshire Regiment. April 1918		
War Diary	Neuve Eglise	01/04/1918	01/04/1918
War Diary	Trenches Douve Sector N.E. Ploegsteert Wood	02/03/1918	04/03/1918
War Diary	Catacombs W of Ploegstoert Wood	05/04/1918	07/04/1918

War Diary	Trenches N of River Lys	08/03/1918	10/03/1918
War Diary	Trenches E of Ploegsteert Wood	11/04/1918	11/04/1918
War Diary	Trenches around Neuve Eglise	12/04/1918	12/04/1918
War Diary	Trenches at Crucifix Corner Near Neuve Eglise	13/04/1918	15/04/1918
War Diary	Locre Chateau	16/04/1918	16/04/1918
War Diary	Trenches near Wolfhoek	17/04/1918	18/04/1918
War Diary	Steenacker	19/04/1918	21/04/1918
War Diary	Jack Camp N of Poperinghe	22/04/1918	25/04/1918
War Diary	Vicinity of Ouderdom	26/04/1918	26/04/1918
War Diary	Trenches 1000 N of La Clytte	27/04/1918	27/04/1918
War Diary	Trenches SE Of Reninghelst	28/04/1918	30/04/1918
Miscellaneous			
War Diary	Trenches N.E of Reninghelst	01/05/1918	01/05/1918
War Diary	Brigade Reserve Trenches 1000 N. of La Clytte	02/05/1917	03/05/1917
War Diary	Trenches E of Hoograaf Cabt W of Reninghelst	04/05/1918	04/05/1918
War Diary	Bivouac N of Steenvoorde	05/05/1918	05/05/1918
War Diary	Billets N of Bissezeele	06/05/1917	09/05/1917
War Diary	Arcis-Le-Ponsart	11/05/1918	23/05/1918
War Diary	Prouilly	24/05/1918	31/05/1918
War Diary	N Bank of R Ardre E of Sarcy	01/06/1918	03/06/1918
War Diary	Bois D'Ecuisse E of Chamuzy	04/06/1918	11/06/1918
War Diary	Bois De Coutron	12/06/1918	12/06/1918
War Diary	Chantereine Farm	13/06/1918	18/06/1918
War Diary	Peas	19/06/1918	20/06/1918
War Diary	Mille-Bosc	21/06/1918	30/06/1918

W095/2243/3

25TH DIVISION
7TH INFY BDE

1ST BN WILTS REGT
NOV 1915 - JUN 1918

FROM 3 INF BDE

To 21 DIV
110 Bde

3rd Division

25th Div

D1
7637

1/Wiltz

Nov 1915

Vol XVI

Nov '15
to
June '18

WAR DIARY
or
INTELLIGENCE SUMMARY.

(Erase heading not required.)

Army Form C. 2118.

Hour, Date, Place	Summary of Events and Information	Remarks and references to Appendices
PLUGSTEERT WOOD 1/11/15	Fine day much useful work done opening 4th Round. Finished WT record who was appointed Intelligence Officer last month. Along with work with Wd Observers & snipers. Situation very quiet.	
5th November	A fine day, much useful stone studding tunnels wrote 6th Roman Train. S.W.B. Ron strength 26 Offrs. 632 O.R. including 1 Offr + 23 men 3rd Roman Train — detached.	1925. 1923.
6th November	A fine day – good work again done by tidying up trenches and draining them. Our snipers were very successful – knocked over 8 Germans – both snoc furnaces and shot down two snipers plates.	
7th November	Batt'n was relieved in the morning by 1st R.S.F. & had a worth done. No casualties. Batt'n went S 20.	

Army Form C. 2118.

WAR DIARY
or
INTELLIGENCE SUMMARY.
(Erase heading not required.)

Instructions regarding War Diaries and Intelligence Summaries are contained in F.S. Regs., Part II. and the Staff Manual respectively. Title pages will be prepared in manuscript.

Hour, Date, Place	Summary of Events and Information	Remarks and references to Appendices
The Piggeries Ploegsteert 7th November	into Brigade Reserve at the Piggeries, with the exception of B Coy which occupied the Enemies lines and took up the Wood. The Chaplain held a voluntary service in the evening.	E.O.
8th November	A fine morning. Two Companies went to Wulverghem for baths - a party of 150 men went out working in the evening. No casualties.	E.O.
9th November to 12th November	Bn. remained in Brigade Reserve at Piggeries, & furnished working parties every evening. No work near firing line. Enemy shelled the 13th Two covered with Lurks [?] hitherto, so many men had colds at the time. Much difficulty was experienced in inoculation & inspiration.	NTS
13th Nov. PLOEGSTEERT	The Bn. relieved 8th L.N.L. in trenches. Relief completed by 12 noon. No casualties.	NTS.
14th " " "	Fine day. Quiet. Wiring done at night. Parapets & drainage worked at	NTS

Army Form C. 2118.

WAR DIARY
or
INTELLIGENCE SUMMARY.
(Erase heading not required.)

Instructions regarding War Diaries and Intelligence Summaries are contained in F.S. Regs., Part II. and the Staff Manual respectively. Title pages will be prepared in manuscript.

Hour, Date, Place	Summary of Events and Information	Remarks and references to Appendices
1915		
15th Nov. PLOEGSTEERT	Fine day. Situation quiet. Sergt. Shuttler A Coy. was killed by a sniper, after firing 5 rounds. —	J.G.S.
16th Nov. — " —	Fine day. Quiet in early morning. — One gun fired at enemy's line to our left opposite the Canadians. Enemy replied but not in force. — At 2.30 p.m. an m. gun opened in demonstration from a cutting not excepting of our patties + 20 Canadians. The Canadian infantry entered German line & captured 3 prisoners. Our gun also opened on enemy's front line. Van gun then returned. —	J.G.S.
17th Nov. — " —	Sharp frost early. Then Cold rain. Quiet day. A Grenadier from one of our big guns on sandbag parapet wounded pte. Webb B. Coy + killed a horse. During night bombers shot 12 Germans & wounded 1. — Z. Coy. hit 2. — Total bag killed 2. — W. 3. —	J.G.S.
18th Nov. — " —	Sharp frost early. Then rain. — At 3 p.m. enemy fired trench mortars along whole Br. front, one of these was accurately located, but our artillery were too slow in opening fire; casualties Pte. Jones J.G.S. B Coy. slightly wounded; night quiet. —	J.G.S.

Army Form C. 2118.

WAR DIARY
or
INTELLIGENCE SUMMARY.
(Erase heading not required.)

Hour, Date, Place	Summary of Events and Information	Remarks and references to Appendices
19th November PAPOT	Frost in morning. Bn. was relieved by 8th L.N.L. & returned to huts at PAPOT. Personal recur — Relief completed at. Strength App. 26. O.R. 636 plus 9 total strength of Bn. including transport & employed men. —	
20th — " —	Bn. employed cleaning mud & drawing round camp. Inspection of Bn. by M.O. & also by medical bound. Frost early, fine day. —	13°/15°
21st — " —	Sunday had good early June day, men in Talbot training Regimental work & erecting Nets Suc. — Lewis num. awfully practised & Bombers & m. gun teams practiced. —	5°/13° 10°/10°
22 — " —	Nothing revonting (practice), M.G. & grenadiers practice. — Frost in morning — Rain at night. —	10°/13°
23 — " —	{ }	
24 PLOEGSTEERT WOOD TRENCHES	Mild morning. Shown Bn. relief completed by 12 noon. — Soup at night greatly appreciated. Save men	0°/5° Two Lewis gun taken to support

Army Form C. 2118.

WAR DIARY
or
INTELLIGENCE SUMMARY.
(Erase heading not required.)

Hour, Date, Place	Summary of Events and Information	Remarks and references to Appendices
1915 25 November PLOEGSTEERT WOOD TRENCHES	Mild & fine morning. Rain later, quiet day. Work continued on dugouts & clay huts. — 3 Officers joined from regimental depot, staying in Officers dugout, arrived yet, remains 340 men to complete. —	M213 (Strength 26th Nov) (Officers 31 O.R. 632)
26th — " —	Rain & snow during day, frost at night. — Very quiet day. 1 patrol out at night, & on 25th scanning enemy wire. Intend to report casualties from improved parapets & C.T. trenches. Enemy snipers unable but seemed no hits. —	M213
27th — " —	Quiet most of night day. Enemy exceptionally quiet. We shelled their line heavily at 12 noon. They replied with a few 7/5 gramps. — Fourteen cadets, all of whom had 8 months service in the ranks, joined for 24 hours instruction in trench warfare. Work carried on at dugouts since. —	M.M.
28th — " —	Useful patrol work done during past 3 nights by 2nd Lts. Brown Sharpe & Corbin. — The exact strength of enemy wire ascertained	

(73989) W4141-463. 400,000. 9/14. H.&J.Ltd. Forms/C. 2118/10.

WAR DIARY
or
INTELLIGENCE SUMMARY.
(Erase heading not required.)

Army Form C. 2118.

Hour, Date, Place	Summary of Events and Information	Remarks and references to Appendices
28th Nov (1/4) PLOEGSTEERT WOOD. (Sunday)	The Germans relieved last night & are active with snipers. Pte Beauchamp M.G. Det. was shot through head at 8.30 a.m. looking over parapet. Men working in trenches, no shells were dropped. Casualties.	
29th Nov. PIGGERIES.	Bn. relieved by L.N.L. returned to Piggeries. "B" Coy. occupied forts in support line. Rained most of day. Situation quiet.	
30th "	Bn. Bathing & fatigues & 8 day Schemes good.	

30/11/15

M. Brown Lt Colonel
Cdg 1st Wiltshire Regt.

1st Bn Wiltshire Regt.

Dec / Vol. XVII

WAR DIARY
or
INTELLIGENCE SUMMARY.
(Erase heading not required.)

Army Form C. 2118.

Place	Date	Hour	Summary of Events and Information	Remarks and references to Appendices
PIGGERIES	1/12		Bn. in fatigues & bathing parades. Artillery bombarded enemy trenches. Shows 0745 to 1045.	
"	2 "		C relieved B in supporting points. Fine day, mild. Casualties: 1 man m.g. Comnd.	
"	3 "		Fatigues. Sent special recce. party out for a nightbattn.	
PLOEGSTEERT WOOD	4 "		Relieved L.N.L. in trenches. Casualties: 2 wounded. Enemy shelled a little.	
"	5 "		Evening trenches & building parapet, enemy very quiet.	
"	6 "		At 11.45 p.m. 2Lt Macklin went out & cut four rows of wire in front of German trenches, 2Lt Clerke (w/ working & 50 men were in readiness to make an attack, "our patrol being told off for separate trenches." At 2.10 a.m. (7th) 2Lt Macklin returned, & reported a listening post just in-ward the Bart row of wire which he consequently cut & outside the wire - As the night had closed to what not concealed enough to surprise the enemy owing to the water in front of the wire & the listening post, consequently at 4.30 a.m. the enterprise was abandoned, 2Lt Macklin cut wire within 4 yds of enemy listening post, & crawled back unobserved.	

WAR DIARY
or
INTELLIGENCE SUMMARY.
(Erase heading not required.)

Army Form C. 2118.

Place	Date 1915	Hour	Summary of Events and Information	Remarks and references to Appendices
PLOEGSTEERT WOOD	Mar 7		Quiet day. Work carried on rebuilding parapets which had fallen in on account of rain.	1915
	8"		Snipers shot 3 Germans including one Officer. Enemy quiet.	1915
PAPOT Pont de Nieppe	9"		Relieved by L.N.L. returned to PAPOT. Sent Coy. in at 3 p.m. 9 Offrs & 230 men H.A.C. joined Bn. to be attached for ten days instruction.	1915
"	10"		Wet day. Bn. went to the baths.	1915
"	11"		Wet day. Whole Bn. on fatigue. One platoon bombing instruction.	1915
"	12"		Sunday. Fine morning, wet later. One platoon bombing. Company musketry. Brigade got 10.30 a.m. 750 yds men needed — Heavy shelling heard 3 p.m. to 4.30 pm. in Ploegsteert direction.	1915
"	13"		Fine day. 4 Platoons bombing remainder on fatigue.	1915

Army Form C. 2118.

WAR DIARY
or
INTELLIGENCE SUMMARY.
(Erase heading not required.)

Instructions regarding War Diaries and Intelligence Summaries are contained in F.S. Regs., Part II. and the Staff Manual respectively. Title pages will be prepared in manuscript.

Place	Date	Hour	Summary of Events and Information	Remarks and references to Appendices
	1915			
PLOEGSTEERT WOOD	16th		Quiet day in trenches much work done — during the night 2/Lt Carlou & 2/Lt Ingram reconnoitred enemy lines. 2/Lt Carlou getting through a gap in wire unobserved — Casualties 1 (killed). L/Cpl Bromhena who was carrying on a.m.g. course was killed by a shell on the road —	
— "—	17th 18th		Quiet days in trenches, weather fine, much work being done, motor flier in afternoon ; Germans retaliated very slightly inflicting no casualties & doing no damage to ourselves. German snipers very active on our left, the Red Machine Gun Officer was killed when looking over parapet on 17th inst.	
— "—	19th		at 4.30 a.m. 2/Lt Carlou & 9 N.C.Os men left suddenly to capture a double sentry post in enemy's front line, which he had reconnoitred on 16th. They entered trench, killed few Germans & threw bombs at a counter attack wounding many of them — One German belt 2/Lt Carlou down, 2/Lt Ge & L/Cpl Ingram shot him. It was most	

WAR DIARY or INTELLIGENCE SUMMARY

Army Form C. 2118.

Place	Date	Hour	Summary of Events and Information	Remarks and references to Appendices
Ploegsteert Wood	19th (Sunday)		Possible to capture a prisoner owing to the rapid counter attack, the Welsh party returned to our trenches at 5.45 a.m. without importance. No machine guns or artillery were fired from either side. At 10 a.m. the Divisional Commander congratulated the Colonel. Bn. was relieved by 1.N.L. & went to Piggeries in Bde. Reserve. No casualties.	
PIGGERIES	20th		"C" Coy went bathing & bomb practice — a draft of 96 joined Bn, mostly men who had been wounded. 2nd Lt Macklin who proceeded with a Military Cross by the Army Commander, for his patrol work on 8th December. Fine day.	1743
— " —	21st		Bathing & fatigues bomb practice for each company. Capt Kimberley left as Instructor in Sniping School, he having been with the Bn since January 15.	1743
— " —	22nd		Strength Offr 32 O.R. 732 Bathing and fatigues	171

WAR DIARY
or
INTELLIGENCE SUMMARY.

Army Form C. 2118.

Place	Date	Hour	Summary of Events and Information	Remarks and references to Appendices
PIGGERIES	1915 23rd		Bathing and fatigues, not day.	S.T.
	24th		Bn. went into trenches and relieved 8 L.N.L. The parapet had suffered considerably through rain. Two casualties in the evening. L/Cpl. Tugwell was attended in the head by rifle bullet and Pte Morgan was wounded while on a listening post. Weather fine after a rainy dawn.	S.T.
PLOEGSTEERT WOOD	25th		Weather very mild. Sunny. No work first all day; a white flag which was shown above their parapet was fired on and withdrawn and opposite the left company a German shouted out a question as to the attitude to adopt, but no reply was given. The repair and drainage of trenches was carried out as usual. The C.O.s Command'r visited the Bn. L/Cpl Tugwell died of wound recvd on the	S.T.
"	26th		Weather mild and sunny. Another quiet day the enemy making no reply to our artillery fire. Work of repairing trenches was continued	S.T.
"	27th		Weather mild; rain. Trench mortars and howitzers bombarded the Bird cage in the afternoon in order to inflict damage on new work there. Enemy retaliated by shelling the vicinity of Fort Boyd. One dugout	

WAR DIARY
or
INTELLIGENCE SUMMARY.
(Erase heading not required.)

Army Form C. 2118.

Place	Date	Hour	Summary of Events and Information	Remarks and references to Appendices
PLOEGSTEERT WOOD	27th		caught fire. There are two casualties; Mr. MILLARD had a shrapnel bullet in the shoulder and Pte Green was wounded in the stomach. In the evening rifle grenades were fired and found to have against the enemy trench; the feeble reply would suggest that the front line was weakly held. As a result of the West Bn Ethorne firing and sending a bomb behind instead of hurling it forward, two men were wounded, one severely. The precaution was taken of clearing the trench before the catapults were employed. The two men wounded are Ptes Rodman and Blair.	JT.
"	28th		Mr Lin Millard much not done in trenches. In the afternoon the enemy shelled the C.T. to the Strand and the Strand itself; two men, Pte Green and Phillips were wounded.	
"	29th		The Bn was relieved by the 8th L.N.L. There was one casualty in the early morning; Sgt. Carpenter and slightly wounded in the head. No casualties occurred during relief. The Bn went back into Divisional Reserve at Papot	JT.

WAR DIARY
or
INTELLIGENCE SUMMARY.
(Erase heading not required.)

Army Form C. 2118.

Place	Date	Hour	Summary of Events and Information	Remarks and references to Appendices
PAPOT	30th		Weather colder. Baking for half the battalion, fatigues for the other half	
	31st		Company drill with practice helmet and bombing and machine gun practice.	77

M. Maurice
Lt.-Colonel.
Comdg. 1st Bn. Wiltshire Regt.

1/1/16

7th Inf. Bde.

25th Division

1st Battn. WILTSHIRE REGIMENT

JANUARY, 1916.

3. 25
1st Miss. Regt.
Jan
Bul XVIII

WAR DIARY or INTELLIGENCE SUMMARY.

Army Form C. 2118.

Place	Date	Hour	Summary of Events and Information	Remarks and references to Appendices
PAPOT	1916 JAN. 1		This day was kept as a holiday by the Bn. only one fatigue party was required in the morning and there were no parades. The men were given a dinner of pork, Xmas pudding and beer and at 5 p.m. a smoker party consisting of six officers and one man, sustained a crowded house at the Romarin Recreation room. At 8 p.m. all officers dined together.	F.T.
"	2		Weather wet. Most of the Bn. on fatigue. Service and Holy Communion 6.30 a.m.	J.A.T.
PLOEGSTEERT WOOD	3		The Bn. went up into the trenches and relieved the 6th Loyal North Lancs. There was considerable shelling while the relief was in progress, but no casualties occurred. The enemy set fire to the thatched roof which was being used as an artillery observation post near the west end of St. Yves. It is quite possible the enemy may have thought that it was being used by a returning party. Weather bright and sunny.	F.T.
"	4		Weather mild. Considerable artillery activity during the day commencing at 12.30 p.m. when the enemy shelled Moated Farm, St. Yves, and Hyde Park Corner. From 2.30 p.m. an hour we bombarded the enemy front line	

WAR DIARY or INTELLIGENCE SUMMARY

Army Form C. 2118.

Place	Date	Hour	Summary of Events and Information	Remarks and references to Appendices
PLOEGSTEERT WOOD	JAN. 4		Opposite trench 123 with trench mortars, rifle grenades and bombs and caused considerable damage to their parapet, but not a single German was seen. It is fairly possible they suspected something and withdrew into their second line. Retaliation came after 11 minutes and for the first half hour was moderately heavy. It then increased in strength and a large number of shells fell in rear of trenches 123 and 120 and along the Fort Boyd line, and also Hunter's Avenue. There were four casualties. Ptes Ashton and Hale (A Coy.), Pte Mussel(?)waite (B Coy.) Ptes Griffin and Hyde (D Company) were slightly wounded, and 4o. Hill (C Coy) suffered from shock. At night we played upon the enemy's damaged trench with machine gun fire and fired 4 rifle grenades, but it is known with what result. 5 Germans were sniped by us during the day.	
	5		In the early morning the enemy fired six trench mortars and some rifle grenades at trench 123, the objective being our standing catapults and mortars, but little damage was done. At noon the artillery registered on the Birdcage	

Army Form C. 2118.

WAR DIARY
or
INTELLIGENCE SUMMARY.
(Erase heading not required.)

Place	Date	Hour	Summary of Events and Information	Remarks and references to Appendices
PLOEGSTEERT WOOD.	JAN. 5		With a 18 & 6" gun. During the morning our Snipers were particularly active at	J.T.
"	6		The day was fine and clear. 3 Germans were accounted for by sniping. L/Cpl. Hughes was wounded by a bullet in the arm whilst asleep in his dug-up. In the morning our artillery was very active; in return the enemy still very mild.	J.T.
"	7		The enemy breached the parapet of the C.T. at top of the Strand. Further work was carried on in Westminster Avenue. The Bn. was relieved by the 8th Loyal North Lancs and went back into Brigade Reserve at the Piggeries, H.Q. of a company proceeding to the Forts Fme la Barre. Oxford and Berks. A Lewis Gun Section was formed.	J.T.
PIGGERIES	8		170 men of the Bn. proceeded to the Divisional Technical School field and were put through gas tests under the supervision of the Chemical Adviser. Altogether 1500 men assembled for this purpose but nothing beyond the ambulance appeared. After waiting for two hours in the field the party returned, ungassed. Fatigue parties were provided by the Bn. in the evening for work on the breastwork behind trench 121. Weather colder.	J.T.

Army Form C. 2118.

WAR DIARY
or
INTELLIGENCE SUMMARY.
(Erase heading not required.)

Place	Date	Hour	Summary of Events and Information	Remarks and references to Appendices
PIGGERIES	9		The same number of men from the Bn. were marched to the Technical School. Field again and this time went through gas. The tubular helmets proved to be exceedingly satisfactory and there were no casualties. In the morning two platoons of C Company relieved the two platoons of B Company in the Forts. The Grenadiers and the Lewis Gun Section paraded for instruction. A voluntary service was held in the Recreation Room at 2:30 p.m.	J.T.
"	10		Weather bright and sunny. Bathing for two and a half companies. Bombing instruction for two platoons of B Company and the usual parade for the Lewis Gun Section. In the evening a fatigue party carried on with the repair of St. Yves C.T. Pte Cornish (C Company) was wounded in the head by shrapnel which burst over Forse la Barre.	J.T.
"	11		Bathing for the rest of the Bn. In the morning two companies had drill with the phosgene tubular helmets. Bombing instruction was given to the available N.C.O's and to the Company Sergeant-major. Two platoons of B Coy relieved the two platoons of C Coy in the Forts	J.T.

Army Form C. 2118.

WAR DIARY
or
INTELLIGENCE SUMMARY.
(Erase heading not required.)

Place	Date	Hour	Summary of Events and Information	Remarks and references to Appendices
PIGGERIES	D.M.		Two Companies practised tubular helmet drill. Usual Lewis gun and bombing instruction. A large party was required for work in the Brewery. Direct upon the Breastwork behind trench 121 here were two casualties. Pte. Parsons was killed & Pts. Hall and Clark died of their wounds and Pte Hawkins was wounded. This was due to a machine gun opening fire from the enemy trench opposite trench 123. Late in the evening 4 enemy shells landed in the vicinity of the Piggeries, the nearest not being more than 60 yards away. The men in the hut N. of the Lane to Piggeries were quickly turned out. One shell actually discharged half of one of the huts. A piece of shell penetrated to roof of the Piggeries and wounded Pte Vines in the foot. There was no further damage. The enemy's intention was destroying his target may have been one of our Batteries or the Piggeries.	Br.
PLOEGSTEERT WOOD	13		The Bn. proceeded to the trenches to relieve the 8th Loyal North Lancs. There were no casualties. A quiet day. Weather fine	Br.

Army Form C. 2118.

WAR DIARY
or
INTELLIGENCE SUMMARY.
(Erase heading not required.)

Place	Date	Hour	Summary of Events and Information	Remarks and references to Appendices
PLOEGSTEERT WOOD	14		Throughout the day the enemy's artillery was very active particular attention being paid to St. YVES communication trench and St. Ethird trench 123, neither of which was in use. Our reply to their fire was very weak, the shells were of small calibre and limited in number owing to the previous drain upon the supply. While the 5th Loyal North Lancs were in the trenches the Bn. suffered no casualties.	127.
	15		Enemy's attitude much firmer. Our sniping is believed to have accounted for three Germans. A draft of 32 men arrived and were sent up to the trenches. Weather very fine.	D.T.
	16		In the early morning considerable progress was made with the opening up of Westminster Avenue, a short length of foot trench being cut in place of the old. A quiet day. In the evening the enemy fired a few rifle grenades against trench 123. We retaliated strongly. In the course of the day two Germans were sniped and it is believed that further casualties were caused by our machine gun in the night.	127.

Place	Date	Hour	Summary of Events and Information	Remarks and references to Appendices
PLOEGSTEERT WOOD	17		A moderately first day. Our sniping accounted for four Germans. S/ Yuss C.T. was shelled in the morning and Fort Boyd line bombed after midnight. In the course of the night Westminster Avenue C.T. was opened up as the result of several works' work.	P.T.
"	18		Weather misty and snowing. Enemy's attitude very quiet. There was practically no sniping and there was no artillery fire until 6 p.m. when Fort Boyd line was shelled in reply to our trench mortars & the Birdcage. The following regimental honours were in the New Year's list :— Military Cross, Capt. Kneller, Lt. Peel & Lt. Gregory. D.C.M. Sgt Elliot. Pte Edwards. Field Ham, Miles and Shingfield.	I.T.
	19		The Bn was relieved by the 8th Loyal North Lancs and went into Divisional Reserve at Papot. No casualties occurred during relief.	P.T.
PAPOT	20		Bathing for three companies: no fatigues except a small party for manning the camp. A Lewis Gun Class was started. Instruction in bombing for the warrant officers and non commissioned officers. Weather fine.	I.T.

WAR DIARY or INTELLIGENCE SUMMARY.

Army Form C. 2118.

Place	Date	Hour	Summary of Events and Information	Remarks and references to Appendices
TAPOT	21		Bathing for the remaining Company. Lewis Gun section parade and firing instruction for the last draft. Morning fatigues in the Bn. sector took most of the available men.	P.T.
"	22		All companies had parades for inspection of rifles etc. and company drill. Many preparations were made for the following day's move.	I.S.T
"	23		The Bn. was relieved by the 7th Seaforths and marched by companies to La Crèche, where the Bn. was billeted for the remainder of the day and the night previous to completing the move on to the following day. A C.E. service was held in one of the barns in the afternoon. Weather, very fine and sunny.	
OUTTER- STEENE	24		At 9 a.m. the Bn. left La Crèche for its Divisional Training area in the Outtersteene district, and after a march lasting two and three quarter hours arrived at the new billets, which were all, with one exception, barns attached to farm houses. Weather colder.	P.T.
"	25		Frosty morning. The companies had half an hour's physical training in their drilling grounds and held inspection of kit clothing	

Army Form C. 2118.

WAR DIARY
or
INTELLIGENCE SUMMARY.

(Erase heading not required.)

Instructions regarding War Diaries and Intelligence Summaries are contained in F. S. Regs., Part II. and the Staff Manual respectively. Title pages will be prepared in manuscript.

Place	Date	Hour	Summary of Events and Information	Remarks and references to Appendices
OUTTER-STEENE			and equipment.	
	26		Usual company parades for physical exercise in the morning. All the N.C.O's except the Warrant officers received instruction from the Regimental Sergeant Major and the subaltern officers paraded under the Commanding officer for communication drill. Football in the Company fields in the afternoon.	P.T.
"	27		Msl usual. Physical Exercise; the N.C.O's paraded under the Regimental Sergeant Major for further instruction and the Subaltern officers had bayonet practise. Football in the afternoon.	P.T.
"	28		The first day of Company training. Physical Exercise. Squad drill without arms. Musketry &c. 12 men per company in addition to the Regimental Gunners received bombing instruction, and 2 men per company besides the snipers received instruction in sniping. In the afternoon there was inter-company football. Weather fine.	P.T.
"	29		Physical Exercise and an hour's squad drill. The Bn. went for a short route march in the afternoon. Football and company cross-country runs. A draft of 7 casualties arrived from England.	P.T.

T/134. W¹. W708—776. 50000. 4/15. Sir J. C. & S.

Army Form C. 2118.

WAR DIARY
or
INTELLIGENCE SUMMARY.
(Erase heading not required.)

Instructions regarding War Diaries and Intelligence Summaries are contained in F. S. Regs., Part II. and the Staff Manual respectively. Title pages will be prepared in manuscript.

Place	Date	Hour	Summary of Events and Information	Remarks and references to Appendices
OUTTER-STEENE	30		There was a Bn. Church parade in the morning at 10.30 a.m. Weather much colder.	177.
"	31		Physical exercises and company training in the afternoon the company final at football were played. D company defeating A by 1 goal to nil. In the morning a fatigue party 100 strong went to Strazeele.	177.
"			Mahon to replace R.E. shed. Heavy artillery heard in the distance from 4 a.m. until 10.30 p.m. — Pte Vinio died suddenly during the night, he was the oldest soldier in the Bn. having 22 years service. —	1725.

W.H.Brown Lt. Colonel
Offg 1/5th Yorkshire Regt.

29/1/16

7th Inf. Bde.

25th Division

1st Battn. WILTSHIRE REGIMENT

FEBRUARY, 1916

Army Form C. 2118.

WAR DIARY
or
INTELLIGENCE SUMMARY.
(Erase heading not required.)

Instructions regarding War Diaries and Intelligence Summaries are contained in F.S. Regs., Part II. and the Staff Manual respectively. Title pages will be prepared in manuscript.

Place	Date	Hour	Summary of Events and Information	Remarks and references to Appendices
	FEB.			
OUTTER- STENE	1		The Bn. went for a route march to Flêtre. Football in the afternoon.	J.T.
"	2		Usual parade for Physical training and company work.	S.T.
"	3		Bn. route march to Strazelle, Borelles, Badelieu and Flêtre. Football.	S.T.
"	4		Physical exercises and company training.	J.T.
"	5			
"	6		Church parade at 10.30 a.m.	J.T.
"	7		Physical exercises and company training. Cross-country running and football.	J.T.
"	8			
"	9		The Brigade was inspected on a route march by the Army Commander, General Plumer. The men were in marching order with packs and the Brigade was accompanied by its first-line transport.	J.T.
"	10		Weather very wet and cold, rendering parades impossible. Lectures were given to the men in their Barns.	J.T.
"	11		Company training. In the afternoon in the football semi-final the Brigade Machine Gun Company defeated D Company of the Bn. by 3 goals to 1.	J.T.
"	12		Company Route Marches. In the morning the Corps Commander, Sir Charles	J.T.

T/134. Wt. W708—776. 500000. 4/15. Sir J.C. & S.

Army Form C. 2118.

WAR DIARY
or
INTELLIGENCE SUMMARY.
(Erase heading not required.)

Instructions regarding War Diaries and Intelligence Summaries are contained in F. S. Regs., Part II. and the Staff Manual respectively. Title pages will be prepared in manuscript.

Place	Date	Hour	Summary of Events and Information	Remarks and references to Appendices
OUTTER- STEENE	12		Brigadier presented the ribbons of medals to the following: Military Cross, Capt. Hartley; Distinguished Conduct Medals, Sgt Loarday, L/Sgt. Ingram, Pte Field. Frozen. Silence and Miles.	
"	13		There was a Voluntary Church Parade at 10.30 a.m.	P.T.
"	14		Physical Exercises and Company training	P.T.
"	15		There was a Bn. route march to Mont des Cats. Weather very cold and snowing.	P.T.
"	16		The Bn. received orders to move to a station of recompots at Romarin; notice arrived at 8 a.m. and the Bn moved from the billeting area at 10.30 a.m. On arrival at Brigade Hd Quarters, Strathtone, information was received that the Strathen was in the nature of a test. After a short route march in a hurricane of mind the Brigade returned to billet.	
"	17			P.T.
"	18		Physical Exercises and Company training.	P.T.

Army Form C. 2118.

WAR DIARY
or
INTELLIGENCE SUMMARY.
(Erase heading not required.)

Instructions regarding War Diaries and Intelligence Summaries are contained in F. S. Regs., Part II. and the Staff Manual respectively. Title pages will be prepared in manuscript.

Place	Date	Hour	Summary of Events and Information	Remarks and references to Appendices
OUTTERSTEENE	FEB 19		A Battalion Route March. Semi-final of Platoon football between winners of platoons in A Coy.	S.A.T.
"	20		There was a Voluntary Church parade. In the afternoon regimental sports were held.	S.A.T.
"	21		A Battalion Route March. Final of inter platoon football in which No 4 Platoon defeated No 7 Platoon.	S.A.T.
"	22		Brigade Operations consisting of a cross country attack on an intrenched position three miles of Merckeghem deep. These operations were carried out in a snow storm.	S.A.T.
"	23		A Battalion Route March in the morning.	S.A.T.
"	24		Company attacks were carried out on the A Battalion bombing trench.	S.A.T.
"	25		A Battalion attack was practised at noon there was a German farmer in Musser demonstration under the Supervision of the Chemical Adviser of the 2nd Army, for the purpose of showing bombs harmless the liquid fire employed by the enemy. In reality made Capt Segrave from the Staff of the 50th. Infantry Brigade joined the Battalion on return to regimental duty.	S.A.T.

T.134. Wt. W708-776. 500000. 4/15. Sir J. C. & S.

WAR DIARY
or
INTELLIGENCE SUMMARY.
(Erase heading not required.)

Army Form C. 2118.

Place	Date	Hour	Summary of Events and Information	Remarks and references to Appendices
OUTTER-STENE	FEB 26		A Battalion Route March. Fighting strength of the Bn. - 29 Officers 717 other ranks.	P.T.
"	27		A Sunday Church service was held. The Division you which I have justice to be ready to move by rail.	S.T.T.
"	28		The Companies held inspection of the Kit Equipment etc and	P.T.
"	29		billets were cleaned up preparatory to an imminent move. Weather much warmer and sunny. There was a Battalion drill march in the morning.	P.T.

Maximum 28. Colonel
O/C 1/9 Wiltshire Regt

29/4/16

7th Inf. Bde.

25th Division

1st Battn. WILTSHIRE REGIMENT

M A R C H, 1 9 1 6

743

WAR DIARY
or
INTELLIGENCE SUMMARY.
(Erase heading not required.)

Army Form C. 2118.

Place	Date	Hour	Summary of Events and Information	Remarks and references to Appendices
OUTTERSTEINE	MARCH 1		Tactical attacks were practised by the companies and bayonet fighting	127
"	2		There was a battalion attack at Outtersteine and a night march. Shortly in the afternoon Capt T.H.H. Kincaid Smith (R.P.I. Fareng) 2nd Cavalry Division joined the battalion and took over the command of D Company. At 7.20 p.m. orders were received, the destination given was Outtersteine in the 5th Corps area. At 8 & 9 p.m. the Battalion was on the road & ready to move to the Brigade starting point which is reached just two minutes late. At 9.50 p.m. the whole of the Brigade had closed up only to discover that they were engaged in practising a night concentration. The Battalion then returned to its billets	
"	3		The numerous lectures were given by Col & Adjutant and other officers on various subjects	170 127
"	4		Company training instructional attacks and trench fighting were carried out. Instructions regarding Parades in the open in particular and lectures were	S. 127

WAR DIARY or INTELLIGENCE SUMMARY

Army Form C. 2118.

Place	Date	Hour	Summary of Events and Information	Remarks and references to Appendices
OUTTER- STEENE	MARCH 4		given in the Barns. An inspection of the Battalion in company with one other Battalion of the Brigade by the Commander-in-chief had to be cancelled	PJT
"	5		There was a Voluntary Church service at 10.30 a.m. It the day	PJT
"	6		Snow in the early morning but by 10 a.m. it had stopped and there had a great improvement in the weather. There was a Bn route	PJT
"	7		march through Strazeele, Merris and Outtersteene.	PJT
"	8		Snowstorms were then very cold only company route marches were possible. There was a Brigade route march through Strazeele Pradelles Borre Flêtre and Meteren	PJT
"	9		The companies held inspections of Kit, Equipment &c and fitted in one cleaned up preparatory to the next days move.	PJT
"	10		The Brigade began its march South and moved into the Robecq area 1 M. of Merville. The Battalion marched away from its billets at 8.15 a.m. and reached Robecq at 1.30 p.m. the route being via Vieux Bergein and Merville. Near Vieux Bergein the Battalion marched past the Corps	PJT

WAR DIARY
or
INTELLIGENCE SUMMARY
(Erase heading not required.)

Army Form C. 2118.

Place	Date	Hour	Summary of Events and Information	Remarks and references to Appendices
ROBECQ	10		Commanders for the last time. The country was exceedingly flat and almost under water.	P.T.
"	11		The Battalion proceeded upon the second stage of the march at 8.15 a.m., the destination being Valhuon, S. of Pernes. After starting through billeting country scouts were reconnoitring wood hills and slag heaps were into view. Valhuon was not reached until 2.15 p.m. in spite of the length of the second march day few men fell out. The village had only been evacuated by the French a few days before, and in consequence the billeting of the first English troops posed a matter of no little difficulty. However, on the next morning the billet had been made habitable. About 10 p.m. a draft of 4? other ranks arrived from St. Pol., of these 42 no less than 36 were men who had either been wounded or sick. Some had been with the 5th. Battalion in the Dardanelles, some were from the 2nd and the remainder had been previously serving with the 1st. The physique showed a great improvement on that of previous drafts, and the men were younger but only 6 had seen no active service.	P.T.

WAR DIARY
or
INTELLIGENCE SUMMARY.

(Erase heading not required.)

Army Form C. 2118.

Place	Date	Hour	Summary of Events and Information	Remarks and references to Appendices
HALHUON	12		There was a voluntary service in one of the farmsheds at 11 a.m. At 12 noon the draft was inspected and distributed to their Companies. During the afternoon the 74th Brigade boxed through the village. Weather sunny and warm.	P.T.
"	13	}	Battalion route march class in the morning.	P.T.
"	14			P.T.
"	15		Battalion route march and instructional attack. A draft of 11 signallers joined the Battalion, part of them from the 3rd Bn. & part from the 8th.	P.T.
"	16		The Brigade continued its march into the 17th Corps area to Bn. proceeding to Ternas, S.E. of St. Pol. The billets had been recently been vacated by the French.	P.T.
TERNAS	17	}	The field training of the Battalion was continued. attacks were carried out & Special attention being given to bombing parties. Weather very fine.	P.T.
"	18			P.T.
"	19		Church parade service at 10.30 a.m. and an inspection of all billets & Battalion route march in which advance and rear guards were practised. A medical inspection of the Companies in the afternoon.	P.T.
"	20			P.T.

Army Form C. 2118.

WAR DIARY
or
INTELLIGENCE SUMMARY.
(Erase heading not required.)

Place	Date	Hour	Summary of Events and Information	Remarks and references to Appendices
TERNAS	21		Company and Battalion training. Washing kit and cltd.	1/JT
"	22		Battalion Route March	1/JT
"	23		The training of the Battalion was continued on the same lines as previously. In the afternoon a most successful cross-country run for the whole Battalion was held. "A" Company joined the winners. Wastage fine but cold.	SSO
"	24		Battalion Route March. In the afternoon bombing was held in one of the barns.	SSO
"	25		Field training continued. The Bombing competition was finished.	SSO
"	26		There was a Voluntary Church Service in the morning. In the afternoon a horse and jumper competition was introduced namely an inter-Company Jumping match with Transport horses and French ponies. The show ended with an engaged in teams, four to the war were selected as representatives of each Company	

Army Form C. 2118.

WAR DIARY
or
INTELLIGENCE SUMMARY.
(Erase heading not required.)

Instructions regarding War Diaries and Intelligence Summaries are contained in F. S. Regs., Part II. and the Staff Manual respectively. Title pages will be prepared in manuscript.

Place	Date	Hour	Summary of Events and Information	Remarks and references to Appendices
TERMAK	26		"D" Company was the winner.	SS0.
	27		} Battalion training. Weather very cold. Football in the	
	28		} afternoons. A draft of 4 + 2 men mostly returned	SS0
	29		} sick recruited from 1st, 2nd & 5th Bns. joined on 29th.	M5
	30			
	31.		The Battalion marched to a field near Tuspei where they were inspected by the Commander-in-Chief - he complimented them upon the way they moved past arms. He thought all the men were looking very fit and wished them all the best of luck. The weather was very fine and much warmer.	SS0.

J.M.Rivers Lt. Colonel
O/C 1st Wiltshires

31/3/16

7th Inf. Bde.
25th Division

1st Battn. WILTSHIRE REGIMENT

APRIL, 1916.

Army Form C. 2118.

WAR DIARY
or
INTELLIGENCE SUMMARY.
(Erase heading not required.)

Place	Date	Hour	Summary of Events and Information	Remarks and references to Appendices
TERNAS	April 1916			
	1.		The Battalion went a Route March, orders had been received that the B⁰ was not to press a certain front until the Corps Commander had arrived for the purpose of inspecting them. After waiting three hours there was still no sign of the Corps Commander and the B⁰ was marched back reaching billets at 3 p.m. In the afternoon a football match was held between Sergt "Sparks" and a Private in the 8th D.N.L. resulted in an easy win for the latter. Weather very fine.	S.E.O.
	2.		There was Church Parade in the Morning. In the afternoon the inter-platoon Football Competition was continued. Weather very fine.	S.E.O
	3.		The training of the Companies was continued. great attention was paid to practice in grenade throwing. In the afternoon a fire broke out in "B" Coy's billets and destroyed a barn. The act -ivities however seems saved by the fire & made h energetic action	S.E.O.

Army Form C. 2118.

WAR DIARY
or
INTELLIGENCE SUMMARY.
(Erase heading not required.)

Place	Date	Hour	Summary of Events and Information	Remarks and references to Appendices
TERVAS.	3.		of the troops.	S.S.O.
"	4.		There was a Brigade Route March through Bonneville during which it was inspected on the march by the Corps Commander. The afternoon was taken up by an extensive enquiry into the causes of yesterday's fire. The Semi-finals of the Inter-Platoon fatigue Tug-of-War were pulled off.	S.S.O.
"	5.		The training of the B's was continued. Washer order.	S.S.O. P.T.
"	6.		Company Field Training was continued.	P.T.
"	7.		Company Field Training was continued. In the afternoon the final of the Inter Platoon was played.	P.T.
"	8.		There was a Battalion route march. In the afternoon the final of the Inter Platoon Tug-of-War was pulled off.	P.T.
"	9.		After Church parade the prizes were given and to the winning team in the afternoon the Sergeants defeated the officers at football etc.	

WAR DIARY
or
INTELLIGENCE SUMMARY.

Army Form C. 2118.

Place	Date	Hour	Summary of Events and Information	Remarks and references to Appendices
TERNAS	9		to Halte	
	10		The Battalion proceeded to Savy on its march into the Support Line. Est of Mart. Lt. Slay Lt. Gorden left the Battalion to take up an appointment as instructor at the 25th. Divisional School at Bena ville.	127.
"	11		[illegible crossed out line] The Battalion relieved the 11th. Lancs. Fusiliers in the Support line N.E. of La Targette. It was preceded in the morning by an advance party consisting of the first relief of the working parties. There were no casualties in the course of the relief. The work taken over consisted mainly of carrying for both French and English mining companies in the front line, and this work continued day and night by means of a series of reliefs which were each of about eight hours' duration. Weather wet and cold.	127
LA TAR-GETTE	12		Mining fatigues went on throughout the day. 1 N.C.O. and 1 man of D Company were gassed in one of the saps through a pump breaking	

Army Form C. 2118.

WAR DIARY
or
INTELLIGENCE SUMMARY.
(Erase heading not required.)

Instructions regarding War Diaries and Intelligence Summaries are contained in F. S. Regs., Part II. and the Staff Manual respectively. Title pages will be prepared in manuscript.

Place	Date	Hour	Summary of Events and Information	Remarks and references to Appendices
LA TARGETTE	12		cont. - Cpl. CULLINAN, F.M. and Pte. SMYTH, R. Lasmy's cottage a altitude was twist. Weather very wet. Lt.Col. BROWN took over temporarily the duties of Brigade Commander, and Major KINCAID SMITH took over the command of the Battalion.	P.T.
"	13		Mine fatigues. There were 4 more casualties, - men suffering from the ef- fects of gas in one of the Saps. They were L/c Payne and Pte. Smart of D Company, Pte. Dudman of C Company, and Pte. Maclean of A Company.	P.T.
"	14		Mine fatigues were continued. Enemy artillery and particularly trench mortars were active on both days.	P.T.
"	15			
"	16		Mine fatigues. Weather much finer. At midnight the French fired two mines in the right sector. There was the tremost, but the attempt was to break in the enemy's Redbout and destroy one of their listening posts. The second effort to capture a prisoner, could not be achieved, as the raiding party was bombed out of the enemy trench. The near lip of the crater was consolidated. The casualties among the Sherwood Foresters consisted of one officer killed	

WAR DIARY or INTELLIGENCE SUMMARY

Army Form C. 2118.

Place	Date	Hour	Summary of Events and Information	Remarks and references to Appendices
LA PARGETTE	16		and several other ranks wounded.	P.T.
"	17		Mine fatigues. During the night there was a considerable amount of bombing after the explosion of an enemy mine. It was thought that the enemy had got into part of the outpost line and blocks were put up, but it was subsequently discovered that the trench was clear. The Lewis m/g of A Company was brought up from the support line and did effective work.	P.T.
"	18		Mine fatigues. An enemy mine, which was blown up, caused very little damage. Two men were wounded. Pte Briton was injured, Pte Hamilton, shock.	P.T.
"	19		The Bn Italian was relieved by the 7th Bn. Sherwood Foresters, and went back into Brigade Reserve at Mont St Eloy. There were no cas- alties during relief. Earlier in the day four men were slightly pressed in a Sap. L/C Penny, Ptes Fletcher, Bancroft and Pontifell of D Company.	P.T.
MONT ST. ELOY	20		There were inspections of rifles, kit &c. in the huts under company arrangements. A concert was held in the evening. Weather, fine.	P.T.

Army Form C. 2118.

WAR DIARY
or
INTELLIGENCE SUMMARY.
(Erase heading not required.)

Instructions regarding War Diaries and Intelligence Summaries are contained in F. S. Regs., Part II. and the Staff Manual respectively. Title pages will be prepared in manuscript.

Place	Date	Hour	Summary of Events and Information	Remarks and references to Appendices
MONT ST. ELOY	21		There were inspections of kit &c. in the morning. In the afternoon upon a ground previously laid out the officers and sergeants went through a practice attack consolidation. At 6 pm a Voluntary Service was held. A fatigue party of 50 men was required for work in rear of the left sector of the Brigade area.	V.T.
"	22		In the morning the consolidation of craters was practised by the companies on ground adjacent to the billets. A small working party went up to a support trench to build dugouts and remained there through the night and next day. Weather very wet.	V.T.
"	23		Services 8th Church of England and Non Conformist were held. In the evening the Bn. relieved the 8th Loyal North Lancs in the right sector of the Bde. area. The relief was completed without casualty. and the night passed quietly. Weather fine.	V.T.
TRENCHES LA TARGETTE	24		Work throughout the day consisted of bailing the trenches, which after the recent rain were in a very bad state. Three of the enemy	V.T.

Army Form C. 2118.

WAR DIARY
or
INTELLIGENCE SUMMARY.
(Erase heading not required.)

Place	Date	Hour	Summary of Events and Information	Remarks and references to Appendices
TRENCHES LA TARGETTE	24		Mine sniped. At 7.35 p.m. the Enemy sprang a mine on the left of the outpost line by a former crater at the top of the GRANGE C.T. and considerable bombing passed for over an hour. The 10th Cheshire Regt. on the left was more deeply involved and sustained several casualties. In the course of the bombing 2/Lt. MAYBROOK, the Bn. Bombing Officer, was killed by a bullet shot through the neck. His body was not discovered until the next morning as he was out in advance of the outpost line by the craters. Two officers were wounded viz. Lt. E.E. BROWN and 2/Lt. K.C. NICHOLS, the former very slightly so that he was able to remain at duty, the latter by a bomb. Casualties among the men were as follows :- Pte. COLES, R. killed, Pte. Coleman, H. and Hemmings, D. wounded.	
"	25		The shelling of trenches was continued. Enemy's attitude : sniping was brisk but general several activity. Two hits are claimed by the Bn. Blasting operations on the front of the Enemy were suspected. Weather very fine.	127

There were two slight casualties, Ptes STONEHAM, H. and WRIGHT, E.A. of B Company

127

Army Form C. 2118.

WAR DIARY
or
INTELLIGENCE SUMMARY.
(Erase heading not required.)

Instructions regarding War Diaries and Intelligence Summaries are contained in F. S. Regs., Part II. and the Staff Manual respectively. Title pages will be prepared in manuscript.

Place	Date	Hour	Summary of Events and Information	Remarks and references to Appendices
TRENCHES LA TARGETTE	26		In the morning some registering took place on the trench railway dump in the Quarries. Enemy Snipers were inactive. One man shot. Work consisted of cleaning trenches and repairing and replacing duckwalks. At night the Bn. had relieved by the 5th. Loyal North Lancs, and went into Divisional Reserve at ACQ. Two men were wounded by bombs Pte FARLEY Two wounded 1/Sgt BENNETT. J and Pte MARTIN. both of D Company by rifle shot.	V.P.T
ACQ	27		There were baths in ACQ for 150 men in the morning. A party consisting of 1 NCO and 4 men. left the Bn. to proceed to the 182nd Tunnelling Company at Mingoval. At 6p.m. the Funeral of Pte. MAYBROOM was held at Mont St. Eloy Cemetery	N.P.T
	28		Company Inspections in the morning and Trollthrowing and gas drill practice. In the evening C and D Companies moved into billets at Mont St. Eloy to replace two companies of the 10th Cheshire Regt. who had gone up to the PYLONES Support line. A working party of 200 men laid cable under R.E. supervision by Bethonval Wood	V.P.T

Army Form C. 2118.

WAR DIARY
or
INTELLIGENCE SUMMARY.
(Erase heading not required.)

Place	Date	Hour	Summary of Events and Information	Remarks and references to Appendices
ACQ	29		Company inspection parade and Lewis Rifle Machine 2/Lt. McKelvey joined the Bn. from the Cadet School G.H.Q. Weather very fine	P.T
"	30		A voluntary Service was held at 11 a.m. During the morning there were Baths for 150 men. In the evening the companies paraded for bayonet drill	P.T

30/4/16

M. M. Brown Lt. Colonel
Commanding 1st. Bn. Wiltshire Regt.

7th Inf. Bde.

25th Division

1st Battn. WILTSHIRE REGIMENT,

MAY, 1916.

WAR DIARY
or
INTELLIGENCE SUMMARY.
(Erase heading not required.)

Army Form C. 2118.

1 Wilts R Vol 22

Place	Date	Hour	Summary of Events and Information	Remarks and references to Appendices
AC &	MAY 1		As nothing have been Company parades to inspections and for Bayonet practice. Working parties were required at night. Weather very fine	PT.
"	2		One party was required in the morning to cattle laying lie to burning the Bn. relieved the 8th Loyal North Lancs in the front line. There were no casualties and the night passed very quietly.	PT.
TRENCHES LA MARGETTE	3		The Enemy was very quiet, but at 4 p.m. sprung two mines one to the right of COMMON C.T. the other to the North of BIRKIN C.T. The firing did no damage to the trenches, the latter blew up a bombing post of the left company and three men were missing. The near lips of both craters were consolidated and rifle fire from the COMMON Crater accounted to several of the Enemy, they retaliated with trench mortar and later with rifle grenade only. Weather fine spent artillery fire. The casualties were as follows :- killed C.S.M. Cool, B Company, and Pte. Bodsworth of the regimental bombers. Missing Pte. Singlehurst and Thacker, D Company. Wounded Sgt Kent, Cpl Allen, Cpl Hitcock, L/C Bourton, Ptes	

WAR DIARY or INTELLIGENCE SUMMARY.

(Erase heading not required.)

Army Form C. 2118.

Place	Date	Hour	Summary of Events and Information	Remarks and references to Appendices
TRENCHES	3		Biggs, N. Elliott, N. Hucbard and Noth, N.I. The flanking Lewis rifles were commanded by 2/Lt. Taylor and Potts, while the consolidating of the BIRKIN craters was under the direction of Capt. Austin and 2/Lt. Sainsbury. That 2 of the COMMON CRS. under Lt. Huntley Stoaza, S.E. Personnel, and 2/Lt. Snelgar and # Coden, the bombing officer. 1/27.	
	4		During the day Enemy was very quiet: work was carried on in the trenches connecting the new craters and the outpost line, and at another steel loophole plates were inserted. At 7.55 pm an enemy mine was sprung just to the South of the already existing crater ad the top of GRANGE C.T. a post of two men was buried and 2/Lt. Clark, D. Company, who was also buried was extracted after ten hours with ill suffered only from bruises and shock. The effect of the explosion was to fill in the already existing craters and form a large platform, the near edge of which was consolidated. By his mine the enemy but himself in a worse position than formerly in the way of sniping. 2/Lt. Sainsbury D Company again did	

WAR DIARY
or
INTELLIGENCE SUMMARY.
(Erase heading not required.)

Army Form C. 2118.

Place	Date	Hour	Summary of Events and Information	Remarks and references to Appendices
TRENCHES LA TARGETTE	4		Good work. The casualties were:- Missing believed killed Pte Hussey and Dudman of C Company, wounded Pte Ellis.	P.T.
"	5		Enemy fired but sniping was brisk and accurate. Hostile working parties were fired on with Lewis rifle and rifle grenades and it is believed that many casualties were caused. Snipers claimed two of the enemy. L/Cpl Roberts was fired on the near edge of GRANGE and BIRKIN craters. Two were two casualties. Cpl Watkins was sniped in the head and Pte. Hulbert suffered from shock.	P.T.
"	6		During the night of the 5th/6th the Bn was particularly active with bomb, rifle grenade, trench mortars and Lewis rifle and by day the snipers were busy. The reply was very great, and the whole day passed without a casualty. On the other hand few of the enemy were sniped and it is believed that some casualties were caused by the night bombing. Work was put in on the fixing of handsteps and strengthening of parapets in the D line and the PIRATES. The posts at the new BIRKIN and GRANGE craters were also	

Army Form C. 2118.

WAR DIARY
or
INTELLIGENCE SUMMARY.
(Erase heading not required.)

Place	Date	Hour	Summary of Events and Information	Remarks and references to Appendices
TRENCHES	7		Strong wind. Weather very fine. During the night of the 6th/7th the Bn was again active with bombs, rifle grenades and Lewis rifles, and fire was directed behind ALBANY CRAFT where work was heard in progress. Throughout the day the enemy's attitude was exceedingly quiet and scarcely a shot was fired. So little did the enemy show himself that only one was sniped. Work was continued on the firesteps and Snapers of P Line and PIRATES. There were five casualties — wounded, Pte. Palmer (B Company), Reynolds (C Company) Davis, Baldwin and Gray of D Company. 2/Lts Howcastle and Richard joined the Bn for duty from the Cadet School, A.H.Q.	P.T
	8		During the night of the 7th/8th the enemy lit up of the CONNEN Crater was rifle-grenaded. By day the Stokes gun registered on the places where the enemy had been working during the night. Lt. S. Brass was killed by a sniper while he was looking over the parapet. This officer who transferred to the Battalion from the A.S.C. in the middle of January, 1916, had done very valuable work in the line previously	P.T

Army Form C. 2118.

WAR DIARY
or
INTELLIGENCE SUMMARY.
(Erase heading not required.)

Place	Date	Hour	Summary of Events and Information	Remarks and references to Appendices
TRENCHES	8		In April, when the battalion was engaged on mining fatigues in the neighbourhood of a Lewis rifle in support of the Stewart Trestle after the explosion of a mine and did most effective work. Later on Easter Monday on the occasion of the GRANGE Crater he was slightly wounded in the head by a piece of bomb which penetrated his steel helmet. After wrapping a bandage over the wound he continued bombing, and did not go down to the dressing station until much later. In spite of his limited experience of trenches he had displayed great coolness and initiative since being in the line. At 7.57 p.m. the enemy sprang a mine between the old and new Craters at the top of BIRKIN C.T. The effect was to fill up the valley between the two Craters and prevent the enemy from enfilading our post. A pro of two men was turned, and new bodies were not recovered in. Pte Drewitt and Moore head of D Company. The new lip was consolidated and a sap pushed out to the north to connect with the crater which was blown up on	

Army Form C. 2118.

WAR DIARY
or
INTELLIGENCE SUMMARY.
(Erase heading not required.)

Place	Date	Hour	Summary of Events and Information	Remarks and references to Appendices
TRENCHES	8		the 3rd. In addition to the two men buried, there was one killed and one wounded.	
		At 6.13 p.m. we sprang a mine N.E. of the top of GRANGE C.T. between the two existing craters. This had the effect of obliterating both craters and forming a crescent shaped crater about 45 yards across and 80 yards in length. It was at least 60 feet deep. After the explosion a Lewis rifle was rushed up, and enfilading fire brought to bear upon a German working party which was fixing loopholes in the northern lip. Good execution must have been done. Work ceased and has not resumed. A sap was run in continuation of GRANGE C.T. to the lip and a lobe cut was made to command the right flank. A further sap bending in a Y shaped fork was run out to the southern extremity, and two loophole plates placed in position. There was no casualty. The casualties for the day were :- Killed, Lt. E.E. BROWN, L/c. CARD, D.H. and Pte. DEERING.G.; Missing, buried by mine debris, Pte. DEWITT, J. and Pte. WOODWARD, T.; Wounded, Pte. CHIDDEY, F. DIXON, C.E. and BALL, J.E.; Wounded on duty, Cpl. MITTEN, W. and L/c GRIERSON, H.C.	17T
	9		Enemy's attitude had quiet ; one Pioneer was sniped, and by the use of armour.	

Army Form C. 2118.

WAR DIARY
or
INTELLIGENCE SUMMARY.
(Erase heading not required.)

Instructions regarding War Diaries and Intelligence Summaries are contained in F. S. Regs., Part II. and the Staff Manual respectively. Title pages will be prepared in manuscript.

Place	Date	Hour	Summary of Events and Information	Remarks and references to Appendices
TRENCHES	9		piercing ammunition the enemy was compelled to leave his Loophole plates. At 7.46 p.m. the enemy sprang a mine N. of the ALBANY C.T. crater. No warning was received earlier in the day of the likelihood of a mine going up at that point, the observers were withdrawn a parts of an hour late earlier and did not return until the new lip had been consolidated. The only casualties were from some period. That night the Battalion was relieved by the 5th Loyal North Lancs. and went back into Brigade reserve in the PYLONES line and in dugouts by the BETHUNE - ARRAS road. The relief passed off without a casualty. Total casualties during tour 1 killed, 1 officer and 11 other ranks wounded, 1 officer and 25 other ranks.	
PYLONES and BETHUNE. ARRAS RD.			While the Battalion was in Brigade reserve, three companies worked by night under divisional orders on a support trench to the P line. This included the whole Brigade front. Small parties from these companies also worked on the C.T. in the right and left Battalion sector of the remaining company two platoons worked on the construction of dugouts in the	

Army Form C. 2118.

WAR DIARY
or
INTELLIGENCE SUMMARY.
(Erase heading not required.)

Instructions regarding War Diaries and Intelligence Summaries are contained in F. S. Regs., Part II. and the Staff Manual respectively. Title pages will be prepared in manuscript.

Place	Date	Hour	Summary of Events and Information	Remarks and references to Appendices
SUPPORT TRENCHES			Pylones trench. The other two platoons went back to Mont St. Eloy with H.Q. details. On the 12th Transport Lt. FOWLER joined the Bn. for duty	PT
	13		Battalion headquarters moved up into dugouts W. of the BETHUNE RD. Weather	PT
			VERY WET.	
	14		Aligned as usual. An additional party was furnished for carrying cable	
	15		Parties were furnished for night work as usual. Weather very fine	PT
	16		There were two casualties, wounded - Pte. MUNDY (C Company) on 15th. Pte OSBORNE on 16th	
TRENCHES	17		The Battalion relieved the 8th Loyal North Lancs Regt. in the front line. The night was quiet. First troops to Bn. bombing activity at the top of COMMON C.T. during which four other ranks were wounded and one was killed. Their wire was killed Pte ROGERS F. wounded. Pte. BANCROFT, WILLIAMS A.E. FOOTE, all of C Company. The following day Pte. WILLIAMS died of wounds. The bombing attack which was made at 15.30 f.m. was repeated at 18.30 f.m. A Patrol went out at 11.30 p.m. and discovered an old sap which ran S.E. from the far side of the COMMON crater. It was believed that the enemy used this	

Army Form C. 2118.

WAR DIARY
or
INTELLIGENCE SUMMARY.
(Erase heading not required.)

Instructions regarding War Diaries and Intelligence Summaries are contained in F. S. Regs., Part II. and the Staff Manual respectively. Title pages will be prepared in manuscript.

Place	Date	Hour	Summary of Events and Information	Remarks and references to Appendices
TRENCHES	17 cont.		was 6 to 831 within bombing distance of the post. Early in the evening the Bn. Bombing Sergeant Sgt. HIBBERD was wounded by an English or shell dropping short in the QUARRIES. Many casualties must have been inflicted on the enemy while the bombing attack was being driven back and again at about 11.30 p.m. when a Stokes gun fired on an enemy working party on the N. edge of ALBANY crater. On this occasion said C.O.s were heard.	197.
	18		Enemy's attitude was quiet. During the day there was registering with Stokes gun and rifle grenades on a new enemy trench which had been dug connecting their left of the BIRDH and COMMON craters. Work was continued on the firesteps and parapet of the P line & trench walks were taken up and cleaned. Another bombing attack which was made by the enemy on the COMMON post at about 8.45 p.m. was driven back. C Company suffered from casualties wounded CSM. WELTON 4/5. LEWIS, Pte. CROOK and BELL. Weather very fine.	
	19		In the early morning at about 2 a.m. the Stokes gun fired on the new	197.

Army Form C. 2118.

WAR DIARY
or
INTELLIGENCE SUMMARY.
(Erase heading not required.)

Place	Date	Hour	Summary of Events and Information	Remarks and references to Appendices
TRENCHES	19		Enemy trench Mortars BIRKIN and COMMON CRATER and can saw woke them in proper to cease. This firing was continued at intervals during the day and attention was also paid to the enemy posts in ALBANY CRATER. Both sides displayed considerable artillery activity in the sector to the left of the Bn line, the ABBEY front being in particular evidence but on this front the enemy's attitude was quiet. At 9.15 p.m. a party of the 5th Loyal North Lancs who had been brought up to assist the 6th Cheshires assaulted the enemy post from R. BROADMARSH CRATER; almost immediately machine gun and trench mortar fire opened all along the Bn front and a large number of bombs were thrown by the enemy towards the GRANGE both the Left company called for reinforcements and rapid rifle fire was opened from trenches P74 and P75. This fire caused the bombing and the fire from trench mortars fire of the enemy to cease. At 9.30 p.m. on receipt of news from the Left Company the rate of fire was reduced and five minutes later the fire was ordered to cease fire. The enemy who	

WAR DIARY
or
INTELLIGENCE SUMMARY.
(Erase heading not required.)

Army Form C. 2118.

Place	Date	Hour	Summary of Events and Information	Remarks and references to Appendices
TRENCHES	19		had been putting a barrage upon the western end of GRANGE C.T. CROSS ST and QUARRIES continued to fire an occasional shell until 1p.m. The 5th. Loyal North Lancs captured the crater and in anticipation of a counter attack the Bn. despatched 60 lives rifles to them as as of their own had been knocked out and he second was firing badly. The rest of the night passed quietly. The casualties mainly from enemy mortar fire were as follows:- Wounded 1/Sgt PONTING, 4/c HILL and Pte. BAUGH of C Company. Ptes. SMOUT and LOVELOCK of D Company suffering from shock. Pte. HARRISON C Company wounded whilst at duty C.S.M. LESTER and Sgt. WOODCOCK During the day work was done on the parapet of P.74 and the draining of VERNON C.T. was continued in the third post on the BIRKIN craters was deepened and shelter provided. Capt. KNUBLEY left the Bn. to take up duties as an instructor at the Divisional Training School, BUNEVILLE. Enemy's artillery was quiet. During the day the Stokes mortars in the line fired	27

Army Form C. 2118.

WAR DIARY
or
INTELLIGENCE SUMMARY.
(Erase heading not required.)

Instructions regarding War Diaries and Intelligence Summaries are contained in F. S. Regs., Part II. and the Staff Manual respectively. Title pages will be prepared in manuscript.

Place	Date	Hour	Summary of Events and Information	Remarks and references to Appendices
TRENCHES	20 cont.		upon the lip of ALBANY Crater and on COMMON crater. The was in retaliation for aerial torpedoes fired by the enemy towards P.75. Several of these also dropped near the outpost line of P.73 and between P.75 and P.75.S. The Sappers Company of the Germans work consisted in building up the parapet of the P line west of VENNELL W.F. of D Company. There was one casualty - killed by a piece of shell L/c	127.
	21		Enemy was quiet until late in the afternoon when about 2.30 p.m. a heavy bombardment commenced upon the Battalion on the left, the 10th Cheshires. Past the P Line of Rue Pector, and RH.33 Ganges and the GRANGE C.T. up to GAS Avenue. About 6.30 p.m. the enemy began to crump a barrage of Lachrymatory Shells on CROSS ST and QUARRIES, the junction of POM C.T. and CROSS ST. marking the right of the Gas area. The gas became particularly dense in CROSS ST where a company of the 7th Rifle Brigade was standing to. After dark the enemy attacked and carried P.79 and P.78 and also reached P.79.S. and part of P.78.S. The Bn. Bombers were dis-	

WAR DIARY or INTELLIGENCE SUMMARY

Army Form C. 2118.

(Erase heading not required.)

Hour, Date, Place	Summary of Events and Information	Remarks and references to Appendices
TRENCHES May 21	pushed to make a block in P.7.F.5. north of LASSALLE C.T. The task of counter-attacking fell to the Bn. reserve the 5th Loyal North Lancs, who were brought up from the Dycombe Line and the BETHUNE RD dugouts. The enemy were forced to vacate the P.5. line but still remained in possession of P.79 and part of P.78. The casualties in the Bn. due to shelling were :- Wounded - Pte. BRISTOW, A. Frances, H. MARE, H. BAR- RETT, W.G. KITLEY, R.A. GODWIN, E.H., BAILEY, R. Pte - L/C STAPLES, J. L/C. BIRD, J. The Bn. Hs still at duty. Throughout the night the companies were repairing the damage done to the P. line by shell fire.	J.77
22	A quiet day, during which the 5th.R.L.Fus. not effective work inflicted claimed two had been consisted of repairing the damage from shell fire and wire was put out in front of the R. post line. The casualties were :- Died of wounds Pte. FRANCIS, H wounded Pte. FOYLE, C. WRIGHT, E.A. MUNDY, H.C. HOULDING, G.	J.77

WAR DIARY
or
INTELLIGENCE SUMMARY.
(Erase heading not required.)

Army Form C. 2118.

Hour, Date, Place	Summary of Events and Information	Remarks and references to Appendices
TRENCHES MAY 23	During the night of the 22nd/23rd rifle grenades and Stokes mortars were fired into the enemy craters & posts. The day was quiet; two Germans were shot and a sniper opposite the top of GRANGE C.T. was silenced. Work consisted in building up the parapet of P.74 and wiring the valley between BIRKIN and COMMON craters; wire was also put up in front of two posts of the right company. Two star rankers of D Company were wounded :- Sgt. EDWARDS.W. Pte. LOVELOCK.C. LOVEGROVE.A.H. COOMBES.A and MARR.A.W.	A.D.T
24	The enemy were able to reach the BIRKIN crater post with cylinder stick bombs and bonus casualties were caused. Many rifle grenades were fired at the outpost line of P.73; these fired in retaliation appeared to do considerable damage. Rifle, S.A.A. & many Field Royal heavy trench mortars at P.74 and P.75 and also at the head of GRANGE C.T. Snipers claimed three Germans. Repairs to the P. Line are	

Army Form C. 2118.

WAR DIARY
or
INTELLIGENCE SUMMARY.
(Erase heading not required.)

Instructions regarding War Diaries and Intelligence Summaries are contained in F.S. Regs., Part II and the Staff Manual respectively. Title pages will be prepared in manuscript.

Hour, Date, Place	Summary of Events and Information	Remarks and references to Appendices
TRENCHES		
24	Carried out and a large amount of wire was put out along the whole front during the night of 24/25 F. The casualties were :- Killed Pte DANIELS. F. (A Company) wounded, Sgt. COOMBES. T. 4/C STRONG. G. L/C INGRAM. F.J. L/C KNEE A.E. PtS CAREY. A. GOWEN. W.H. AND J. L/C KILLICK. W. died of wounds later. There were all of D Company One sniper was also wounded Pte WHITE. F. and one Bomber Pte HUNTLEY. A.	
25	Enemy snipers were more active. There was the usual firing of Stran[?] pound and rifle grenades, to some appearing to be very successful. What were believed to be a kind of rocket grenade was fired on the right company's front. The snipers claimed three of the enemy. Work on the right of the 24/25 F. Consisted chiefly of putting out a considerable amount of wire in front of outpost and reserve lines, and of repairing damage done by hostile mortar fire. In the C/4 Company in order to shield bombing posts a latter wire back screen was	127.

(73989) W4141—463. 400,000. 9/14. H.&J.,Ltd. Forms/C. 2118/10.

WAR DIARY or INTELLIGENCE SUMMARY

Army Form C. 2118.

(Erase heading not required.)

Hour, Date, Place	Summary of Events and Information	Remarks and references to Appendices
TRENCHES	25. Sector A. At about 11 p.m. a considerable number of casualties were caused among ration parties by an accident which occurred at the railway dump. One of the mules struck against an old French aerial torpedo which was lying close to the track. The projectile exploded, and there were many killed and wounded of this Bn. and of the 3rd Wor-cesters Regt. Beyond these casualties two men of the centre company were wounded by a rifle grenade. The casualties were:- Killed. Pte. Renade J. Wounded L/C Irons S. L/C Collier F. Shute T. Pte Wabb G. Cruse S. Gibbs H. King A.T. Love-lock H.C. Cox A. and Drummer Dunne F. Hosp-idal, able at duty:- R.S.M. Parker S.J. Pte. Read J. in the line the night passed very quietly.	
	26. 7m from the [strikethrough] 2 inch trench mortar in the afternoon drew heavy retaliation from the enemy who replied by firing from a heavy trench mortar once in about every two minutes for one and a half hours. Damage was done to the trenches but no casualties were caused	W.P.T.

Army Form C. 2118.

WAR DIARY
or
INTELLIGENCE SUMMARY.
(Erase heading not required.)

Instructions regarding War Diaries and Intelligence Summaries are contained in F.S. Regs., Part II. and the Staff Manual respectively. Title pages will be prepared in manuscript.

Hour, Date, Place	Summary of Events and Information	Remarks and references to Appendices
TRENCHES 26	Beyond this the enemy showed little activity but sniping was far too brisk. 10/16 wiring during the night of the 25/26th. Two flying matters were dropped in common c.T. between the outpost line and retrenchment. The outpost line of the cross companies have half of it in places to put better cover from hostile sniping. On the night of the 26/27th the damage done to ORANGE C.T. by trench mortar fire was repaired, and further was put out in front of the centre and left companies. There were four casualties: Rifles Runciman WOOD C & D Companies. Any thicker traces wounded. Sr ALFORD.? D Company. Pts PIKE M.4. and BURT.E. of B Company. The night passed very quietly. Watson, Jnr. The enemy's attitude had normal. In the evening his usual brigade fire upon the right company was attended by strikes but the sniping was far too brisk while he put each company officers. Between them climate have hit five of the enemy, two of whom were known to be an officer. We succeeded of repairing the damage done by trench	9 T.
27		

Army Form C. 2118.

WAR DIARY
or
INTELLIGENCE SUMMARY.
(Erase heading not required.)

Instructions regarding War Diaries and Intelligence Summaries are contained in F. S. Regs., Part II. and the Staff Manual respectively. Title pages will be prepared in manuscript.

Hour, Date, Place	Summary of Events and Information	Remarks and references to Appendices
TRENCHES	27 Mortars in the centre company and at the top of GRANGE C.T.. The parapet of the attachment in front of D 78 was strengthened and the portion of trench that were known in front of the BIRKIN post was continued. There were two casualties – wounded, Sgt. EVANS E.Q., Cpl. HORSLEY H. of R Company. It was also reported from the 17th. Tunnelling Company, R.E. that Pte. HER-BERT.C. D Company, attached to that company, had been wounded. The night was quiet except further wind and rain storm.	
	28 During the night of the 27/28th. while wiring was in progress there was a considerable amount of enemy machine gun fire which delayed work; no one was hit. There was little sniping on the part of the enemy. Several two Germans were claimed to have been hit in the evening. The top of GRANGE C.T. was damaged by shell and trench mortar fire, and repaired at night. General repairs of the D and support trench were carried out. Their parties were engaged on clearing out the P.S. line	17.T.

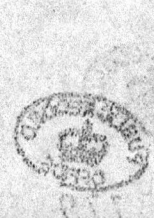

Army Form C. 2118.

WAR DIARY
or
INTELLIGENCE SUMMARY.
(Erase heading not required.)

Instructions regarding War Diaries and Intelligence Summaries are contained in F. S. Regs., Part II. and the Staff Manual respectively. Title pages will be prepared in manuscript.

Hour, Date, Place		Summary of Events and Information	Remarks and references to Appendices
TRENCHES	28 cont.	There were Six casualties :- Wounded Cpl. HICKMAN. H. Ptes. ROBINSON. H. STONE. W. ANNETTS. T. Fighting strength officers 26, other ranks 670. Actual numbers in trenches Off 17	SPT. O.R. 520 men
	29	On the night of the 28/29th. a patrol went out from the right company to within 15 yards of the hostile post on ALBANY CRATER, and threw bombs into it. the same was repeated half an hour later. the enemy replying with oyster shaped bombs at intervals between 5 a.m. and 9 a.m. The enemy fired trench mortar and howitzer shells at the top of GRANGE C.T. and concentrate.da. maze was done. The sniper claimed by Germans. not done. further wiring by night: The RE line on the direction of P.73/74 was continued and deepened: a trench was completed connecting No 2 ALBANY post and the advanced post in the M.P. of water the clearing of the Support line was continued. There were Slight casualties during the day. Wounded Cpl. WALTERS. G. L/Cpls. HARRIS. C. DAVIS. T. GILLETT. H. Ptes. HILLIER. E. LUCAS. W.T.	

WAR DIARY or INTELLIGENCE SUMMARY

Army Form C. 2118.

Hour, Date, Place	Summary of Events and Information	Remarks and references to Appendices
TRENCHES 29 cont	SHEPPARD, C. and MOOHAM, G.	127
30	During the night of the 29/30th a party was sent on to repair the damage done to GRANGE C.T. by shell fire. Little swing could be done in the morning the GRANGE C.T. was again shelled and during the afternoon several rifle grenades were fired into it. Our B.M. of P.75 (& German) was shot twice over sniping was very persistent. Repairs to parapets and parapet wire carried out on the P3 line and posts on the P3 line were continued. The sniping in left centre and Redoubt companies was relieved by the 10th Cheshire Regt. The support company went East to A.C.D., the left company to MONT ST. ELOY, while the centre company moved into the P3 line as Brigade Reserve and worked on this line during the night. The right company remained in the line. The night passed very quietly, there being only one casualty. Pte. NEVILLE P. a B_n Runner wounded. During the 29th and 30th all company HdQrs in	

Army Form C. 2118.

WAR DIARY
or
INTELLIGENCE SUMMARY.
(Erase heading not required.)

Instructions regarding War Diaries and Intelligence Summaries are contained in F.S. Regs., Part II. and the Staff Manual respectively. Title pages will be prepared in manuscript.

Hour, Date, Place		Summary of Events and Information	Remarks and references to Appendices
TRENCHES	30	The two wire companies & Bde. H.Q. in QUARRIES by composite Coy.	S.T.
	31	A fine day. Work of laying of wire L continued. Relief of the right company by the night company. During the night of the 30/31st. much work was done on the R.S. line. In the evening the right company was relieved by a company of the 5th. Seaforths. The company & Bde. reserve moved from the R.S. line and both companies marched back to MONT ST ELOY. R. & Lieut. E. had casualties during the tour were as follows — R. & Lieut. 6. Died of wounds 9. Wounded 63 and wounded still at duty 5. making 2" in all.	S.T.

M.J. Brown 2/Lt Colonel
c/g 12th Middlesex Regt

31/5/16

7th Inf. Bde.

25th Division

1st Battn. WILTSHIRE REGIMENT,

JUNE, 1916.

W.T. 253
1-7-16

1 will

Army Form C. 2118.

WAR DIARY
or
INTELLIGENCE SUMMARY.
(Erase heading not required.)

Instructions regarding War Diaries and Intelligence Summaries are contained in F.S. Regs., Part II. and the Staff Manual respectively. Title pages will be prepared in manuscript.

Hour, Date, Place	Summary of Events and Information	Remarks and references to Appendices
ACQ JUNE 1	On the night of May 31/June 1st three Coy Comdrs fell in the Bn Parade Ground & the O.C. Bn (Lt. Col. Mont. Of Bay), when he was not satisfied, following suggestions as Bn marched into the Divisional training area instructed	PT
CHELERS JUNE 2	The Bn was spent in fitting down to new billets (with the exception of 3 officers & a Sergt. of no. 2 Cheshire Regt. from the 2nd East Hampshire Regt. arrived on duty with Bn Pm	PT
JUNE 3-13 (inclusive)	During this period the training of the Bn. in open war fare tactics was carried out with the exception of Sundays, an average of 9x hours work in the open was maintained on the Divisional training area. to the Mm of CHELERS. On June 3,5 and 6 the training was under Comdrs arrangements: this included bayonet fighting the practice of advance in artillery and deployed formation	

Army Form C. 2148.

WAR DIARY
or
INTELLIGENCE SUMMARY
(Erase heading not required.)

Instructions regarding War Diaries and Intelligence Summaries are contained in F. S. Regs., Part II. and the Staff Manual respectively. Title Pages will be prepared in manuscript.

Place	Date	Hour	Summary of Events and Information	Remarks and references to Appendices
CHEERS	JUNE 8 - 13		On June 7 and 8 this company work was detended to Bn attack practice, special attention being given to artillery formations and extended order. the cooperation of Lewis rifles and bombers was also practised. On June 9 and 10 the whole Brigade practised the capture of the second enemy line after passing through the first, and on the following day the capture of a 3rd & 4th strong points to rear of the 3rd enemy line. On June 12 and 13 a Divisional scheme was practised, - the capture and consolidation of the third enemy line by troops passing through the first and second lines. On the second day the attack was carried out in the presence of General GOUGH. During this period reinforcements to 12 officers and men arrived as follows:— Officers June 3. 2/Lt STRAYSON and 96 P. BALES. June 6. 3/Lt CARLETON, JEFFRIES, SANDS, STOCKBRIDGE, TROUGHTON June 7. 2/Lt CLEGG, HAYWARD, STARKEY. Men June 2 40 2/1 2nd HANTS REGT. June 6 75 OR. June 12 70 OR and June 13 53 OR	

2449 Wt. W14957/M90 750,000 1/16 J.B.C. & A. Forms/C.2118/12.

Place	Date	Hour	Summary of Events and Information	Remarks and references to Appendices
HEBUTERNE	JUNE 3-13		The draft, contrary to previous experience, consisted chiefly of men who had seen service in the country before, and, as a consequence, their physique was of a higher standard. The fighting strength of the Battalion was now raised to Officers 42. Other Ranks 939.	797
PENIN	14		The Battalion received orders to march South, and moved with Brigade at PENIN for the first stage. The daylight-saving scheme came into force at midnight.	797
BARLY	15		From PENIN the Bn. continued it's march at 9 a.m. and arrived at BARLY, 10 M. of DOULLENS, at 3 p.m. Only this new file and so such, and they reported the Bn. late in the day. Divisional orders announced the following award for conspicuous gallantry in the trenches N.E. of MEUVILLE ST MAAST on the 31st of May, and 8th May, when hostile mines were exploded 12 yards of the trench held by "D" Company: — MILITARY CROSS MILITARY MEDAL 2/Lt. SAINSBURY. Sgt. COLLIER F. C.S.M. WOOD J. and L/C STAPLES T. for Annual The half yearly gazette also announces the awards of Distinguished Conduct Medals to good work in the trenches E. of YPRES during the latter half of 1915.	797

Army Form C. 2118.

WAR DIARY
or
INTELLIGENCE SUMMARY
(Erase heading not required.)

Instructions regarding War Diaries and Intelligence Summaries are contained in F. S. Regs., Part II. and the Staff Manual respectively. Title Pages will be prepared in manuscript.

Place	Date	Hour	Summary of Events and Information	Remarks and references to Appendices
BARLY	16		Only company inspections of kit etc were held. A draft of 49 other ranks from the 1st Dorset Regt. arrived for duty with the Bn. This brought the fighting strength of the Bn. to 956 other ranks.	J.T.
	17		In the morning company training was carried out in the wheat orchard of the village. This included bayonet fighting and practising bivouac drill. Rifles dark the battalion marched to GEZAINCOURT arriving 9 a.m.	J.T.
GEZAINCOURT	18		Killed at about 1.30 a.m. on the morning of the 18th. The men worth up the peak part of the day to be a perm on the museum draft were inspected by the Commander 5 Officers at 6 p.m. a voluntary Church Service was held. After dark the battalion marched to HALLOY. LES-PERNOIS arriving in billets at 2.30 a.m. Their most officers joined the battalion for duty. Viz D.F.BROWN, E. BUTLER, H.R. SAUNDERS.	J.T.
PERNOIS	19		There were only short afternoon parades for the companies, bayonet fighting, machine and Lewis gun instruction to Lewis rifle were given.	J.T.
	20		During the morning officers and N.C.O's of all companies were given lessons in fighting in an estaminet from the Army Gymnastic Staff. From 3 p.m. to 5 p.m. Company training was carried out on the Role. Raining as a raid on the village, the advance to contact and subsequent assault were practised. The last hour was devoted to bayonet fighting.	J.T.

2449 Wt. W14957/M90 750,000 1/16 J.B.C. & A. Forms/C.2118/12.

WAR DIARY or INTELLIGENCE SUMMARY

Army Form C. 2118.

Place	Date	Hour	Summary of Events and Information	Remarks and references to Appendices
PERNOIS	27		During this period company and Battalion training was continued. Particular attention was paid to the development of initiative and leadership in the Section commander, and to fire control by the junior N.C.O's. The reference to the assault and the assault itself were practised first by single companies and then by the whole Battalion, and the part played by specialists such as Lewis Gunners, Signallers and Bombers and by carrying and mopping up parties, was also demonstrated. In the meantime a considerable attention was given to bayonet fighting, and the services of a Sergeant Major of the Army Gymnastic Staff were utilised for instructing the officers and N.C.O.s. This instruction was then passed on to the men.	SJT
	28		Very little was done during the day. On the night of the 28/29/6/16 the Battalion marched to PUCHEVILLERS	SJT
PUCHEVILLERS	29, 30		The training of the companies to bayonet fighting and fire control was continued and several route marches were played in order to develop the speed and stillness of the men. On the night of 30th 30th July 1st the Bn marched to MARIEUX in the forward area of impending operations.	SJT

M Brown Lt Colonel
Cdg 1st Wiltshire Regt

30/6/16

7th Bde.
25th Div.

1st BATTALION

THE WILTSHIRE REGIMENT

JULY 1916

WAR DIARY or INTELLIGENCE SUMMARY

Army Form C. 2118.

1st Wiltshire Regt.   VOLUME XII

Place	Date	Hour	Summary of Events and Information	Remarks and references to Appendices
Various	1st Sept 1916	9 a.m.	The day was spent resting after the previous night's preparations being in rest to the coming offensive.	
	2nd		A full kit inspection. Shall Company in battle order was inspected by the G.O.C. Church Parade & Gen. L.S. Grenfell was buried.	
	3rd		At 3.15 p.m. we were ordered to proceed to Kestrelville. At 10 p.m. we were to proceed to our new line on AVELUY Road, to frisk Battn. HQ being in Bouzincourt. The intention was for B Coy on the right & C Coy left to attack with two platoons each up to the Battle H.Q. They were then to push forward through the Bn to the 20 dublin Fusiliers in FULBROOK. At 9 p.m. the Battn. moved off and when the Strat. shell carried chieflyon to the Right Battn Bomben Coy to Karboy (16 in all) (6 platoons required) the D & C Companys moved up from the front line trenches & Captured the ENEMY 1st line at 2 platoons up to 2 platoons back. B Coys were in support in Johnson st. up to Carlyle Av. C.T. Coy were in support. Battn HQ at Camp Hill Post. Att 11 p.m. Manchesters relieve 1st Wilts to Right of Pr. Snow line Regt.	5-5-y
	4th		The men were all in Cledius Right up to Bangor. The D Company extended to fight of the N & relieved the Manchesters. At 6 a.m. the enemy attempted to bomb in to Birchy Trench our right flank. About 12.30 a.m. we ceased the attack. 150 yds of newly dug trench was all that the enemy were in, It has been reported the troops were afar at of our bombs from a front line. It was found that after the attacks could not advance to heavy artillery & machine gun fire. Killed 1. Wounded 11. Capt A Lee.	3-50

WAR DIARY
or
INTELLIGENCE SUMMARY

(Erase heading not required.)

Army Form C. 2118.

Place	Date	Hour	Summary of Events and Information	Remarks and references to Appendices
[illegible] Salem	5/5		Enemy continued shelling heavily after mid-day when were received the [illegible] whilst B was to move up to [illegible] the enemy trench in the Redoubt Salem [illegible] a way to an attack on the enemy position which very strongly held [illegible] to [illegible] for [illegible] a Redoubt. Early in the attack we advanced to [illegible] outskirts of [illegible] and here were some 200 yards [illegible] to [illegible] the actual advanced trench of [illegible] changed to 300 yards. [illegible] advance was made to the [illegible] our Camp advance. [illegible] to be accompanied by [illegible] on left an Coy on right. B Coy [illegible] of the [illegible] company [illegible] the attack was being carried out in the following [illegible]. [illegible] A Coy [illegible] 3 platoons, 1 platoon in support. Two platoons A B Coy were occupied in the out-skirts attacking company. Two platoons of [illegible] Company on [illegible] [illegible] [illegible] B were in support. The attack was to the [illegible] to the [illegible] of the [illegible] had afterwards changed to 7 p.m. [illegible] 1/2 an hour The [illegible] whose artillery bombardment has to be [illegible] 6 officers attacked, made [illegible] [illegible] [illegible] at 7 p.m. our 1st [illegible] advanced [illegible] Capt R. Linley [illegible] [illegible] on the [illegible] [illegible] Capt D Carpentier left with R. [illegible] on the left [illegible] Company. [illegible] Right way Capt R B [illegible] [illegible] [illegible] advance then objective [illegible] [illegible] what her [illegible] [illegible] [illegible] the left. [illegible] [illegible] by [illegible] [illegible] for hidden [illegible] [illegible] [illegible] [illegible] [illegible] [illegible] the objective here his officer [illegible] [illegible] to [illegible] [illegible] immediately [illegible] second [illegible] a very [illegible] Company attack [illegible] of [illegible] [illegible] Company coming to [illegible] [illegible] platoon [illegible] [illegible] [illegible] [illegible] [illegible] first back it an [illegible] of about 30 to 40 yards.	550

Army Form C. 2118.

WAR DIARY or INTELLIGENCE SUMMARY

Place	Date	Hour	Summary of Events and Information	Remarks and references to Appendices
Leipzig Salient	5th (ctd)		C Coy on the right, were followed by the enemy bombing parties up the trench. They were driven back towards Grenade Alley(?) but the bombers' bombs ran out and they had to retire. All the Company officers having been casualties and many men killed, Lieut. Brown caught up some bombs in a blanket & rushed up the trench to Grenade Alley where he met two blocks already erected by the enemy. He attacked them but was driven back. Pte Caton(?) threw Jacob's ladders across these blocks & Lieut. Brown made a fresh attack & succeeded in taking the first block. A bombing officer came up & assisted him to attack the second block which he captured & consolidated. (All the officers of his party were wounded). Lt. Hollwart, 2/Lt Troughton, 2/Lt Stokey, Lt. Penny & the attacking company were all hit by this time. Abbey(?) Miller, shiftly(?) after this, on their way back from the German trenches, found some Coy HQ officers wounded, and carried any(?) they could. Captain(?) A.E.J. Collins(?) of B Coy had been killed. 2/Lt Ridyard was killed, Captain A.W. Stokes returned in command. B Coy on the left, followed by D Coy attacking dugouts killed Coy R.W.? Holmes Capt R.L. Buckley Lieut. Glieu(?). After the attack formed up with Captain R. ? Ball had arrived at a dugout killed Capt S.G. Byles & Lieut Shapland(?) had been taken to B team Shelter ? we found the B team shelter full of wounded. Pte men Killed 20, Missing 22, Wounded 158. Other ranks killed 20, Missing 22, Wounded 158. After the attack, Missing (where killed 2).	S.S.O.

Army Form C. 2118.

WAR DIARY or INTELLIGENCE SUMMARY

(Erase heading not required.)

Place	Date	Hour	Summary of Events and Information	Remarks and references to Appendices
Map 3/9 Sailly	1/7	[illegible]	On the advance being [illegible] the captured trench communication was now opened up to C.T. with A Company. Who were holding the line behind C. [illegible] Company here refused about 5 a.m. & went back to T. [illegible] Street, relieved the at 7.30 a.m. by no Company the captured trench. 3rd Worcestershire Regiment took their place in Wood. Casualties (were roughly) as follows:— Carries out the 1st attack Lt. Sandys. [illegible] attn. Lt. Pennycoke. Killed — Colonel Brown, Capt [illegible] Kate [illegible] 2/Lt. Starker. Wounded [illegible] Lt. Holman Capt Taylor JR [illegible] Throughout the day the enemy carried on intermittent bombing kept Rifle Grenades, Shelling was continued. [illegible] attack at [illegible] Map 3/9 Not the same intense bombing, brought up [illegible] to the [illegible] Saillet. C & D Companies here as a [illegible] replied on the night [illegible] on the evening C & D taking up from the Coy in the line. A Company were placed in Reserve taking up 5th July. A Company [illegible] B Company the 3rd [illegible] Regt [illegible] 2 companies of the British Fusiliers relieved. 4 Companies to Reserve in 3rd [illegible] Support the line. [illegible] attack another [illegible] morning lifted to N.C.R. [illegible] attack. About 6 a.m. on the Regiment to the [illegible] but, the enemy attacked by D Company on the Repton Regiment. While the [illegible] [illegible] Hostile Counter attack was beat off. The Regiment held a very violent Counter attacks [illegible] the trench captured by C Company in commenced about	[illegible]
4/5 7/7	12.15 a.m.			

WAR DIARY
or
INTELLIGENCE SUMMARY

Army Form C. 2118.

Place	Date	Hour	Summary of Events and Information	Remarks and references to Appendices
[illegible]	7th	1.15 am	Enemy attempts to shell trenches from the [illegible] but light flares likely broke down the enemy [illegible] but the first six [illegible] were turned back [illegible] which [illegible] further [illegible] the enemy [illegible] to [illegible] officer into [illegible] found [illegible] [illegible] [illegible] the attack [illegible] [illegible] [illegible] to our [illegible] [illegible] [illegible] [illegible] [illegible] casualties [illegible] 5.30 am. Company from [illegible] attempted to [illegible] the attack on the left were [illegible] to [illegible] [illegible] the operation were [illegible] observation [illegible] [illegible] by [illegible] [illegible] to make the assault [illegible] 9 [illegible] the attack was [illegible] in 2 [illegible] each consisting of 3 platoons [illegible] [illegible] [illegible] platoons [illegible] in reserve. At 9.30 am the [illegible] [illegible] 30 [illegible] [illegible] and [illegible] [illegible] [illegible] 30 [illegible] [illegible] advanced [illegible] and [illegible] [illegible] captured the objective by surprise [illegible] [illegible] [illegible] enemy did not seem to have [illegible] [illegible] [illegible] [illegible] as [illegible] of our men [illegible] [illegible] [illegible] [illegible] [illegible] [illegible] had been placed in [illegible] [illegible] [illegible] [illegible] on [illegible] [illegible] which has [illegible] 9 [illegible] [illegible] 30 [illegible] [illegible] [illegible] to [illegible] [illegible] attack by [illegible] [illegible] in our [illegible] [illegible] [illegible] [illegible] the [illegible] [illegible] of the [illegible] [illegible] the enemy machine gun [illegible] during our advance, [illegible] the [illegible] killed [illegible] [illegible] 2 Offrs. 9 [illegible] Class 9 [illegible] wounded [illegible] left 7 L Class 9 [illegible] [illegible] [illegible] close to [illegible] of [illegible] [illegible] [illegible] [illegible]	

WAR DIARY or INTELLIGENCE SUMMARY

Place	Date	Hour	Summary of Events and Information	Remarks and references to Appendices
[illegible]	7th	1 pm	[Handwritten entry largely illegible due to faded handwriting] ... the attack ... taken ... Germans ... machine guns and 23 were ... tanks ... fifteen tanks would ... I accepted ... could disable but being too long ... attacked very little over ... to increase ... another from the left flank ... No great difficulty was experienced until about 3.30 p.m. when the enemy opened a terrific bombardment with high explosive ... our ... for retaliation ... support of the British ... design faltered and ... the enemy captured trenches & a ... at ... dropped bombs to about 5 Runner posts ... ... advance about 180 ... two comp of the 3rd Bn. were to support ... had been guiding parties ... Cavalry patrols were sent ... and near the two officers ... Capt R & Rouille ... 2 Lt Clegg ... Such an stiff ... was also ... down to ... chief objection ... was ... Pvt ... Shillin ... the Germans also ... but ... A+B Coys & our ... Lt A.H.B. Morris Rees ... officers and killed ... Carthalthen, and Dr L Capt R C Buller ... 2 Lt S.J Teny (A Coy) would ... Regt ... 2 Pethr wounded ... & attached ... about ... ... wounded. (See Appendix) 2 Lt Mitchell [?] passed ... the Regt. ... ... L. Capt Davis & 3/Lt Mitchell went into dugouts of Chester Cross.	
[illegible]	8th	2 a.m.	At 2 a.m. orders were received from Bn. to move to Mr. Corner & Archer Woods by 7 a.m.	8/12/11

WAR DIARY
or
INTELLIGENCE SUMMARY

(Erase heading not required.)

Army Form C. 2118.

Place	Date	Hour	Summary of Events and Information	Remarks and references to Appendices
Avelay Wood	8th	7 a.m.	Lieut. G. Robb has taken over the Battn. whilst the Bn. is resting. In the C.O. Capt. J Blair. In the afternoon proceeded to Kinville to take over. Lieut Col F.S.H.Bn. B. receiving instructions to move to Kinville.	H.L.Q.H.
	9th		12th Sept the Bn. marched with 7 Bn. to Kinville on war office. Battn spent the day resting. C. Coy went through its Battle Organisation & Coy fighting strength - about 300.	H.L.Q.H.
Kinville	10th		a 32 b 61 c 45 d 66	
		4.20 pm	Honing Rifle Inspection Inspection. Post intention of Physical Drill & Bn. while Bn. had still into fatigue & carrying parties were absent. The others were working for 13 hours.	H.L.Q.H.
		5.30 A.M.		
Roch. Ell	11th		Day was spent resting - Parades consisted of Physical Exercises and French course of instruction to see there was a shell free there.	
	12th		The Bns. found carrying parties of men unloading ammunition &c. Railway.	
	13th		The Bn. moved into support to 5th Brigade in de Bocelle where they occupied old German dugouts. There was some shelling in	SSS

Army Form C. 2118.

WAR DIARY
or
INTELLIGENCE SUMMARY
(Erase heading not required.)

Instructions regarding War Diaries and Intelligence Summaries are contained in F. S. Regs., Part II. and the Staff Manual respectively. Title Pages will be prepared in manuscript.

Place	Date	Hour	Summary of Events and Information	Remarks and references to Appendices
LA Boisselle	14		The Bn. remained in LA Boisselle and carried on the 3rd line trenches in Rgt. Major J. Stevenson Ryan finishing came to take over command. In the afternoon the Bn. was relieved wholly by a Hampshire Bn. of the 74th Brigade, and marched to the Lake just east of St Albert - where the men bivouaced.	S.S.V.
Albert	15		The day was spent in minute inspections. The Bn. moved off at 9.30 p.m. and marched to Forceville - where it spent the night in Billets.	S.S.V.
Forceville	16		The day was spent resting. Lt Col. A. Richardson came to take over command - Major Stevenson Ryan rejoining 2nd Bn. R.F.	S.S.V.
"	17			S.S.V.
	18		The Bn. marched off at 7.20 am to Baouval - the weather was very hot - but the march was very good. No one fell out.	S.S.V.

WAR DIARY or INTELLIGENCE SUMMARY

Army Form C. 2118.

Place	Date	Hour	Summary of Events and Information	Remarks and references to Appendices
Beauval	19.		Battalion spent the day resting. Nothing of importance occurred.	Appx.
"	20.		The Bn. marched at 2 p.m. to BOIS-du-WARNIMONT where they remained in huts.	Appx.
Bois-du-WARNIMONT	21		Battalion remained in the woods. The day was spent training. O working party was sent off to ENGLEBELMER WOOD (100 men and 8 NCOs under Lt. D.T. Brown and 2/Lt. Butler). at 7.30 a.m. Col. Richardson went to command 5/th S. Lancs. Regt. Capt. Gifford took command.	Appx.
"	22.		Battalion still at Bois-du-WARNIMONT. Capt. Gifford went to take with the other Commanding officers in Brigade. Nothing was spent in training. 2/Lt. Readshaw joined Battalion woods in the evening.	Appx.
			4th Bn. from 20. H. Russots having obtained his commission from these regiments. Bn. moved to Pt. Venechin East of HAMEL at 10.30 a.m. and relieved the 2/Royal Fusiliers. Trenches were very quiet. Capt. Russell was Officer of the strength of the Bn.	Appx.
TRENCHES (HAMEL)	23rd		having been transferred to England from Hospital.	Appx.
"	24th		Lt. O.T. Adam proceeded to R.F.C. to be trained. Situation in trenches very quiet. One man was wounded. Draft of 32 O.R. joined Bn. in the trenches.	Appx.
"	25th		Major Freeman of 3rd Cheshire Regiment was attached to Bn. for course of duty in the Trenches. Situation very quiet with exception of a few trench mortars & front line Reserve Companies went up to front line in the evening and put out wire in front of Mens.	Appx.

Army Form C. 2118.

WAR DIARY
or
INTELLIGENCE SUMMARY
(Erase heading not required.)

Instructions regarding War Diaries and Intelligence Summaries are contained in F.S. Regs., Part II. and the Staff Manual respectively. Title Pages will be prepared in manuscript.

Place	Date	Hour	Summary of Events and Information	Remarks and references to Appendices
Tranchée (Hamel)	25th		Front Line Bequeath new front line and connected new line with new support line with Sap 8.	
"	26th:		Lt. Adams was struck off strength of Bn. having proceeded to England to undergo a course necessary to obtain a pilot certificate with R.F.C. The Germans had ranged perfectly on shells into around Bn. H.Q. Several incendiary shells were sent into MESNIL. The casualties caused by these for twenty four twenty, work was continued as in previous night. Patrols were sent out during night and patrols from Durvin met patrols as in previous night. The Day was quiet, the enemy shelled top O.P. trench line with French mortars in the evening. Work was carried on as before as previous night. Patrols were sent out on the right and left front flanks of the right Coy: in the night, there was wire cut away to the front of Prisoners to right.	
"	28th		Situation was very quiet. Few prisoners during the night were unsuccessful in getting to a convoy of transport in French Station road. Bournemouth returned to Beaucourt. 1 man was killed and 9 men wounded.	

S.S. Ogilvie Lt Col
Commanding 1st W Yorks Regt
2.9.7.16

7th Brigade.
25th Division.

1st BATTALION

WILTSHIRE REGIMENT

AUGUST 1 9 1 6

Attached :- Reports on Operations 21st & 24/25th

WAR DIARY or INTELLIGENCE SUMMARY

1 Wilts
Vol 25

Place	Date	Hour	Summary of Events and Information	Remarks and references to Appendices
MAILLY WOOD	29/7/16		The Battalion was relieved in the trenches by the 2. N. Lancs Regt. Bn: arrived at Hubbound at about 7 p.m. The day was very quiet in the trenches. A few s'g shells fell around MESNIL during the relief. 50 men were attached to H: 2522 Tunnelly coy: for duty.	
	30/7/16		The day was spent in rest. Baths were allotted to Companies throughout the day. Major Heseman, attached for instruction, left the Bn: for England. The Bn: carried on with training throughout the day. One officer, 2/Lt Watson and 5 N.C.O's left the Bn: for the Divisional Recruiting School at BERTRANCOURT. Fatigue party returned to Battalion from BEAUX EQUIS.	
	31/7/16		Training was carried on during the day. Baggage fatigues furnished, shooting at Rangs etc: 2/Lt D.J. Brown left Bn: for 4th Army Trench mortar School at VAUXHEUREUX. 2/Lt Griffiths left and 1 N.C.O left Bn: for Div: anti-gas school at BERTRANCOURT.	
	1st August		The usual Training was carried on and in addition companies furnished attacks. 50 men of D Coy relieved their men of C Coy who were attached to Tunnell: coy:on and 24 men of C Coy under 2/Lt Butler relieved men acting as escort to German Prisoners at BEAUX EQUIRE. The Commanding Officer and 2 Coy: Commanders reconnoitred	
	2nd		the position the Bn: would take over in case of an enemy attack.	

WAR DIARY
or
INTELLIGENCE SUMMARY
(Erase heading not required.)

Instructions regarding War Diaries and Intelligence Summaries are contained in F. S. Regs., Part II. and the Staff Manual respectively. Title Pages will be prepared in manuscript.

Place	Date	Hour	Summary of Events and Information	Remarks and references to Appendices
MAILLY WOOD	3.8.16		Bn. spent day training. A new training ground was used to test the methods that have been encountered. 2/Lt SHERWOOD left Bn. for the Div Bombing School at BERTRANCOURT. 5 NCOs also proceeded to Bombing school. One man left Bn. for Lewis Gun course at ETAPLES. 2/Lt BUTLER and 29 men of C company returned Bn. from BELLE EGLISE.	
"	4.8.16		The Bn. spent the day training. The weather was very hot and fires broke out of importance everywhere. Battn. was attached to Battalion at METHOD.	
"	5.8.16		Bn spent 2 hours of the day training, and rested for the remaining hours. The General of the 11th ESSEX Regiment visited Colonel Ogilvie. [illegible] and [illegible] [illegible] [illegible] the GREEN LINE (position to hold in case of attack by enemy). The Battalion was relieved by the 11th ESSEX regiment at about 10. a.m. and proceeded by companies to BOIS ESS - ARTOIS. There was a church parade at 5.30 p.m. in the afternoon.	
BUS-en-ARTOIS	7.8.16		The Bn spent the day training. The regimental Chaplain rejoined the Battalion. There was a regimental football match held in the evening against the R.A.M.C. attached to the Guards Divn. The result was 4 goals to nil in the Battalion favour.	

2449 Wt. W14957/M90 750,000 1/16 J.B.C. & A. Forms/C.2118/12.

WAR DIARY
or
INTELLIGENCE SUMMARY

(Erase heading not required.)

Instructions regarding War Diaries and Intelligence Summaries are contained in F.S. Regs., Part II. and the Staff Manual respectively. Title Pages will be prepared in manuscript.

Place	Date	Hour	Summary of Events and Information	Remarks and references to Appendices
Bois les Côlois	8th August		The Battalion spent the day training. The weather was very hot. Nothing of importance occurred.	
"	9.		Four hundred men left camp at 5.25 am for fatigue, filling in ENGLEBEMER. The remainder of the Battalion trained.	
"	10.		Drilled by a drill instructor from the Guards. The Commanding officers and other officers left in camp attended an exhibition in bombing attacks at D.H.Q. Three hundred men left camp at 6.25 am for fatigue, filling in ENGLEBEMER. The signal training was carried on during the day. There was a demonstration in the cooperation of Stokes Mortars, Mills Rifle Grenades and Smoke bombs by 3rd GUARDS BDE, near BEAUCQUESNE which was attended by the C.O and Bombing Officer.	
"	11.		The Battalion moved to SARTON at 11.0 am. Route. BUS les ARTOIS, LOUVENCOURT VAUCHELLES and SARTON. 500 men were again required for similar fatigue as on 9th & 10th insts. There was inspection of the men kit on arrival at SARTON. The C.O. inspected all officers in the afternoon.	
SARTON	12.		His Majesty the King passed through village of SARTON at about 11.0 am. The Battalion lined the main street extremes and cheered as His Majesty passed to the	

INTELLIGENCE SUMMARY

(Erase heading not required.)

Instructions regarding War Diaries and Intelligence Summaries are contained in F.S. Regs., Part II. and the Staff Manual respectively. Title Pages will be prepared in manuscript.

Place	Date	Hour	Summary of Events and Information	Remarks and references to Appendices
SARTON	12th		Water cart. The usual training was carried out after this. The fatigue party returned from Bus-lès-ARTOIS.	
SARTON	13th		The usual training was carried on. There was a voluntary church service at 9 a.m. In the afternoon there was a Bn route march held by Capt Ravenscroft. The route was SARTON - THIÈVRES - ORVILLE - SARTON.	
	14th		The Bn spent the day Coy, Platoon, Section, Squad, Company drill &c. Nothing occurred of importance. Capt Hammond & 2/Lt Rudd proceeded to England on special leave.	
	15th		The Bn moved to PUCHEVILLERS by companies at 8 minute intervals. 1st Coy moved at 6 a.m. The last Company arrived at the lines at PUCHEVILLERS at about 8.30 a.m. Later in the day there was a foot inspection by companies.	
PUCHEVILLERS	16		The Battalion spent the day training, two Coys training in the camp, bombing, wiring &c, and two coys on the MARIEUX road doing coy training. J Macklin proceeded to England on special leave. The Bn trained in the evening. In the evening at 6 p.m. the Bn moved to HÉDAUVILLE by companies moving at 5 minutes interval. The Route was TOUTENCOURT - HARPONVILLE - VARENNES - HÉDAUVILLE. The Bn arrived in their billets at about 10. p.m.	
HÉDAUVILLE	18		The Battalion took over a portion of the line at ILLAPEIS SALIENT. An advance party of 100 men (9th Huss Btlg) of 7.30 am The Remainder of the Battalion proceeded to the trenches by companies at 5 min interval, the relief being first Coy starting	

INTELLIGENCE SUMMARY

(Erase heading not required.)

Instructions regarding War Diaries and Intelligence Summaries are contained in F.S. Regs., Part II. and the Staff Manual respectively. Title Pages will be prepared in manuscript.

Place	Date	Hour	Summary of Events and Information	Remarks and references to Appendices
HÉDAUVILLE	18th		at 7.45 a.m. the last company arrived. The trench about midway on the left of our front line was quiet on the whole. The enemy shelled French positions on our left of front line.	
THIEPVAL LEIPZIG SALIENT.	19th		The day was fairly quiet. The enemy shelled our front line intermittently throughout the day. 2/Lt Birtwell with 5 NCOs left the trenches for a Bombing course. There trench held by the Bn near the same as those held at the beginning of July. A & C Companies were in the front line, A on the left and C on the right. D Company was in support to C. B Company were in reserve in OBAN AVENUE behind Bn HQ.	
"	20th		The day was moderately quiet on the whole. The enemy shelled front line and around Bn H.Q. every now and then. The weather was fine and clear.	
"	21st		Nothing of importance happened in this day. The enemy used trench mortars on our front line. Our artillery bombarded the enemy trenches during the afternoon. In the evening the enemy sent some lachrymatory shells over Battalion Head Quarters and on our front line. Often were warned for trench to attack.	
"	22nd		Our artillery was active all day. B Company was warned up from OBAN AVENUE to NOMAN'S ALLEY. The attack was made at [illegible] past 6 p.m.	

INTELLIGENCE SUMMARY

(Erase heading not required.)

Place	Date	Hour	Summary of Events and Information	Remarks and references to Appendices
LEIPZIG SALIENT	22nd		The objective was the line from (R.21.c.10.63) – (R.21.c.9.0.) The attack was to be by C Coy on the left and D Coy on the right, the two companies were together with the GLOUCESTER Regiment (4th) on the right. The British guns were putting a very heavy barrage on our objective, our own very nearly reached our barrage when it lifted eastwards. The objective was found. A block was established about 50 yards up the tunnel from R.20.9.0 – R.20.D.2.6 and duly consolidated. The enemy shelled our trenches throughout the night. Lewis guns & casualties amounted to roughly 90. Our front and support trenches were shelled at intervals during the day. Lt STRAWSON was wounded in the arm in the morning, 2/Lt WITHINSON was wounded in the eye. Our guns bombarded the enemy trenches during the day and the following night.	
"	23rd		The following operation order was received in the early morning. "The Bn with the 2nd WORCESTER regt on our right will [?] and consolidate the line R.21.c.40.65, SE-78 & R.21.D.07, 26,35,64 & 65.30." In preparation	
"	24th		Two companies of the L N Lancs Regt were placed at the disposal of this Bn. These coys were used mostly for carrying ammunition &c up to the front line throughout the operation.	

INTELLIGENCE SUMMARY

(Erase heading not required.)

Place	Date	Hour	Summary of Events and Information	Remarks and references to Appendices
LEIPZIG SALIENT.	24th		The attack commenced in proper. An intense artillery bombardment was put on the line R.31.c.40.65 - R.31.D.80.25 and the enemy's defences in an area N.of the line at 4.10 p.m. Martelmann The 7th & 75th Bde STOKES mortars bombarded the area R.31.C.40.65,55. 67,66, 40.55 and also point 76. at 4.10 p.m. In this Bn. the attack was carried out by A Coy: on left, B Coy in the centre and D Coy on the right. C Company was in support. A&D Companies assaulted at 4.12 p.m. the artillery barrage lifted Northwards and cleared the line R.31.D.65.30, 64, 35, 26, 07; R.31.C.97, 76, 55, 40.65. At 4.15 p.m. Progress on the 4 hour left was slow, but on the right the position was gained and consolidation started immediately. Casualties were heavy, amounting to about 320. St officers were lost, 5/Lt BUTLER being killed. 5/Lt GILBERT, wounded, however, was slight and he carried on. The Commanding Officer Lt-Col. SS GYLBEE, was hit by a bomb on the leg, his wound, however, was slight and he carried on.	
"	25th		Shelling continued on both sides. The consolidation of our trenches was completed.	

Place	Date	Hour	Summary of Events and Information	Remarks and references to Appendices
LEIPZIG (SALIENT)	25th		The 2 Coys of 8th Loyal North Lancashire Regiment in our alignment relieved two of our companies which returned into bde held the 2nd line. It was decided not to attack at the alignment left of 8th in front line. It was decided not to persist in the 24 hr. Leipzig Salient with a counter attack without troops, and owing to the shortage put any fresh troops who were unable to had attention paid to them. The remaining two companies of the 8 K.N. Lancs relieved the two other two	Lt-Colonel Dawson 1st Bn Wiltshire Regt.
"	26th		of our Regiment battalion at about 7 a.m. The Battalion spent the day in the Bluff as they were relieved, fresh men were sent for the Bn to march back to HEBUTERNE & working parties. The last of the Bn arrived at HEBUTERNE at 1:30 p.m. The remainder of the day was spent resting.	
HEBUTERNE	27th		Baths were allotted to the Bn at HEBUTERNE and HETTE UX. These were for inspection in the afternoon.	
"	28th		The Corps Commander inspected the Brigade at 10 a.m. at HEBUTERNE and thanked the officers and men for the work they had done in the recent operations. The Bn moved to BOUZINCOURT, after starting by Scotch Express marched, and reached BOUZINCOURT about 11:30 a.m. The Bn were encamped in huts, the officers in billets.	

INTELLIGENCE SUMMARY

(Erase heading not required.)

Place	Date	Hour	Summary of Events and Information	Remarks and references to Appendices
HEADQUARTERS BOUZINCOURT	29th August		The Bn started the day by training. At 10.30 am a message came from the Brigade ordering the commanding officer to proceed to 75th Bde H.Q. at Riegsy Valley. The Bn had to stand by ready to move off at a moment's notice. During the afternoon a message arrived which cancelled the orders of the former message. An official photographer arrived but owing to the dull weather condition failed to take pictures. The commanding officer returned from 75th Bde H.Q. after receiving orders with reference to the Bn with the operation arrangement requested to assist the 75th Bde in their operation ordered to start at dawn on August 31st. The Bn was to proceed to ENGELBELMER & the following morning.	
"	30th "		Preparations with regard to the attack to be launched tomorrow continued. In the afternoon however news came in that the Bn was to hold fast from to Division and stating that it was hoped that the Bn would not move that day. Owing to the fact a message arrived that the weather operations had been postponed for at least 24 hours further & at dawn. The rain proved very further parades.	

Report on Operations
undertaken by 1st Bn The Wiltshire Regt
on the 21st July 1916.

On the 20th July I had received
oral instructions that my Bn
would make an attack in conjunction
with the 143rd Brigade on the South.
All preparations in the nature of
dumps - bombs and stores were
made - and trench steps were
procured. At about midday on
the 21st July I received orders
in writing to capture trench
R.31 c 63 - 90 X1 A 79 - 68.
and to push bombing parties
along trenches R 31 c 90, X1 B 19
and along X1 A 79 - 98. to
join hands with the 4th Gloucesters
attacking from the south.
C and D Companies were
selected to do the attack. C Coy
received orders to assault across
the open from trench "Cat" Street
while D Coy. was to bomb from
point 68 and get into touch
with C Coy on its left and
with the 4th Gloucesters in front.

A Flame Thrower had been put at my disposal and I had decided to utilise it at the K Sap to play down the trench leading to point R 31 c 90. This was duly installed but orders were received later that the Flame Thrower should not be used.

I had also under my command a Hydraulic Push-pipe under the charge of Lt Matheson R.E. This was employed at Sap L [about X1 A 6 8] with the object of boring under the German block and blowing it up. Zero was at 6·0 pm - and at 5·59 pm C. Coy left their trench - formed up in the open. At 6.0pm plus 45 seconds the Push-pipe was exploded with complete success - blowing up the enemies block and forming a ready made communication trench almost as far as X1A 79.

At 6·0 pm + 1 minute was the hour ordered for the assault by my Regiment.

The attack was made in two waves by C. Coy at about

30 yards apart. The waves went
forward right under our barrage
and had even to be stopped mom-
entarily to allow the barrage to
lift. The men were into the trench
with hardly a casualty.
At the same time D Coy on the
right rushed down the trench
formed by the explosion from the
Push-pipe, and almost immediately got into touch with both
B. Coy and the 4th Gloucesters.
Clearing up parties (detailed beforehand) bombed such dugouts as had
not been blown in by our Heavy
Artillery. Owing to the speed of
the assaulting troops and the
surprise effected by the Push-pipe
there was practically no opposition
Some Germans were killed in
their dugouts and a few were
bayonetted. Several prisoners were
taken but it was impossible to
ascertain the exact number as they
became mixed with those taken
by the 4th Gloucesters.
Some rifle and machine gun

was opened on the assaulting troops from the line R31c76 to R31d.26. but was quickly silenced by our Lewis Guns. An enemy machine gun is believed to have been put out of action here.

The Regimental Snipers were posted in advantageous positions from which they could cover the assault. They claim six hostile snipers.

The fire of our Artillery was most accurate and destructive and many Germans were found dead in their trenches - killed by shell-fire.

The co-operation of the Stokes Mortars under Captain Harrison D.S.O. was again most valuable.

The success of the operations was largely due to the care and forethought of 2nd Lt. A.D. Brown commanding C Coy and his Coy. Sergt. Major G. Filor.

Consolidation and wiring was proceeded with as quickly as possible. The enemy remained very inactive save for some

machine gun fire.
Casualties were very slight being 1 Officer 2nd Lt E. H. Butler wounded and about 33 OR killed and wounded

Sholto S. Ogilvie Lt Col
Commdg 1st Bn. The Wiltshire
Regt.

22/8/16.

No of prisoners taken and passed through Brigade HQ was about 40 others were sent direct to Corps Collecting Station

1st Wilts

Report on Operation 24/25

Report on Operations
by 1st Bn The Wiltshire Regiment
on the 24th & 25th ~~July~~ August 1916

On the 23rd ~~May~~ August I received
oral instructions that the Regt
should be prepared to assault
and capture the German trenches
R.31.C. 45 - 76 - 97 - 07 - 26 -.
~~as~~ All preparations were accord-
-ingly made and supplies of
Bombs and SAA ~~&~~ were procured
and forward dumps of R.E.
material ~~&~~ were made. On the
night of 23/24 August orders
in writing were received confirm-
-ing the previous oral instructions.
~~The~~ Two companies of the 8th
Loyal North Lancs were put
at my disposal for the attack.
~~From the disposition of the troop~~
Later the same night orders were
received postponing the attack.
~~The attack was~~
The date of the attack was
finally fixed for the 25th August
zero being at 4.10 pm.
The disposition of the troops
was as follows: A Coy on the

and ½ of D Coy in the centre and B Coy on the Right. The remaining two platoons of B Coy formed the carrying parties for D and B Coys, and a platoon of C. Coy was sent to C. A Coy to assist in carrying as the latter Coy. had already suffered heavy casualties. The three remaining platoons of C. Coy were held in reserve in Bow Street. The two Companies of the HLI were used to garrison the line.
The attack was somewhat complicated by the fact that B & D Companies were making an attack from trench to trench while R Company was bombing up trenches on the left flank. The distance to be covered was about 300 yards and the troops received orders to advance under the barrage of our guns.
2nd Lt Mackenzie RE superintended two pipe-forcing jacks which had been put at my disposal for the purpose of blowing up the blocks in the two enemy trenches on the left flank. Owing to the fact that one of these had been from already exploded

They were not placed at this [?] proved to be the last of my [?] Report - there in by the [?]

by a shell, sticks of ammonal had had to be laid near the blocks under cover of darkness the previous night.

B & D Companies received orders to assault in two waves at 30 yards distant while A Company's attack was assisted by a small detachment assaulting P point R31c5.8 & across the open from R31c5.4.

The hostile trenches were bombarded during the day and at 4.10 pm an intense fire was opened on the objective and gradually lifting so as to clear the trenches by 4.15 pm.

At 4.10 pm B & D Coys left their own trenches and advanced 150 yards to a line of pistol tins previously put out to mark where the men should form up for the assault.

At 4.12 pm the jacks were exploded and R Company advanced down their enemy trenches.

At 4.14 pm B & D Companies assaulted from the line of Pistol Tins, and at 4.15 pm reached and captured the enemies trench. The trench held a considerable number of enemy who showed fight and some trench fighting ensued. The enemy in the trench were killed or made prisoners while those who tried to leave the trench and return to their lines in rear were all shot. Touch was almost immediately got with the 8th Worcestershire Regt on the right and A Coy on the left. The carrying parties pushed up H Sap from point 63 and kept the front line supplied with all that they required.

On the left. A Coy experienced great difficulty from the outset. The enemy concentrated immediately an intense fire on their bombers causing heavy casualties. They were however successful in their attack on the trench leading up the old road to R 31 c 7.6. In the trench however on the extreme left leading to R 31 c 4.8. They met with resistance from the beginning — and failed to progress further than about 50 yards. I ascribe this lack of complete success to the two following causes.

(i) The heavy casualties caused by the hostile shelling just prior

to the attack. (The officers and several
N.C.O.s became casualties at this
time).

(ii) The pipe-pushing jacks
were exploded too soon – so that the
assaulting troops had to proceed slowly
down the trench in order to avoid
running into our own barrage – instead
of taking the objective at a rush.
The explosion of these jacks has
the effect of a small mine and
at once brings every one of
the enemy from his dug-out –
so that it becomes absolutely vital
to rush the trench immediately
after the explosion with the
greatest possible speed.
Heavy bombing went on all day
in this left sector
with varying fortune – but only
slight progress could be made.
Consolidation of the trenches gained
was proceeded with without
speed.

That night passed quietly but
the next day the whole of the
Leipzig Salient was shelled
with the utmost persistency

and from about 2.30 p.m. with great intensity.

At 6 p.m. I had ordered a further attack upon the extreme left but this could not be carried out owing to the terrific barrage on the trenches. It is my firm conviction that the enemy were contemplating a very serious counter-attack at about 6 p.m. that day and that it was only frustrated by the very heavy intense fire of our artillery at this time. The speed with which the heavy artillery action was due to the use of pigeons carrying the message at the required hour.

The conduct of all ranks was beyond praise throughout. They had had but little sleep or rest for over five days an had already made one attack. Captain J. Deane-Drummond R.H.G. in charge of a Machine Gun Squadron rendered me invaluable assista

[margin note:] I do not think anyone wants to know in the slightest, be all that from the 20th as to the messages by the pigeon from the vredom form.

throughout - taking charge of parties which had lost their officers and N.C.O's - organising bombing and blocking of trenches and in every way helping by his fine example and leadership.

Certain points have now arisen with reference to bombing and the clearing of dugouts which I am making the subject of a separate Report.

Sholto S. Ogilvie
Lt R.S.

Commdg 1st Bn The Wiltshire Regt.

26/8/16

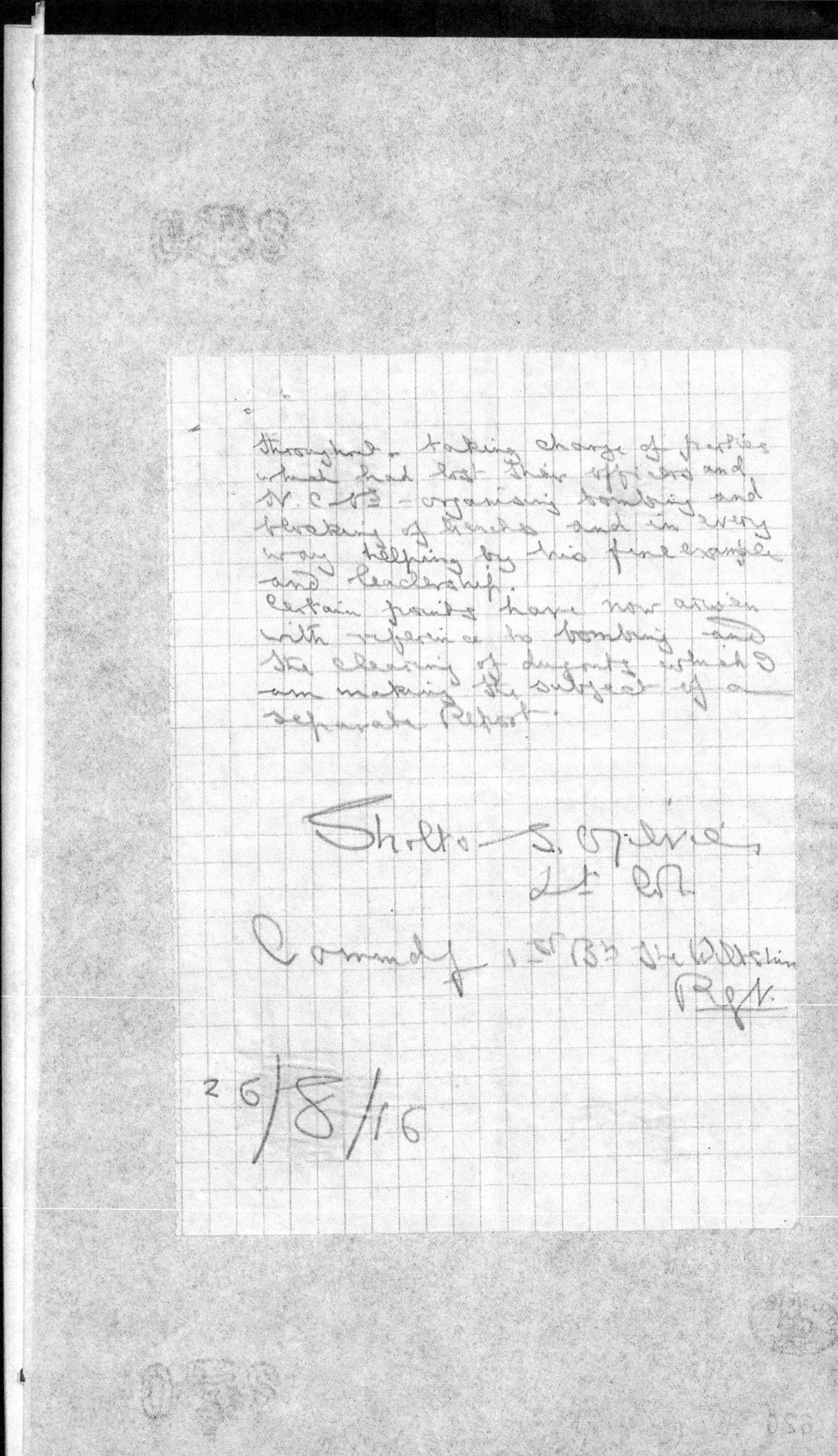

7th. INFANTRY BDE.
25th. DIVISION

1st. WILTSHIRE REGT.

SEPTEMBER 1916.

Army Form C. 2118.

WAR DIARY
or
INTELLIGENCE SUMMARY

(Erase heading not required.)

1/WILTS
SEPTEMBER 1916

Place	Date	Hour	Summary of Events and Information	Remarks and references to Appendices
BOUZIN-COURT.	31st		The Bn. turned out for Physical Training in the morning before breakfast orders were received to the effect that the Battalion would not move towards the trenches. An attack practice was carried out in the morning and evening. In the afternoon, an inter-platoon football competition was arranged and played. The winning platoon was from A Company.	
"	Sept 1st		The Bn expected to move to the trenches, but orders were received at 9.30 a.m. that he must could take place that day. The Battalion had morning training until 12.30 p.m. The Commanding officer visited the 4th Brigade Head Quarters in the morning. In the afternoon, the companies played football. A v B and C v D Companies. In the evening at 6 p.m. there was a conference in which Commanding officers discussed the coming operations with the G.O.C. Division. At 8.30 p.m. the Battalion carried out a practice attack. The officers and N.C.Os of the 1st Border regiment looked on.	

WAR DIARY
or
INTELLIGENCE SUMMARY

(Erase heading not required.)

Army Form C. 2118.

Place	Date	Hour	Summary of Events and Information	Remarks and references to Appendices
BAIZIN COURT.	Sept. 2nd		Orders were received from Brigade for Officers and N.C.O's to visit the trenches of the OVILLERS sector with a view to relieving the 74th Brigade. The Commanding Officer spoke to the Battalion at 10 a.m. and there was a meeting of Company Commanders afterwards at H.Q. Mess. Orders were received for the Bn. to march to CRUCIFIX CORNER at 1.15 p.m. by companies at 5 minutes interval. The 1st of	
AUTHUILLE WOOD. ANZAC	p.m.		The Battalion reached CRUCIFIX CORNER at about 3 p.m. The men stayed in dugouts under a bank. At 11 p.m. the Bn. moved up to the trenches.	
			Orders had been received previously that the Bn. would take the trenches R.31.c.75, R.31.d.45, R.31.d.07. and that after reorganisation would take the trenches R.31.c.4.6, R.31.a.5.9, R.31.a.55, R.31.a.93, R.31.a.94, R.31.a.95, R.31.b.D.3, 2.3, 32, 31, 51, 50, R.31.d.79, 98. Later on the night of the 2nd-3rd written orders were received that the only attacks to be made were upon the lines R.31.c.46 to R.31.a.55, and upon R.31.c.7.6 to R.31.a.91. R.31.d.4.4.	
TRENCHES LEIPZIG SALIENT			R.31.d.07. It was stated that both the flanks of this Bn. were exposed. The Bn. arrived in position in trenches at 2.30 without a casualty inspite of heavy shelling. The intense bombardment began at 5.10 a.m. and the troops moved up	

Place	Date	Hour	Summary of Events and Information	Remarks and references to Appendices
TRENCHES LEIPZIG SALIENT	3.10		of the trenches and found up about 50 yards off and entrenched upon their opposite. As soon as they had left the trench they were met by a heavy "whizzbang" fire and about at the same time machine guns from right and left opened upon them. Our right Company (D) state that they got into the enemy trench and were wiped out by our own barrage which did not lift in time. The centre and left companies report that their lines were enfilading [?] from both flanks. By the time they reached their objective they were so manouevrably inferior to the enemy. The left company [?] and occupied into trenches and made a block there. The few men of the other companies who reached the enemy trench were forced to take away to their lack of numbers. The time position was not known at this time and [?] reactor Company was sent up to strengthen the line but so far as I can ascertain they were unable not to broken gun fire from the enemy. Shortly after the CO officer commanding right and centre companies reported that they were seen to be a general	

WAR DIARY or INTELLIGENCE SUMMARY

Army Form C. 2118.

Place	Date	Hour	Summary of Events and Information	Remarks and references to Appendices
Tranchée d'Opaque Support Trench	3.7. 5.7.07 Sunday		Work continued steadily and very few men had the chance how pulled. The Commanding Officer was hit by a bullet in the leg. No other officer casualties. At about 11 a.m. orders were received that the Battalion should proceed and small parties to BOUZINCOURT, which was not unlocked in by nightfall. The Battalion arrived at their billets at about 5 p.m.	
Bouzincourt	4.7.		Billets were allotted to the companies. There was a knock roll at 12 noon. Football was played in the afternoon by the men. Nothing else occurred on that day.	
"	5.7.		The Battalion did Physical Training in the early morning. At about 7.45 a.m. orders were received to continue the Bn that the Brigade would move to POTTE & LEAVILLERS at 9 p.m. Further orders were received at 11.30 a.m. stating that the Bn would move at 2 p.m. to LEAVILLERS by companies at 5 minute interval. The Bn arrived in billets at about 8.45 p.m. after a very heavy march in the rain. This command of the Bn was taken over by Major FRIZELL on 3rd R. Berkshire.	

2449 Wt. W14957/M90 750,000 1/16 J.B.C. & A. Forms/C.2118/12

WAR DIARY
or
INTELLIGENCE SUMMARY

Army Form C. 2118.

Place	Date	Hour	Summary of Events and Information	Remarks and references to Appendices
LEALVILLERS	6th Sept		The morning was spent by the companies in inspection parades. In the afternoon football was played by the men on level ground as they could find. Nothing else of any importance occurred.	
LEALVILLERS to RAINNEVILLE	7th		At 9.10 am the Bn. moved to RAINCHEVAL by double companies with a distance of 300 yards between each marching party. The Battalion arrived at billets at about 10.30 am. The command of the Battalion was taken over by Lt. Colonel FINLAY. Major TROTT left the Battalion in the early afternoon. The Bn. spent the rest of the day resting.	
RAINNEVILLE	8th		The Bn. spent the morning resting. In the afternoon at about 2.30 pm the Divisional Commander inspected the Battalion in a field near the transport lines.	
	9th	11.30 pm	A Bus left Bn. HQ. for AMIENS. Six officers in the Bn. went in it. The Bn. left the Bn. HQ. quarters. I don't know the exact route they went but we all did men together until the orders of route were for the first after, HOUEN - ESAINT - PUCHA - MADONVILLE via SENLINS- - MOQUERIE - AMIENS - ESAINT-	
COISY			The Bn. reached their billets at about 2.30 pm. They were	

WAR DIARY or INTELLIGENCE SUMMARY

Army Form C. 2118.

Place	Date	Hour	Summary of Events and Information	Remarks and references to Appendices
HARDIN-VAL	10th		C of E voluntary church service at 5.45 p.m.	
	11th		The Bn. marched to BEAUMETZ by the route via ACCOCHES – OUTRE BOIS – LA MAISON D. At about 2 p.m. each Battalion halted for an hour for dinner. Bn. reached about 6.10 p.m. Arms for a shower & following days in billets at 9.20 p.m.	
BEAU-METZ	12th		At 8 a.m. the Battalion marched to COULOMVILLERS via LONGEVILLERS. Killed which lead for HA'. Arms and officers. The remainder left the day was spent in rest.	
ACHEUX VILLERS	13th		NAVAL arms to MANDREUVRES The morning was spent in cleaning up billets and inspection of kit etc. The remainder of the day was spent in rest.	
	14th		The Bn. was a parade the whole morning from 9 to 1 p.m. Companies did Physical Training, Arms Drill etc. In the afternoon the usual inter-Coy football.	

WAR DIARY or INTELLIGENCE SUMMARY

Army Form C. 2118.

(Erase heading not required.)

Place	Date	Hour	Summary of Events and Information	Remarks and references to Appendices
COULON-VILLERS	15th		The Bn paraded in the morning from 9.0 a.m - 1 p.m. Physical Training, Arms drill, Bayonet fighting was the work done. In the early afternoon the men played football. At 6 p.m. there was a Boxing competition.	
"	16th		There was a class of instruction in Box respiration at the Division Gas School to which the 2nd in command, M.O. 1 officer per company and 2 N.C.Os per company, went. The Bn. spent the day training. There was a lecture at 5.30 p.m. by Major Kincaid-Smith.	
"	17th		At 10 a.m there was a church of England parade. In the afternoon the Bn played football. At 6 p.m. the Boxing competition was continued. A draft of 13 men arrived. All had been out before.	
"	18th		Morning parades were cancelled owing to the bad weather. There were lectures under company arrangements throughout the day. There was a lecture at the B.E.F. Reading room by Major Kincaid-Smith at 5.30 pm. The day was very wet. There were lectures during the morning by under Company arrangements. In the afternoon, the weather cleared and there was a Brigade Boxing competition. The regiment had 4 representatives, one of whom won his weight. At 5.30 p.m. there was a lecture at the B.E.F Reading Room at 5.30 pm.	
"	19th			

Army Form C. 2118.

WAR DIARY
or
INTELLIGENCE SUMMARY
(Erase heading not required.)

Instructions regarding War Diaries and Intelligence Summaries are contained in F. S. Regs., Part II. and the Staff Manual respectively. Title Pages will be prepared in manuscript.

Place	Date	Hour	Summary of Events and Information	Remarks and references to Appendices
COULONVILLERS	20th		Baths were allotted to the Bn at DOMQUEUR. at the rate of 80 per hour. The remainder of the day was spent in training. There was a regimental football match against the 1/7th R.Lancers which resulted in a win for this Bn. 7 - 0 goals. Eight officers joined the Bn: three had been to this Bn before.	
"	21st		There was a inspection of the Bn: by the B.G.C. at 9.0 a.m. Bn: Lobby which was presented there onto were then search. The morning were spent in training to the afternoon there was a Bn. Sports and in the evening a regimental football match against the 2nd Worcesters which this Bn: won (1-0).	
"	22nd		The morning was spent in training. In the afternoon there was a Brigade cross country run. A draft of 15 men arrived in the morning all of whom had been out before.	
"	23rd		The Bn. trained all the morning and the remainder of the day was spent in rest.	
"	24th		There was a church parade at 10 a.m. Baths were allotted to go to the 5th Bn: at DOMQUEUR at in the afternoon. Stores were received for an	

2449 Wt. W14957/M90 750,000 1/16 J.B.C. & A. Forms/C.2118/12.

WAR DIARY
or
INTELLIGENCE SUMMARY

Army Form C. 2118.

Place	Date	Hour	Summary of Events and Information	Remarks and references to Appendices
CONDON-MARK y HARDINVAL	25R		The Bn moved to HARDINVAL via LONGVILLERS - BERNAVILLE - BIENVILLERS. Starting at 7.15 a.m. The Bn arrived in billets at about 1.30 p.m. Rest of the men slept in fields under bivouac sheets. Bivouac were arranged by a march in the next day.	
HARDINVAL y RAINCHEVAL	26R		The Battalion moved to RAINCHEVAL via HEM - PUZEAUX COURT - HERISSART - TERRAMESNIL y BEAUQUESNE. The Bn halted for an hour for dinner, and arrived in billets at 4 p.m. 6 officers joined the Battalion. Two officers went to ACHEUX to witness an experiment in intensive	
RAINCHEVAL	27R		digging by 6 South Wales Borderers. The morning was spent in inspection of clothing, kits etc. In the afternoon Arms Company practised in trench digging, use APPROVES. 6 Lieutenants G.S.O. were given at HEADQUARTERS by a Lecturer learnt by recent engagements. 11 officers from the Bn. attended it. A draft of 15 men arrived at about 9 p.m. All ⁂ belonged to their regiment.	

J.R. Finlay Lt.Col.
Comd. 14Batt. R.Warwick Regt.

7th Inf. Bde.

25th Division

1st Battn. WILTSHIRE REGIMENT

OCTOBER, 1916.

1/6 Wiltshire Regt: 108 27
1 W Wilts

Army Form C. 2118.

WAR DIARY
or
INTELLIGENCE SUMMARY

(Erase heading not required.)

Place	Date	Hour	Summary of Events and Information	Remarks and references to Appendices
RAINCHEVAL HEDAUVILLE	Feb 29		The Bn. moved from RAINCHEVAL – HEDAUVILLE, starting at about 8 a.m. The proceed with rain the whole march. Billets were reached at 11.30 a.m. Lt. Col. Philby went over with the Brigadier and other O's C. Battalions, carrying about 8 p.m. that the Battery was to be taken over in the following day, on the afternoon. The Colonel and Company Commanders went out to see the trenches. They returned at about 6:30 p.m.	
HEDAUVILLE	20th		The Battalion moved to the Trenches East of POZIERES at 2 p.m. and attacked place at Strong pts. No. Bn. was in support to the X Cheshire Regiment which was striking in STUFF redoubt and HESSIAN Trench. The Disposition of the trenches were as follows: A+B Coy in JOSEPH'S Trench, C Company in CONSTANCE Trench and D Company in DANUBE Trench. 12 officers were left behind as B team. There were no dug outs except in DANUBE Trench where shelters for the Bn. & the HQ was open shelters to the Trench and company commanders & great practice bay. 14 officers and men of each company reconnoitred the line. A Staff of 2 Officers and 52 men others at H.Q. train front. The weather was very wet all day. The Bn. spent the day & support Trenches. At 6 p.m. orders were received for the Bn. to relieve the X Cheshire Regiment in the line. The relief started at 8 a.m. J. Bn. and were completed by 1.0 a.m. C+D Companies took up the front line to STUFF Redoubt. A Company in HESSIAN Trench and A Company in 2nd LRN Trench.	
TRENCHES NR POZIERES	30th	1.0 A		

Army Form C. 2118.

Instructions regarding War Diaries and Intelligence Summaries are contained in F.S. Regs., Part II and the Staff Manual respectively. Title Pages will be prepared in manuscript.

WAR DIARY
or
INTELLIGENCE SUMMARY
(Erase heading not required.)

Place	Date	Hour	Summary of Events and Information	Remarks and references to Appendices
Trenches STUFF Redoubt	October 3rd		Bn HQ. was situated near MIDWAY trench at R.27.d.5.5. Lieut Col. Finlay left the Bn sick. The command was taken over by Capt Austin. The day on the whole was quiet, but our own infantry & enemy trench at 4.30 p.m. for about 1 hour. Enemy retaliation on our front and support trenches. The weather was wet and the trenches extremely muddy.	
"	4th		The weather was very wet and trenches in a worse state than the previous day. Purnip guns were active throughout the day. Particularly on HESSIAN trench and ZOLLERN trench. Enemy fire was not anything that serious. Relief were detailed and did not arrive until lines at 11 p.m.	
"	5th		The weather was dull but no rain. The trenches were drier but still very muddy. Enemy stellen was quite busy throughout the morning but in the afternoon fairly quiet. In the evening at about 10.30 p.m. Bn attacked from brigade.	
"	6th		Watering was received from brigade. The day was on the whole quiet and drier. There were received for the & Cheshire Regt to relieve this Bn to the him nothing of importance occurred.	
"	7th		The Bn was relieved at about 2 p.m. onwards by the 8 (Cheshire) Regt and proceeded back to JOSEPH trench, CONSTANCE trench and SANDOE trench. Bn HQ.	

2449 Wt. W14957/M90 750,000 1/16 J.B.C. & A. Forms/C.2118/12.

WAR DIARY or INTELLIGENCE SUMMARY

Army Form C. 2118.

Place	Date	Hour	Summary of Events and Information	Remarks and references to Appendices
SUPPORT TRENCHES SOUTH OF THIEPVAL	7th		was situated in Danube Trench. The attacked operations orders were received.	
	8th		The Battalion spent this day in support trenches. The weather was very cold & consequently the operations planned for this day was postponed. The 8th Royal North Lancashire Regt relieved the 10 Cheshire Regiment in the line. As regards shelling the day was fairly quiet. Our heavy guns shelled front North of STUFF REDOUBT.	
	9th		An attack on STUFF REDOUBT was carried out by the 5 Cheshire Regiment in accordance with the operation orders dated October 7th. The attack was in every way successful. The objectives were gained and lines established North of points 18.39 and 17. The Battalion was in immediate support with one company in ZOLLERN Trench in holding line, one company was in R32.b.7.6. ALG & ZOLLERN and it HQ Company in the trench near pt R32.b.7.6. ALG & ZOLLERN Trench was called upon to form the birivouac and HESSIAN Trench. This company was detailed to hold Bainbridge posts. B Coy was also called up to hold this line. A company was used for carrying parties &c. D company and Headquarters A Coy & ZOLLERN Trench.	
	10th		The Battalion was relieved by the 8th Lancashire Regt at about 2 pm	

Army Form C. 2118.

WAR DIARY
or
INTELLIGENCE SUMMARY
(Erase heading not required.)

Instructions regarding War Diaries and Intelligence Summaries are contained in F. S. Regs., Part II and the Staff Manual respectively. Title Pages will be prepared in manuscript.

Place	Date	Hour	Summary of Events and Information	Remarks and references to Appendices
SUPPORT Trenches	10		The Bn. went back to CONSTANCE DUMP and JOSEPH Trench.	
& THIEPVAL	11th		The Bn. spent the day to support Trenches. In the evening orders were received for the Bn. to relieve the 20th R.F. Inniskillings Regt. in the left sector of the line.	
	12th		The Bn. relieved the Inniskillings at about 2 am. "A" Company were in the front line, "B" Company were to the front line and to B.Hq were in ZOLLERN Trench. "C" and "D" Companies were in SCHWABEN Trench. Bn. Hqrs were situated in ZOLLERN Trench. The day was quiet. We received shelling. Lt Colonel A.E. Williams left this battalion. Regt. took over command of the Bn.	
Trenches	13th		The weather was dull. The morning was quiet to the battery of the enemy however HESSIAN Trench and Bn. Hq. were heavily shelled by 5.9's. at about 3 pm. the men up ratest at spread a ground at 7 pm. very few casualties were sustained.	
ANZAC DUMP R.E. DUMP	14		The battery was quiet and the weather was dull. In the afternoon at	

2449 Wt. W14957/M90 750,000 1/16 J.B.C. & A. Forms/C.2118/12.

WAR DIARY
or
INTELLIGENCE SUMMARY

Army Form C. 2118.

Place	Date	Hour	Summary of Events and Information	Remarks and references to Appendices
Trenches left of STUFF REDOUBT	14th	2.46 pm	The 11th H.L.I. & 11th L.N.L. Fusiliers Regiments assaulted the MOUND in the enemy. The objective was taken and about 90 prisoners secured. C Company of the regiment was called up to the 5th Lancs to carry bombs etc to STUFF REDOUBT. An tally a ZOUAVE trench was ordered to proceed to STUFF relief of neighbouring forces.	
	15th		The Bn. was relieved by the 8th Border Regiment, 75th Brigade at about 8 pm, and proceeded to DONNET post. The day was spent in rest. 2 officers Lieut Brown and Lieut Tooley joined the Battalion	
	16th		The morning was spent in training and the afternoon in rest. wiring of importance happened	
	17th		The morning was spent in training, but about 10.30 am F.S.O.I visited the Bn. and warned us the Commanding officer that the Bn would have to go to the trenches to hold the line while the 74th Bde came in to support him	

Place	Date	Hour	Summary of Events and Information	Remarks and references to Appendices
BENNET'S POST	17th		Before an attack. Orders to this effect were received from Brigadier at 1"45 PM and the Bn started off immediately and moved to 11th Lancashire Fusiliers in the Right Brigade sector of the line. C.O. arrived at 11th F2. H.Q. their ⸻ advised us to go to the HQ in ZOLLERN redoubt. Arrived there it was found that there it was occupied by the 10th Bn Cheshire Regiment. The Commanding officer then returned to former HQ 11th LF H/Q was completed by about 9.30 p.m. The Bn were bus to H. 74th Rifles. G draft of 47 men arrived at the Transport.	
Trenches ALBUQUET ?TOWN?	18th		The day was spent in the Trenches. The weather was very wet. Headquarters to the scheming ?Bn? was relieved again by 11th Lancs Fusiliers and withdrew to ZOLLERN ASSEMBLY, FABECK ⇢ CONSTANCE trenches & 372 PATRICK trench. Bn HQ moved to those occupied by 10th Cheshire Regiment.	
	19th		Operation orders were postponed. In the evening the Battalion headquarters were to take over the front line. The relief started at about 6.30 pm. and came in through on the night of 19/20. A draft of 52 men arrived at the Transport	

Place	Date	Hour	Summary of Events and Information	Remarks and references to Appendices
	20		Relief of front line by the Battalion was completed by about 5:30 a.m. The weather had cleared and was fine, the frosty & sunny. The day was quiet thro' the whole.	
	21st		The Engineers were relieved in the front line by units of the 74th Infantry Brigade and reliefs were (except B Company) to CONSTANCE & PYS 2 PATRICIA Trench. B. Hqrs were at R.28.c.7.3. B. Coy Hqrs were in a trench just behind front line. The men supported the 74th Bde who were ordered to attack REGINA Trench at 12.6 p.m. The attack was carried out in accordance with orders. Operation orders issued were Left see attached. Tools & repairs and refreshly constructed had Mr. Green, framer, helped that 74th Bde Hqrs the members being about 400. C Company to FIR STREET. Casual was observed tho' about 1 hour after the attack that the attack had stopped it. A Coy supplied an escort of 1 Officer + 1 N.C.O. to take German prisoners	

War Diary or Intelligence Summary

Army Form C. 2118.

Place	Date	Hour	Summary of Events and Information	Remarks and references to Appendices
TRENCHES NR MOUQUET FARM	21st		back. The remainder of A Coy and D Company spent the rest of the day with carrying parties for the S.M.R. reinforcements up to the frontline. The infantry had nuisance fire and he found certain rarely less steady and nearly thus at the previous days. A strength of 84 men arrived as transport.	
	22nd		The Bn withdrew from the trenches and proceeded to BOUZIN-COURT. Orders were received from 7th Inf Bde for the Bn to strictly to Officers post. He was in a chief adviser. The place we'll take to the was mostly [illegible] and BOUZINCOURT and as our destination but day's march. At [illegible] Coy arrived at D Company's small in the remainder of the 7th Bde less 1½ you there. At D Company arrived their journey back as about it home and arrival at BOUZINCOURT at 2 and 3.60 p.m. ("D") Coy came into the trench line was relieved by the QUEENS 1st 5th Bn. 1½ Relieved at about 4 pm and by 11 pm the retired back at 11½ Division at about 4 pm and by night the retired back at about 7.30 p.m.	
BOUZINCOURT	23rd		The Bn moved to @ RUBEMPRÉ via HEDAUVILLE, VARENNES, HARPONVILLE, RUBEM-COURT & HERISSART. The Bn started at 6.30 am and by companies with 300 yards interval between batteries each. There was a half hours to arise and	

WAR DIARY
or
INTELLIGENCE SUMMARY

Army Form C. 2118.

Place	Date	Hour	Summary of Events and Information	Remarks and references to Appendices
BOUZINCOURT to RUBEMPRE	23rd		10 a.m. for breakfast. RUBEMPRE was reached at 1 p.m. the afternoon. Here we is free time for men.	
RUBEMPRE to GEZAINCOURT	24th		The Bn. moved to GEZAINCOURT via VADENCOURT & ROSSEL and BEAUVAL starting at the 7.20 am with 20 its distance between companies. The Bn. arrived at GEZAINCOURT at 12 noon. A halt of 8 min and 1 Bn fans culminate dinner 12.30 pm.	
GEZAINCOURT	25th		Battalion war allotted to the Br. Indian Car and 12.30 pm of Divisional Reserve & of the Bn. are offered for use. D, C & B companies billeted. A company in hut.	
"	26th		Parades under company arrangements were ordered but the bad weather made it impossible for them to be held. In the afternoon the Battalion turned up on the street of the billets for a brief inspection by the Commander in Chief. 2/Lt. S.F. TERRY resumed the duties of acting adjutant in place of Lt. HILL who had filled the post since the middle of July.	I.J.
	27th		As the weather was again bad orders were given in billets and company parades were cancelled.	I.J.

2449 Wt. W14957/M90 750,000 1/16 J.B.C. & A. Forms/C.2118/12.

Army Form C. 2118.

WAR DIARY
or
INTELLIGENCE SUMMARY
(Erase heading not required.)

Place	Date	Hour	Summary of Events and Information	Remarks and references to Appendices
GEZAINCOURT	OCT. 28		There was a short Bn. route march in the morning. Instruction in bomb throwing was given to 6 partially trained men per Company. Mothers unsifted	177.
"	29		There was a Voluntary Church Service in the morning. The sig. sec. spent in preparing for a train move into the 2nd. Army area. The train at	
"	30		midnight, the Bn. entraining at DOULLENS BAILLEUL, the station of detrainment, was reached about 11 a.m. on the 30th., and the Bn. marched into billets near PAPOT and ROMARIN.	127.
PAPOT	31		There were Company parades for two hours in the morning. Special attention being paid to gas helmet drill. There were two bomb throwing for the 6 men per Company who were instructed at GEZAINCOURT. The Commanding Officer inspected the employed details of the Bn. at 11 a.m. Subsequently all arrangements were made for the move of the Bn. into Rec. Reserve area on the following day.	

31.10.16

Williams Lt.Col.
Cdg. 1st Wiltshire Regt.

SECRET

7th INFANTRY BRIGADE OPERATION ORDER No. 158.

Map Reference, K.36 - M.33, 1/10,000,   Copy No. 4

& Operation Trench Map, 1/5,000.   7th October 1916.

INTENTION

1. In conjunction with operations by the 3rd Canadian Division on our right, the 10th Cheshire Regt will to-morrow assault and occupy the whole of STUFF REDOUBT and gain the line R.21.a.80 - 12 - R.20.b.90.15 which will be held as a strong observation line, in accordance with plan arranged between B.G.C. and O.C. 10th Cheshire Regt.

   1st OBJECTIVE.- Line R.21.c.87-58-38-18.

   2nd OBJECTIVE.- Line R.21.a.80-12- R.20.b.90.15.

2. **RELIEF** For this operation the 10th Cheshire Regt will relieve 1st Wiltshire Regt in trenches in Right Sector to-day.

3. The Artillery Programme will be issued later.

INFANTRY ACTION

4. Before ZERO the Bombing Posts at R.21.c.85.80, R.21.c.75.75 and R.21.c.18 will be withdrawn to R.21.c.97, 87 and 26 respectively.

5. At ZERO plus 3 minutes the 10th Cheshire Regt will assault the first objective. At ZERO plus 7 minutes the second objective will be assaulted, a strong bombing party at the same time pushing down from R.21.c.97 towards R.21.a.80 to meet a bombing party which will proceed simultaneously from R.21.c.58 towards the same objective.

MOPPING UP

5.a. Strong "mopping up parties" parties must be detailed to clear up trenches running in a Northerly direction from R.21.c.38 and 18.

CONSOLIDATION

6. All ground gained must be exploited and held. Strong observation points will be established at R.21.a.80-12- R.20.b.90.15 and strong points in the main defensive line at R.21.c.97-58-38-18. The latter should be made to contain a garrison of one platoon. These protective measures must be executed with the greatest energy immediately the objectives are gained.

   To assist in the construction of strong points, 1 Officer and 10 sappers, 130th Field Coy. R.E. will be placed at the disposal of O.C. 10th Cheshire Regt, and will report at his battle Headquarters (R.21.c.44) one hour before ZERO. The R.E. should not be sent forward until O.C. 10th Cheshire Regt is satisfied that his final objective is held. One loopholed plate will be carried forward by the party detailed to consolidate each strong point.

7. **MACHINE GUNS.**

   In addition to the Artillery Barrage, the 74th Infantry Brigade will assist by covering the right flank of the attack with machine gun fire from HESSIAN TRENCH, on REGINA TRENCH from R.31.b.35 to the junction of REGINA TRENCH with STUMP ROAD.

   The 117th Infantry Brigade, on our immediate left, will as far as possible cover the left flank of the attack by directing machine gun fire along STUFF TRENCH in the direction of point R.20.b.85.

   O.C. 7th Machine Gun Company will arrange for eight guns, in position in SKYLINE TRENCH, to fire on the following targets from ZERO onwards :-

   (a) R.21.a.75 traversing west to R.20.b.94 (3 guns).
   (b) Trench from R.21.a.05.50 to R.20.b.95 (1 gun).
   (c) Trench from R.20.b.94 to 8.5 (1 gun).
   (d) Traversing fire along STUFF TRENCH in R.21.a. and R.20.b (3 guns).

   The two guns in position in STUFF REDOUBT will, as soon as the

/ second

second objective is gained and consolidated, be moved forward to the northern face of STUFF REDOUBT between R.21.c.58 and 38 to repel counter-attack.

8. **STOKES MORTARS.**

From ZERO hour 7th Trench Mortar Battery will fire on STUMP ROAD from R.21.c.85.60 northwards, and on trenches :-
   R.21.c.75.75 to 5.8.
   R.21.c.38   to R.21.a.12.
   R.21.c.18   to R.20.b.9.4.
Positions of guns will be selcted with a view to bringing enfilade fire to bear on above trenches, and fire will conform to the lifts of the Field Artillery Barrage.

9. **DUMPS.**

The following dumps have been formed, forward of the Brigade dump at R.32.b.98 :-
   (a) R.27.c.5.5 (including rations and water).
   (b) R.27.a.3.7 (including shaped corrugated iron sheets and loopholed plates).
   (c) R.21.c.45 (including wiring materials).
A reserve of 50 two-gallon tins of water will also be established at the Brigade dump at R.32.b.98.

10. **SUPPORTS.**

1st Wiltshire Regt will be held in readiness to support 10th Cheshire Regt, moving one company into ZOLLERN TRENCH between points R.27.a.59 and R.26.b.88, and one company into MIDWAY LINE between points R.27.c.77 and 89. These companies will be in position one hour before ZERO. The remaining two companies will be in position in trenches R.27.c.54 to R.32.b.98, and SCHWABEN TRENCH from R.32.b.98 to R.26.c.9.3, at the same hour.
Routes to STUFF REDOUBT must be carefully reconnoitred from the above positions prior to the hour of ZERO.

11. **LIAISON.**

O.C. 1st Wiltshire Regt will detail from his "B" Team two Officers to act as liaison officers between this Brigade and the Brigades on our flanks. They will report at the headquarters of the 74th Infantry Brigade and 117th Infantry Brigade, respectively, one hour before ZERO.
   Headquarters 74th Infantry Brigade.........MOUQUET FARM
   "   117th   "   "   ....Q.29.d.45.50.

12. **CONTACT PATROLS.**

Positions of advanced troops will be shown to contact patrol aeroplanes by red flares, burnt in the trench. Should flares not be available troops will wave helmets and flags (the latter will be carried for use in emergency) to indicate their most forward positions to R.F.C. observer who will draw attention by sounding the KLAXON HORN.
Artillery boards (2 feet square and pained red and green in vertical halves) will be placed behind the furthest advanced positions occupied.

13. **COMMUNICATIONS.**

The Brigade Signalling Officer will arrange for the necessary communication by means of telephone, visual and pigeons.

14. **MEDICAL.**

The advanced aid post is established at R.27.c.5.4.

ADDENDA AND CORRECTIONS TO 7th INFANTRY BRIGADE

OPERATION ORDER. No. 158.

SECRET

Copy No. 4

7th October, 1916.

1. **ADDENDA.. ARTILLERY PROGRAMME.**

The Artillery Programme for the attack of 10th Cheshire Regt will be as follows:-

At Zero
- (a) Intensive barrages. On line R.21.b.63, R.21.central, R.21.c.8580 - 57 - 37 - 17 - R.20.d.85.
- (b) On line R.21.c.58 - R.21.a.80.
- (c) On line R.21.c.8580 - R.21.a80.
- (d) On and immediately in front of REGINA Trench in R.21.a. and b.
- (e) On and immediately in front of STUFF Trench in R.20.b. and R.21.a.
- (f) On area in R.20.d. and B.
- (g) On lines R.21.c.18 - R.20.b.85 and R.21.c.38 - R.20.b.95.

At Zero plus 3 minutes. Barrage (a) will roll gradually backwards at the of 50 yards a minute to the line R.21.b.63 - R.21.central - R.21.c.89. - A.50. 30, 00.
Barrages (b) and (c) will lift to R.21.a.80.
Barrages (d),(e) and (f) will remain.
Barrage (g) will lift to 100 yards North of R.21.c.18. and 38.

At Zero plus 7 minutes. Barrage (a) will continue to roll gradually Northwards at the rate of 50 yards per minute to the line R.21.b.63. - A.82. - 14 - R.20.b.9540. D.74.
Barrages (b) and (c) will lift to a Point 100 yards beyond R.21.a.80. and remain on STUMP Road North of this Point as far as R.15.c.60.
Barrages (d),(e) and (f) will remain.
Barrage (g) will roll gradually Northwards to points R.21.a.14. and R.20.b.94.

At Zero plus 12 minutes. Barrage (d) will lift to 100 yards North of REGINA Trench.

At Zero plus 14 minutes. Barrage (d) will return to REGINA TRENCH.

At Zero plus 30 minutes. Rate of barrage fire will gradually decrease.

Heavy Artillery will bombard selected points under arrangements to be made by G.O.C., 11th Divisional Artillery.

G.O.C.,11th Divisional Artillery will arrange for a Heavy Trench Mortar to bombard STUMP Road North of R.21.a.76. for 30 minutes from Zero hour.

para.2.

2. NEW TRENCH.

If 10th Cheshire Regt has gained its objective, a new trench will be dug tomorrow night, under Divisional arrangements, between STUFF REDOUBT and R.20.d.01.

O.C., 3rd Worcestershire Regt will establish a line of observation posts as soon as practicable to cover the above line, and will provide the necessary covering party to protect the R.E. digging party.

3. TRAFFIC.

The New Communication Trench running from R.27.c.54. to its junction with HESSIAN TRENCH at 21.c.38. will be used for UP Traffic only, runners, and linesmen. All down traffic will proceed across country.

4. LIAISON.

O.C., 1st Wiltshire Regt will establish Liaison with O.C.10th Cheshire Regt by sending an Officer to the latter's Battle Headquarters. half an hour before Zero

5. ROCKETS.

Supporting troops of 10th Cheshire Regt will carry forward a Supply of S.O.S. Rockets.

6. CONTACT PATROLS.

A Contact Aeroplane will fly over the Area of attack from 12.30 p.m. Infantry will light flares at 1.20 p.m., and at any time later when the Aeroplane lights a White flare on Sounds a KLAXON HORN. Troops will also Wave helmets and flags.

7. ZERO HOURS.

Zero hour for attack by 3rd Canadian Division is 4.50 a.m.
Zero hour for attack by 10th Cheshire Regt is 12.50 p.m. In no circumstances will mention of ZERO HOURS or of tomorrow's Operations be made on the telephone.

***

CORRECTIONS.
MACHINE GUNS.
Para.7.

117th Infantry Brigade will now cover the Left flank of the attack with Machine Gun fire along LUCKY WAY. Fire will not be directed South of this Trench.

Captain,
Brigade Major, 7th Infantry Brigade.

Copy No. 1. Brigade Major.
" " 2. Staff Captain.
" " 3. 3rd Worcester Regt.
" " 4. 1st Wilts Regt.
" " 5. 10th Cheshire Regt.
" " 6. 8th L.N.Lancs Regt.
" " 7. 7th Trench Mortar Battery.
" " 8. 7th Machine Gun Company.
" " 9. 25th Division "G".
Copy No 10. C.R.A.25th Division.
" " 11. 130th Field Coy R.E.
" " 12. C.R.A.11th Division.
" " 13. 74th Infantry Brigade.
" " 14. 117th Infantry Brigade.
" " 15. 7th Canadian Brigade.
" " 16. Bde Signalling Officer.
" " 17. Arty Liaison Officer.
" " 18. War Diary.

War Diary

3rd Worcestershire Regt.
1st Wiltshire Regt.
Xth Cheshire Regt.
8th L.N.Lanc. Regt.
7th Machine Gun Company.
7th Trench Mortar Battery.
7th Brigade Signal Section.

7th I.Bde Misc. 544.

The following message has been received from the G.O.C. Reserve Army.

The B.G.C. wishes it to be circulated to all ranks and himself wishes to congratulate the whole Brigade on their splendid work in the trenches during the past fortnight.

"Please convey the congratulations of the Army Commander "to the 25th Division on the excellent arrangements made and the "dash and gallantry displayed by the troops in the operations "carried out in the neighbourhood of STUFF REDOUBT during the last "few days".

[signature]

Captain,

15/10/16.
Brigade Major, 7th Infantry Brigade.

SECRET.

Copy No. 9

74TH INFANTRY BRIGADE OPERATION ORDER NO. 83.

Reference 1/5,000)   H.Q. 74th Infantry Brigade.
Operation Map.   )   17th October 1916.

1. The Brigade will attack, capture and consolidate REGINA TRENCH from R.23.a.03 to R.22.a.38 (roadway inclusive) on October 19th. Zero hour will be notified later.
The 75th Brigade will attack on the left of 13th Cheshires, and 39th Division on left of 75th Brigade. The 18th Division will attack on the right of 11th Lancashire Fusiliers.

2. Attack will be carried out as follows:-

   UNIT.   OBJECTIVE.
   13th Cheshires.   R.22.a.38 to R.22.b.08 (exclusive).
   9th L.N. Lancs.   R.22.b.08 (inclusive) to R.22.b.44 (Railway inclusive).
   11th Lancs. Fus: R.22.b.44 (exclusive) to R.23.a.03. (inclusive).

   Infantry will attack as follows:-

   Each Battalion in three waves.
   First wave - Two Companies in line in fighting order, with two Mills bombs per man.
   Second wave - One Company in line with five Mills bombs.
   Third wave - One Company in line with five Mills bombs.
   Each man of third wave will have a pick or a shovel tied on his back in the proportion of 1 pick to 3 shovels.
   If third wave cannot carry enough tools, a proportion of second wave will also carry them in a similar way.

   Thirty yards distance between waves.

3. PREPARATORY RELIEFS.
   1st Wilts will relieve 11th Lancashire Fusiliers today in the line. Platoon guides at OVILLERS CHURCH at 2 p.m.
   All three attacking Battalions will move up to the line on night of 18th/19th October. Relief to be completed by 5 a.m. 19th instant.
   Details of relief to be arranged between O's.C. concerned.

4. 2nd Royal Irish Rifles will hold the line in HESSIAN TRENCH from TWENTY THREE ROAD (inclusive) to R.22.c.37 moving in to unoccupied portion at Zero hour.
   1st Wilts will be withdrawn into reserve at ZOLLERN, ASSEMBLY and HIGH TRENCH by 5 a.m. on 19th October.

(2)

5. BOUNDARIES:- Parallel lines running S.W. from frontages of objectives.
O.C's will make all necessary preparatory dispositions in their sectors for the attack and arrange for forward dumps as required.

6. Two machine guns will be placed at the disposal of each O.C. attacking Battalion and two guns at disposal of 2nd Royal Irish Rifles.

7. Two Stokes Mortars are placed at disposal of each O.C. attacking Battalion.

8. A rolling barrage will be established at Zero.
All likely Machine Gun positions in rear of enemy trench will receive special attention.
The attack <u>must</u> closely follow Artillery barrage as this is essential to success.

9. Outposts will be pushed out in shell holes 100 - 150 yards in front of captured line immediately after assault.
O.C. 11th Lancashire Fusiliers will arrange for defence of his right flank after assault, and will push bombing parties along REGINA TRENCH eastwards to meet bombing parties of another Division which will commence working westwards from about R.23.a.3½.

10. It is essential that wire, after Artillery preparation, is carefully inspected and kept cut.
O's.C. attacking Battalions will satisfy themselves that wire opposite their Units is thoroughly cut.

11. Directly after assault the following Communication Trenches will be cut by Battalions as follows:-
    13th Cheshires from a suitable point to join into GUNPIT TRENCH.

    9th Loyal North Lancs - R.22.b.28 - R.23.a.11.

    11th Lancs. Fusiliers from a suitable point to R.22.d.40.95.

12. Prisoners will be sent back to HESSIAN TRENCH, where O.C. 2nd Royal Irish Rifles will arrange to send them back under small escorts to Brigade Headquarters.

    O.C. 1st Wilts will detail a party of about 25 men to be at Brigade Headquarters to escort prisoners further to the rear.

[handwritten: What time?]

(3)

13. Watches will be synchronised by Signals at 9 a.m. on October 19th.

14. ACKNOWLEDGE.

Issued at 2pm
Through Signals.

Captain.
Brigade Major.
74th Infantry Brigade.

Copy No. 1 to 25th Division.
" " 2 " - do -
" " 3 " 11th Lancashire Fusiliers.
" " 4 " 13th Cheshires.
" " 5 " 9th Loyal North Lancs.
" " 6 " 2nd Royal Irish Rifles.
" " 7 " 53rd Infantry Brigade.
" " 8 " 75th Infantry Brigade.
" " 9 " 1st Wilts.
" " 10 " G.O.C.
" " 11 " Brigade Major.
" " 12 " War Diary.

7th Inf. Bde.

25th Division

1st Battn. WILTSHIRE REGIMENT

NOVEMBER, 1916

Army Form C. 2118.

WAR DIARY
or
INTELLIGENCE SUMMARY.
(Erase heading not required.)

Hour, Date, Place	Summary of Events and Information	Remarks and references to Appendices
PLOEGSTEERT WOOD 1st November	Bn. relieved 8th L.N. Lancs in trenches by day, relief completed 2 p.m. moving to T.S. trenches only 425-0. The Bros Cyclists were sent to Clobit Support line, all 4 Coys. 4 m.gs in firing line. Enemy very quiet here. Heavy rain at night.	N/S
— 2nd Nov.	Heavy rain all day, trenches + C.T. trenches falling in. Col. Hillier who came out with 1 the Bn. killed owing to dugout falling in.	N/S
— 3rd Nov.	Very heavy rain nearly every day out in these trenches falling in. Men wet but cheerful. Two Germans shot by snipers. Enemy shelled left Coy. cmpires. No casualties for October. No outline for October.	N/S

Army Form C. 2118.

1st Bn Wiltshire Regt

Vol 28

WAR DIARY
or
INTELLIGENCE SUMMARY
(Erase heading not required.)

Place	Date	Hour	Summary of Events and Information	Remarks and references to Appendices
PONT DE NIEPPE	Nov. 1		The Bn. moved early into Brigade Reserve at PONT DE NIEPPE and relieved the 8th DEVON REGT.	J.T.
	Nov. 2-6		During this period the Bn. remained in Bde. Reserve. There was practice in bomb throwing for selected men from the companies, and the Lewis Gunners paraded for instruction under 2/Lt. SMITH who was appointed Bn. Lewis Gun Officer. Sniping parties were repaired for work in the Bde. forward area during the greater part of the day, and this work took about half the battalion, with the result that company parades were rendered impossible. Lt. McDONNELL (5th WILTS REGT.) joined the Bn. for duty on the 4th. The weather throughout was mild and unsettled.	J.T.
TRENCHES LE TOUQUET Sector	7		The Bn. relieved the 10th CHESHIRE REGT. in the left subsector of the Relief was completed by 1.30 p.m. We had no casualty. There was considerable rain during the day, and work chiefly consisted of repairing trenches which had fallen in. The Snipers	J.T.

Army Form C. 2118.

WAR DIARY
or
INTELLIGENCE SUMMARY
(Erase heading not required.)

Instructions regarding War Diaries and Intelligence Summaries are contained in F. S. Regs, Part II. and the Staff Manual respectively. Title Pages will be prepared in manuscript.

Place	Date	Hour	Summary of Events and Information	Remarks and references to Appendices
TRENCHES	8		Both sides were quiet throughout the day. The enemy fired a few shells in the neighbourhood of RESERVE FM and caused one casualty. Pte. BRANT, of A Company, wounded. About dawn a hostile working party was dispersed by Lewis gun fire from the right company. During the day Lt.y. m.g. were active by supporting upon damages, stationed and the enemy was observed taking rations out of this front line. The Regimental Sniper claimed one hit. There was no other casualty. Lt. EVANS (C Co) wounded at B.T.	
	9		A confused bombardment of three minutes' duration by Divisional Artillery and Stokes Mortars was carried out at 4.30 a.m. upon the Divisional front, to strikers being the German front and support lines. It was planned to inflict damage upon hostile working parties. Gas was also discharged except upon this Brigade front where the discharge was cancelled at the last moment. The retaliation was slight. trench mortars and field guns opening fire. Previously about 4 a.m. Lewis gun fire from the right company had caused three or four casualties in an enemy working party opposite. Throughout the day both sides were quiet. At night patrols went out from the centre and left companies, found the enemy wire very strong, and heard the enemy busily working in his front line talking out wire, working and repairing his parapet. No hostile patrols could be seen.	
		*	Insert. 7/4.7 J. W. GUNNING was wounded but remained at duty.	

WAR DIARY or INTELLIGENCE SUMMARY

Army Form C. 2118.

Place	Date	Hour	Summary of Events and Information	Remarks and references to Appendices
TRENCHES	9		The Company continued drainage work in front line and C.T's and in attack places. The parapet was strengthened. Reinforcements & other parties joined the Bn. for duty. Weather much improved also.	
	10		Both sides still very quiet. During the night 9/10/16 the Lewis Gunners harassed hostile working parties and must have caused casualties. Rifle which was not heard a great deal of use in mopping in enemy's front line, hammering in particular was evident. In the morning and afternoon great use of artillery was displayed by the enemy but otherwise he was inactive. Not a Hun was observed mainly of drawings and leaving handshake there there had recently	S.9.T.
	11		Weather still dry. A quiet day: the Regimental Snipers claimed two hits, making parties in each cat suffering. Between 10 p.m. and 10.30 p.m. a confused far distance and bombardment was carried out on the Divisional front. The officers from the enemy's C.T. elected points and back areas. No gas appeared to accompany the enemy off. Stop. No gas stand alarm could be heard on time after the discharge. The Retaliatory fire was slight, only field guns and French mortars firing. Employed, but these were a considerable amount of rifle and heard up to 10th. Regimental Snipers claimed 5 hits.	S.9.T.

WAR DIARY or INTELLIGENCE SUMMARY

Army Form C. 2118.

Place	Date	Hour	Summary of Events and Information	Remarks and references to Appendices
TRENCHES	11		Machine gun fire. Fire was first opened at 10.35 p.m. and the right front without event. The Bn. suffered no casualties either from the gun or the hostile artillery fire.	J.T.
	12		A very quiet day: the regimental snipers claimed two hits and in addition this was inflicted upon an enemy working party by Lewis gun fire to right by 11/12th Hants opposite the right of the Bn. sector. The work of parapet repair and improvement continued throughout the day. Reinforcements, Six other ranks. Joined the Bn. for duty. Weather, mild and rainless.	J.T.
LE BIZET	13		The Bn. was relieved in the morning by the 1st Cheshire Regt. and went into Bde Support. This meant that two companies and Headquarters were billeted in LE BIZET, the other two companies were split up to form garrisons for supporting points behind the Bde Front	J.T.
	13-18		During this period the Bn. remained in Bde Support. No incidents of any sort happened on the Bde front. In the mornings the two companies at LE BIZET held parades for Physical Training, Bombthrowing instruction and gas respirator drill. The whole Battalion was able to have baths and was fitted out with the hot respirator which took the place of the one P.H. helmet. Small drafts arrived for duty with the Bn. at the following

WAR DIARY
or
INTELLIGENCE SUMMARY

Army Form C. 2118.

Place	Date	Hour	Summary of Events and Information	Remarks and references to Appendices
LE BIZET			Casualties:- 15 O.R. other ranks, 17th 8 other ranks. There were 3 casualties on the 18th. Pte. PARKES, H. (D Company). On the 14th, Lt. J. McDONNELL eff. the Bn. for duty with the 7th Bde. Trench Mortar Battery. On the 15th 17 other ranks from A Company left the Bn. for permanent work with 2 Prisoners of War Company. Capt. J READER being in Command of the party. C.S.M. THOMAS W.G. was slightly wounded but remained at duty. The weather throughout was variable, but towards the end grew very cold.	D.T.
TRENCHES	19		The Bn. relieved the X the Cheshire Regt. in the left sub sector of the LE TOUQUET Sector. The day passed quietly.	
"	20		There was hostile artillery and trench mortar activity on the left of the Bn. Sector. Attention being paid to GAP "F" and the CONVENT. 8 rifle grenades fired in the morning from GAP F bought in return retaliation on the Bn. on the left. One enemy sniper was active and one airman. Work throughout the day consisted chiefly of repairs in the fire line, the scrapers were in places strengthened and the duckboards raised and repl. There was one casualty in B Company. Pte. BURCH, G. — Wounded. 2/Lt. LEWIS, L.G. joined the Bn. for duty and was posted to C Company. Weather dry and cold.	D.T.

* Insert under 18th. Reinforcement arrived: 2/Lt. MATHINSON, L.H. and GIBSON, H.W. and ten other ranks.

WAR DIARY or INTELLIGENCE SUMMARY

Army Form C. 2118.

Place	Date	Hour	Summary of Events and Information	Remarks and references to Appendices
TRENCHES	21		During the morning and afternoon many small trench mortar bombs fell in rear of G.T.O. "F" on the left of the Bn. Sector and also in rear of the Bn. on the left. Our own trench mortars were slow in opening reply, but fire and many bombs failed to explode. In the early morning a hostile machine gun was observed outside the trench and was fired on. When hit were claimed by one of our sentry posts. Work: further repairs to parapet and drainage of front line; inverson of [...] frames in the fire line; wire in front of line was strengthened in several places where weak. There were two casualties in the day. Pte. CLEVERLY, W. (C Company) killed by an enemy sniper. Pte. MITCHELL, G. (B Company) wounded.	J.T.
"	22		Enemy artillery was active in the afternoon, when several shrapnel shells fell near RUTTER LODGE on the extreme left of the Bn. Sector. Other shrapnel fell burst over No Man's Land near the enemy's line there over, three leading to the supposition that he was ranging on No Man's Land. Our snipers were active; two claims for the day made - 2 enemy snipers hit. 1 enemy sniper silenced, two periscopes smashed. There was the usual patrolling at night. By the enemy appeared to be much more active in this respect. 2/Lt M.W. AWDRY of B Company was accidentally wounded while cleaning a revolver. Weather fine.	J.T.

WAR DIARY or INTELLIGENCE SUMMARY

Army Form C. 2118.

Place	Date	Hour	Summary of Events and Information	Remarks and references to Appendices
TRENCHES	23		A post where one sniper claimed two hits. The usual work was carried on.	Maps
"	24		2/Lt. OGILVIE rejoined the Bn. There was a continued artillery and trench mortar bombardment on the left edge of the Battalion area. About midday damage and effects on the moral were not heavy and first line and communication trenches. The Battalion had but very scant cover and no casualties. Then artillery and trench mortar fired only upon the right and left company fronts. Thereafter the day was quiet.	P.T.
PONT DE NIEPPE	25		Bn. was relieved by the X/X Cheshire Regt. and went into Brigade Reserve at about 5 pm. No casualties. Men rested during what little leave to Battalion on duty.	P.T.
"	26		A Pay Parade was held in the morning. The men rested during the rest of the day.	P.T.
"	27		The G.O.C. Division gave away presents to those who had distinguished themselves. Namely C.S.M. FLON (S Coy) Sgt. AVERY. S Sgt. VINE (C) L/C. BIRD and L/C SMITH (Bn H Q Orderlies), Pte BEGGON and WHITBREAD (Snipers), Pte MOSCOP (Signallers) and Pte EVANS (of B Coy Stretcher-Bearer). On that day and until the Bn. remained in PONT DE NIEPPE large working parties were supplied for work on the defences, front line and VA Yao roads. R.E. Supervision.	P.T.
"	28-30		These working parties took away for the greater part of the day about half	

Army Form C. 2118.

WAR DIARY
or
INTELLIGENCE SUMMARY
(Erase heading not required.)

Place	Date	Hour	Summary of Events and Information	Remarks and references to Appendices
	30		The Battalion were able to have baths in the mornings instruction in Bomb throwing was given to the few men left in camp. Weather during this period remained fine.	A7

Williams Lt. Colonel,
Comdg. 1st Wiltshire Regiment.

30. 11. 16

7th Inf. Bde.

25th Division

1st Battn. WILTSHIRE REGIMENT,

D E C E M B E R,   1 9 1 6.

Army Form C. 2118.

Vol 29

WAR DIARY
or
INTELLIGENCE SUMMARY

(Erase heading not required.) 1st WILTSHIRE REGT.

Place	Date	Hour	Summary of Events and Information	Remarks and references to Appendices
TRENCHES LE TOUQUET	DEC. 1		Maj Br. & relieved the 16th Cheshire Regt in the line - without casualty. There was slight trench mortar activity during the day several bombs falling in rear of the right company and evidently aimed at new work nearly completed. Bombardments absent.	A.T.
"	2		The enemy again devoted his attention to the ground in rear of GAP D and in the neighbourhood of ESSEX FM. He was active rather shelling this ground between 10 a.m. and 12 noon and 2.30 p.m. and at 3 p.m. little damage was inflicted on defences and no casualties were incurred. Our artillery fire was ineffective. Our snipers claimed two hits. Pvc was one casualty: 29/2 Pte. TREMAYNE J.G. wounded, but remained at duty.	A.T.
	3		The enemy's artillery and trench mortars were active during the day particularly in rear of GAP D and in the neighbourhood of HARNIAN'S AVENUE. BATTERMASTER RUN, PVE FOLK AVENUE etc. from 4.15 p.m. to 4.45 p.m. there was a heavy bombardment of these parts. But little material damage was done and no casualties were caused. Our observations were also in camp and post. The snipers claimed one hit. Lt. R.F.T. HAYWARD was admitted to hospital sick.	A.T.
	4		A very quiet day, during which the repairs to the parapet and check trading were continued. 9/11 (C.S.M. of C Company) Pte TILOR took up the duties	

WAR DIARY or INTELLIGENCE SUMMARY

Army Form C. 2118.

Place	Date	Hour	Summary of Events and Information	Remarks and references to Appendices
TREN CHES	5		of an officer in D Company. Another very quiet day on the part of both sides. In the afternoon the 7th Bn. took over a portion of the 7.R. Bn. line; the 2nd S/Lancs Regt. relieved the left, centre and support companies of this Bn. and this Bn. took over on front line company taken from the 8th L.N. Lancs. on the right. The distribution of the line left two companies of the Bn. in the front line, one company became support company in the neighbourhood of PRIEST FM and one coy. became reserve company in SEVEN TREES AVE and BUNKER FM. No front line work was carried on by the reserve company. There was no casualties during the relief was completed by the evening.	97 97
"	6		but in the early morning of the 6th 2 G. Lewis was wounded. A quiet day, during which the usual trench repair work was carried on. Sniper claimed two stres.	97
"	7		Bn. was relieved by the 10/CHESHIRE REGT. and went into Brigade Support at 2E BIZET and in the forward supporting Bnt. there were no casualties	97
LE BIZET	8-12		During this time the Bn. was not engaged in Bde. Support, providing garrisons for the supporting points and having both our two companies in LE BIZET. A certain amount of training was possible. The Corporals and Lance Corporals attended courses	97

Army Form C. 2118.

WAR DIARY
or
INTELLIGENCE SUMMARY
(Erase heading not required.)

Place	Date	Hour	Summary of Events and Information	Remarks and references to Appendices
	12		The R.S.M. for instruction. Classes for Lewis Gun instruction and Bayonet fighting were also held. There was an allotment of baths and day for the Bn. and a few fatigue parties were required for work.	
	13		On the 11th reinforcements, 114 other ranks, joined the Bn. for duty. Owing to a fair proportion of casualties the majority of the men, however, had not been out before.	
			Capt. L.H. HORNCASTLE proceeded to the 74th. Bde. for instruction. Is Staff duties. Notification was received that 2nd Lts. RENDER, HORNCASTLE and BROWN and Lt MACANN were appointed Acting Captains from dates in July and August.	B.T. 127. P.T.
TRENCHES	13		The Bn. relieved the 10/ CHESHIRE REGT. in the line. The day passed quietly.	P.T.
"	14		No activity on the part of either side. Repair work in the front line was carried on throughout the day. Reinforcements 10 other ranks joined the Bn. for duty, made up of 7 to signallers and 3 bombers. Weather mild.	
			At about 1.30 a.m. a raiding party of the enemy (10 strong) attacked a front line bombing post, killed Pte. GULLIVER (C Company) and wounded and took prisoner Pte. GOODWIN and was then repelled. During the periods 9.30 a.m.—10 a.m. and 3.15 p.m.—3.45 p.m. there was a continued artillery and trench mortar bombardment for ourselves	J.T.
	15			

WAR DIARY or INTELLIGENCE SUMMARY

Army Form C. 2118.

Place	Date	Hour	Summary of Events and Information	Remarks and references to Appendices
FRICOURT	15		along the Divisional Front. The 2nd French Mortars were employed for wirecutting. The 18 pdr. Batteries and the Howitzer Battery carried this trench destruction fire and were to the case of the field guns engaged against the enemy's parapet where the gaps who made in the wire, whilst the trench destruction was employed against known enemy trench works parapet. Good shooting was made and the bombardment appeared to be effective. The enemy's retaliation was slow to commence and only of moderate strength. It consisted largely of Trench Mortars, but the trench and heavy mortar bombs fell to fair of the defences which were unoccupied. Little material damage was done and no casualties were caused. Whizzbangs to the Tambour trenches to fire line were much cut. Petit Bovins and men were brought back into Dugout trenches in consequence little work was done in the trenches. Between Fricourt and Péronne the enemy were hit by Regimental snipers.	
	16-17		This period passed quietly, sniping and bombing much activity. The usual amount of wire was carried out daily, and a certain amount of work upon the trenches.	

Army Form C. 2118.

WAR DIARY
or
INTELLIGENCE SUMMARY
(Erase heading not required.)

Place	Date	Hour	Summary of Events and Information	Remarks and references to Appendices
	19		Men had one ½ hour of light scavenging Drill. Whilst on a working party on the 17th Bn. PALMER, H. (B Company) was wounded.	
	20		The Bn. was relieved by the 10/Cheshire Regt. and went back into Bde. by platoons & reserve. Route and LBR 30 A & 31 at 5.57 & 27 their routes formed the Battalion for duty casually. Wounded accidentally as the Bn. Bombing School - Pte. PUNTER, H. (A Company).	V.P.T.
	21		There were company parades to the area conferred in & sight during the morning. NCO's attended instructional parades in the morning and afternoon under the R.S.M.	V.P.T.
	22		The Bn. was relieved by the 8th (Loyal North Lancs) Regt. and moved into Bde. Reserve at DEPOT. A draft of 3 other ranks joined the Bn. for duty. The Bn. supplied a large number of fatigue parties for work in & near of the front line. The parades were possible except for Lewis Gun Class.	V.P.T.
	23		The Bn. in the afternoon moved to BOIS DE METRE. The town having passed by Perm. street to Beuvry. Bn being at an outpost of the outlets in the Sect.	V.P.T.
	24		Musaufelius Regt. The Bn. again supplied large working parties for work under the superv[ision] of the R.E. Company. In the afternoon a concert and cinema show was given	V.P.T.

WAR DIARY
or
INTELLIGENCE SUMMARY

Army Form C. 2118.

Place	Date	Hour	Summary of Events and Information	Remarks and references to Appendices
PONT DE NIEPPE	25		To the satisfaction of the Bn. by the 25th Divisional Pioneer Troops in the Divl. Baths at PONT DE NIEPPE. The Bn. was excused all fatigues for the day. In the morning Church parades were held; there was a Christmas dinner for the men in the evening. Men preserved. If then marched to meet the Bn. for duty. Weather mild.	1 P. 1 P.
TRENCHES (LE TOUQUET)	26		The Bn. relieved the 15 Cheshire Regt. in the line. The relief commenced 8 a.m. The day passed quietly, and there was no casualty.	
"	27		A quiet day, during which the usual trench work, sandbagging, drawing &c. was carried on. Rifles had a certain amount of firing was done in front of the right company trenches. Other ranks reinforcements joined the Bn. for duty. There was no casualty. Pte. BUCKINGHAM. 27 (C. Coy.)	
"	28		Another quiet day. Routine side showing much activity. There was the usual amount of sporadic work carried out in the front line trenches by the 28th British and a Lieutenant and 2737. Me. CARTER. W (3 Coy) was killed by a Chance rifle bullet. At night when men were being sent out in front of the right company trench #223 F. Pte. McCAS. J.R. was killed by a sniper, working by the aid of a bare light which shone from the trenches.	

WAR DIARY or INTELLIGENCE SUMMARY

Army Form C. 2118.

Place	Date	Hour	Summary of Events and Information	Remarks and references to Appendices
TRENCHES (ST JULIEN)	28 Sept.		Employed normal nights improving the trench & light approaches & any other work in the enemy's support line. There was	A.7
"	29		Between 2 p.m. and 2.30 p.m. a detachment of our R.E. assisted by Artillery (Lyddite and How. (Sm). Stokes Mortars and 2" Mortars of the Brimay & R.F. and Trench Mortar Battery strafed strong point C.10.d.6.9 and C.4.d.3.u & Kent 30 N.W. of N.E. line Hooplines). The enemy's retaliation consisting of light and heavy trench Mortar fire was chiefly directed against SUSSEX and KENTISH FM GRD'S and just N of the head of LONG AVENUE. No casualties were caused; the whole of the front line had previously been thinned out, and the men withdrawn to support trenches. During the operation a regimental sniper shot one of the enemy in the trench line from O.P. "D".	
			Otherwise the day was quiet. In the morning 29630 L/C DOSSING E. (D. Cy.) was wounded, but remained at duty.	
"	30		At about 3 a.m. two of the enemy entered the trenches of the left company and were challenged by a sentry in the nearest bay, who was uncertain whether they were our own patrol or one of the enemy. As answer was given the Sentry fired and L/C that one of the enemy fell. The other two ran and disappeared. There was no damage and no activity during the day.	

War Diary or Intelligence Summary

Army Form C. 2118.

Place	Date	Hour	Summary of Events and Information	Remarks and references to Appendices
TRENCHES	30		At night the Coys were patrolled as usual, and an officer's patrol went out from the right company at 10 a.m. On the morning of the 31st to examine a point in the enemy line where a "Hammerwerfer" position was suspected. It had been had was no work in progress, and the patrol could report nothing. During the day the enemy was quiet: a sniper was observed firing up in his line where an injured Germans who had been killed	
	31		On the trenches had been fairly quiet. No action was taken on our part. On our artillery was active during the morning. The howitzers in particular, kept firing well shots in the right company sector between the front and support lines. As a result of the second shell falling short there were 1 Killed: 26/198 Pr. DAWKINS, A.T. (Down? orderly in "B" Company) Killed. 32/77 Pr. SAUNDERS R. 32/71 Pr. KERRY, F.E. Wounded— 9249 Pt. HULL, W.B. SAUNDERS and 32/75 Pr. STROUD, W. Pr. worthy of note that since this Bn had been in this area not a single casualty had been caused by shell fire. Reinforcement, 40 other ranks joined the Bn. to-night, 10 N.C.O. & 1 men from 3 Bn. to-reform 1 N.C.O. and 1 N.CO. joined the Bn. from the 1st Bn. SIT Bn. Having previously served with the Bn. 1 Ordinary Strength of Bn. on 31st Inst. — 18 Officers — 702 other ranks.	

S.S. David Major
Cmdg. 1 Wiltshire Reg.

WAR DIARY
or
INTELLIGENCE SUMMARY
(Erase heading not required.)

Army Form C. 2118.

Vol 30
1st Wiltshire Regt

Place	Date	Hour	Summary of Events and Information	Remarks and references to Appendices
LE BIZET	JAN 1st 1917		The Bn. was relieved in the line by the 15/Cheshire Regt. and went back into Bde. Support at LE BIZET. On Dec. 31st. 48 other ranks, reinforcements joined the Bn. for duty; a large number of these men were from the Royal Warwickshire Regt. 2/Lt. N.R. HINTON (late 4th H.A.C.) joined the Bn. from 9th I.B. Cadet School on 30th Dec. 1917. During this period the Bn. remained in Bde. support. There were small fatigues brought, and there was all given to one company at a time. Thus leaving 3 companies free for company parades and training during the morning. The remaining company provided fatigues for the supplies being found. The running parades included physical training bayonet fighting arm drill instruction in Company and Platoon, throwing into a.m. now the recruit drafts were given live bomb throwing practice. On the 4th there was an outbreak of what was judged to be German measles in the Bn. A considerable number of men were isolated and a whole Pn. was naturally inspected in the evenings, the medical authorities decided that it was not German measles and quarantine was not instituted.	
			Bn. on the following day was to have baths and had all clothing and parades until to be held. The New Year's Eve Afterwards welcomed the names of Major W.M. AUSTIN	

Place	Date	Hour	Summary of Events and Information	Remarks and references to Appendices
TRENCHES	7		2nd R.S.M. PARKER, V.T. — both awarded the Military Cross. On the 6th inst. reinforcements, N.C.O.s & men, saved, joined the Bn. for duty. Lt. S.S. Fowler reported the Bn. from hospital. Lt. Watt returned from hospital & D to Bn.	P.T.
	8		Recd. an. released to 10th Cheshire Regt. to be mea. Rn. the day passed quietly. A quiet day. During other the usual minor work, sandbagging and draining was carried on. In the early morning our men were killed by an enemy sniper. 24191 Pte. Jones, E. of A Coy. Another was wounded but remained at duty. 3/1897 Pte. Warder, R.C.C. The following officers joined the Bn. for duty. 2/Lt. C.H. Atkinson, 2/Lt. G.S. Clarkson, 2/Lt. (R.A.M.C.) B.B. Hillings	P.T.
	9		Another quiet day, with intermittent enemy shelling, not on the maintenance of the trenches was continued. There was one casualty, wounded but remained at duty — 22869 Pte. Harman, G.H.	P.T.
	10		The writers and stores kitchens & dugouts took place between 11 a.m. and 2 noon. The officers being to many 5 mile front. Support line and C.T's. Efforts to repair temporary front line entrances have for the an a. The whole of the Bn. front line having previously been returned.	P.T.

WAR DIARY or INTELLIGENCE SUMMARY

Army Form C. 2118.

Place	Date	Hour	Summary of Events and Information	Remarks and references to Appendices
TRENCHES	10		out. There were no casualties from the shelling. The shots appeared to be effective in damaging the wire and parapet, and in the course of the ... were sent out from the right and centre companies to ascertain as far as possible the extent of the damage done. In the morning Lieut. C.L. USHER was wounded by an enemy sniper while himself sniping. One man was also wounded. 2nd Lt. LIGHT (3 Dn.) ※ Two officers joined the Bn. for duty: Lt. C. SAINSBURY who had previously served with the 1st Bn., and Lt. M.J.G. BIGWOOD who had done duty with the 2nd Bn. It had become about this time quite a practice with the Enemy to throw bombs into his own wire, not only often during daylight and it was apparent that he recognised in good a network newly wired draft.	
"	"		A quiet day, weather much colder, snowing at times causing visibility to ... poor. Good draining work was done and the usual work on the ... course of the trenches was continued.	/37

※ Lieut. The man was wounded but remained at duty. 2/Lt C.M. ROGERS (M.C.J.)

Army Form C. 2118.

WAR DIARY
or
INTELLIGENCE SUMMARY
(Erase heading not required.)

Place	Date	Hour	Summary of Events and Information	Remarks and references to Appendices
TRENCHES	12		A quiet day, during which the usual work of repairing trenches was continued. There were two casualties: 10468 Pte. HUGHES. W (C Coy) killed, and 28672 Pte. READ. R. wounded. Men joined the Bn. for duty.	B.J.
"	13		The Bn. was relieved by the 10/Cheshire Regt. and went back into Brigade Reserve at PONT DE NIEPPE. There were no casualties during relief. Weather very cold, causing the trenches to collapse at many places. In the afternoon a Cinema Show was given to all who had not been able to attend a Christmas or Concert owing to fatigues. Kit inspections were held in the afternoon. Lt. J.R. TAYLOR rejoined the Bn. for duty.	B.J.
PONT DE NIEPPE	14		Two Church Parade services were held, the first for B and C Companies, the second for A and D Companies. A Battalion Brothers Section was once again formed under Lt. SAINSBURY.	B.J.
"	15, 16		The greater part of the Battalion was taken to working parties at different points in the Brigade forward area under R.E. supervision. The Battalion Bombers were available for parade, but the companies had very few left in. On the 15th, C Company proceeded to the Divl. Infantry School at METEREN for a Hachment for a week. On the 15th 9.L.T. W.E. LUDFORD joined the Bn. for duty.	V.J.

Army Form C. 2118.

WAR DIARY
or
INTELLIGENCE SUMMARY

(Erase heading not required.)

Place	Date	Hour	Summary of Events and Information	Remarks and references to Appendices
DE SEULE	17		The Bn. was relieved by the 8th. BORDER REGT. of 74th. Inf. Bde. and marched to DE SEULE Camp; at the same time the whole Brigade came out of the line and moved into a Divisional Training Area for a fortnight's hard training.	A.T.
"	18		Little was done on this day owing to weather conditions rendering parades impossible. Company Inspections were held in the morning and Men who bathe at PONT DE NIEPPE for the whole Battalion during the afternoon and evening.	V.D.T.
"	19		There was a Battalion Route March in the morning through LA CRÈCHE and STEEN WERCK. Independent parades were held in the afternoon rallies and Snipers, and two Lewis Gun classes of 12 men each were formed under the Lewis Gun officer. On the evening of the 19th. and 20th. B Company held Boxing Competitions in the Regimental Canteen. Weather very cold.	V.D.T.
"	20		Company Parades were held in the morning or found in the vicinity of the Camp. The Bn.'s to Trench Attack was practised by each Company in turn, and parades also included Physical Training.	A.T.

Army Form C. 2118.

WAR DIARY
or
INTELLIGENCE SUMMARY
(Erase heading not required.)

Instructions regarding War Diaries and Intelligence Summaries are contained in F.S. Regs, Part II. and the Staff Manual respectively. Title Pages will be prepared in manuscript.

Place	Date	Hour	Summary of Events and Information	Remarks and references to Appendices
DE BULE	20		Bayonet fighting and Squad Drill. In the afternoon a Regimental Soccer Team defeated the 42nd. Signallers, R.F.C. at BAILLEUL.	/AT
"	21		2/Lt E.J. BREWER reported and 2/Lt T.G. FAITH joined for duty. Only a voluntary service was possible. Owing to the limited available accommodation. This service was taken by the Senior Chaplain 25th Division.	/AT
"	22		The morning programme consisted of Battalion Foot Ball, followed by independent company parades. In the afternoon C Company returned to the Battalion from the Swanned Infantry School. The personnel of the Bn. to form band was strengthened by the addition of 15 drummers who returned from the 5th Wiltshire Regt.	
"	23		Company training in the BREAD to BRUAY areas was carried out on the Divisional Training Area.	/AT
"	24		Battalion Foot Match followed by the normal programme of work. The whole Battalion marched to the Divisional Training Area and practised the capture of two objectives, a front line with its immediate support trenches and a Second Line. Skeleton work from Special Duties, the support	/AT

Army Form C. 2118.

WAR DIARY
or
INTELLIGENCE SUMMARY.
(Erase heading not required.)

Instructions regarding War Diaries and Intelligence Summaries are contained in F. S. Regs., Part II. and the Staff Manual respectively. Title Pages will be prepared in manuscript.

Place	Date	Hour	Summary of Events and Information	Remarks and references to Appendices
DE SEULE	25		to rush out just previous to the assault and the upon enemy to ascertain front and support. headquarters to push on down communication trenches and establish blocks. The signallers to establish telephone communication with the section when captured. The men were to fight on and carry out tasks in the construction of the objective. The scheme was carried out twice and the Battalion then marched back to Camp. 4th. C.F.G. Tomes joined the Bn. for duty from the G.H.Q. Cadet School.	(S.T.)
"	26		There was a Battalion route march in the morning followed by independent company parades.	
"	27		Inter-sport parades were held in the morning upon receipt of a warning that large working parties might be called for shortly. C and D Companies were required for work of an urgent nature upon the defences in the PLOEGSTEERT Sector held by the 74th Infantry Brigade. These companies left camps at 1.35 p.m. and returned at 5.30 a.m. on the 29th. A draft of 35 other ranks joined the Battalion for duty, conducted by M/L STRIBLING	
"	28		A Company was at work during the morning "m" to PLOEGSTEERT Ash. stable. C and D companies rested. There was a voluntary Church service at 11.30 a.m. (S.T.) "m" this evening B.C and D Companies were all required for work on the Def.	(S.T.)

2449 Wt. W14957/M90 750,000 1/16 J.B.C. & A. Forms/C.2118/12.

Army Form C. 2118.

WAR DIARY
or
INTELLIGENCE SUMMARY
(Erase heading not required.)

Instructions regarding War Diaries and Intelligence Summaries are contained in F. S. Regs., Part II. and the Staff Manual respectively. Title Pages will be prepared in manuscript.

Place	Date	Hour	Summary of Events and Information	Remarks and references to Appendices
DE SEULE	28		Opened line, north and east of PLOEGSTEERT WOOD. There continued till moved at 10 a.m. on the 29th.	BT
"	29	5.30 p.m.	A Company continued with their task and were away from 7 a.m. until the afternoon. In the morning the wire parades for Bombers, Snipers and Bomb signallers and the Lewis Gun Classes in the afternoon took up were allotted to all H.Q. details B.C. and D Coys carried on with their work during the night of the 29th/30th.	BT
"	30		There was the morning work for all A Company; parades were held for Bombers, Snipers and the Specialists. In the evening B and C Companies were required for work in the PLOEGSTEERT sector.	BT
"	31		Parades for Specialists were held and for A and D Companies until the air movements. In the evening B Company had taken over the greater part of the day. B and C Companies worked while their officers were noting the 74th R.B. also which was to be taken over by this Battalion on February 2nd.	BT

S.S. Ogilvie Major
Cap I/Wiltshire Regt.

WAR DIARY
or
INTELLIGENCE SUMMARY

Army Form C. 2118.

1 Bn K.R. Rifles
J. Knott Sgt.
Vol 17 31

Place	Date	Hour	Summary of Events and Information	Remarks and references to Appendices
DE SEULE	FEB. 1st		Two Companies were required for a morning's work upon the defences at PLOEGSTEERT WOOD. The remaining two companies and the Specialists held short parades in the morning.	P.T.
PLOEGSTEERT WOOD	2		The 7th Inf. Bde. relieved the 74th Inf. Bde. in the PLOEGSTEERT WOOD Sector and the Bn. moved into Brigade Support and occupied huts and farm billets in the wood and in its vicinity.	P.T.
"	3 - 6		During this period the Bn. remained in Brigade Support and it was found possible to hold short parades in the wood for Box Respirator Drill, Instruction in Bomb throwing, Bayonet fighting etc. Two Lewis Gun classes were formed, one of men, the other of officers. Only two fatigue parties were called for, for carrying tiles and mortar ammunition. Officers and N.C.O.s made themselves acquainted with the front and support lines of the Brigade Sector, and the means of approach. The weather remained cold, but fine.	
"	6		The Bn. relieved the 8th L.N. Lancs Regt. in the line; two Companies garrisoning the front line, and two the support defences the KEEPER'S HUT BREASTWORK line. In the evening 7Lt. R.E.E. OKYRNE was killed	

Place	Date	Hour	Summary of Events and Information	Remarks and references to Appendices
TRENCHES	6		While looking over the front line parapet, on this same day 26515 Pte. Lewis H. was accidentally wounded while under instruction at the Bolo Bombing School.	
	7. 8		These two days passed quietly, and it was suspected that a Saxon Regiment had taken over the line, a change attributed to the enemy's part firing quick-firing aircraft. His aeroplanes were particularly active, while our anti-aircraft was weak. During the afternoon of the 8th, our heavy mortar and howitzer gun registered upon the enemy's defences in the neighbourhood of FACTORY FM., North of the Br. Rd. this was in view of a proposed raid at this point, in which C Company was to take part. On the evening of the 8th C Company was withdrawn from the line and billeted in the Piggeries, preparatory to a short period of training for the raid. There was one casualty on the 8th. 9.45 P.M. Andrews W. T.A. Coy. wounded.	
	9.10		The 9th passed quietly; only a small amount of junk could be done owing to the frozen condition of the ground. On the morning of the 10th a slight snow-storm was raging. At 2.9.22 Cpl. Burton A. (D Coy) was wounded by the enemy trench mortars and	

WAR DIARY
or
INTELLIGENCE SUMMARY

Army Form C. 2118.

Place	Date	Hour	Summary of Events and Information	Remarks and references to Appendices
ROMARIN	10 cont.		In the afternoon the Battalion was relieved by the 8th L.N. Lanc. Regt. and went into Brigade Reserve at REGINA CAMP.	
	11		Voluntary parades were held in the morning for all denominations. Company parades were held for inspection of kits etc.	
	12-14		During this period the Battalion except for C Company which had moved into billets at PONT DE NIEPPE, remained in Bde. Reserve. Kit Company parades were held in the mornings; only the small working party was called for in the evenings for work on WESTMINSTER AVE. In the meantime C Company was preparing for a raid which was eventually to be carried out on the 17th. The scheme was practised each day upon ground near REGINA CAMP. The enemy's front and support lines being denoted by flags.	
	#		In the afternoon of the 14th. the 2nd Bn. (less C Company) relieved the 8th L.N. Lancs Regt. in the line: the relief was effected without casualty.	
	15,16		Preparatory to wire-cutting bombardment by artillery and trench mortars preparatory to the impending daylight raid, two days passed without incident as far as this Bn's sector was concerned. There was very little retaliation on the enemy's part in reply to our persistent bombardment.	

WAR DIARY or INTELLIGENCE SUMMARY

Army Form C. 2118.

Place	Date	Hour	Summary of Events and Information	Remarks and references to Appendices
	15/9		On the night of the 15/16th instant, the enemy was busy repairing the gaps cut in his wire, and to ensure that sole gaps were made the same artillery programme had to be produced until the last possible moment. On the night there were two casualties: Wounded still at duty, 15090 Pte. MILLER, J. "A" Coy. - Wounded. 9'91 4/C. STRONG, G.	
	17		The raid was carried out in conjunction with a party of the 10/Cheshire Regt. (200 in strength). The objective allotted to the Brigade being the enemy's defences to and of FACTORY Fm, to East of Fig in cluded. Zero hour was 10.40 a.m. the frontage seemed to be taken quickly by surprise and his trenches were passed with but slight loss. The objectives were reached, with the exception of FACTORY Fm where stout resistance was offered. Slinchens U/w Fm & the Enemy were found. It is believed that about 20 Germans were killed in these Fm's. Strong machine gun nests cursed by the U Fm. No prisoners were taken and no identification was secured. The casualties returned were killed: + other ranks, 26 Wounded, 1 Died of Wounds, 1 Missing, the majority of these were caused by hostile machine gun fire, which was brought to bear upon the parties as they returned to our lines.	

Army Form C. 2118.

WAR DIARY
or
INTELLIGENCE SUMMARY
(Erase heading not required.)

Instructions regarding War Diaries and Intelligence Summaries are contained in F. S. Regs., Part II. and the Staff Manual respectively. Title Pages will be prepared in manuscript.

Place	Date	Hour	Summary of Events and Information	Remarks and references to Appendices
TRENCHES	1917.		The Battalion was relieved by the 1st/5th Bn. K.S.L.I. Lancs. Regt. and moved from the Brigade Support in PLOEGSTEERT WOOD. There were no casualties during the day.	
PLOEGSTEERT WOOD	9th –21st		During this period the Battalion remained in Brigade Support. No fatigue parties were called for, and so it was possible to hold Coys. Company parades in the morning. On the afternoon of the 20th, C Company moved up to ST ANSELM. DRIVE into Close Support to the 4th Worcester Bat. talion, the 3rd Worcestershire Regt. in consequence of the withdrawing of one of their companies for duty at the Divisional Infantry School. On the 20th Lt. D.F. Brown proceeded to Battalion to duty. On the 20th Officers of the 2nd. Bn. New Zealand Rifle Brigade reconnoitred the Battalion Area in view of the Brigade relief which was to take place on the following day.	
	22nd		The Battalion was relieved by the 2nd Bn. New Zealand Rifle Brigade and proceeded to DE SEULE Camp for the night.	
MONT DES CATS	23rd		The Brigade moved into to MONT DES CATS Area for a period of training. The Bn. left DE SEULE at 10 a.m. and marched via BAILLEUL and METEREN to billets on the S. and W. sides of MONT DES CATS. No men fell out on route in spite of	

Army Form C. 2118.

WAR DIARY
or
INTELLIGENCE SUMMARY
(Erase heading not required.)

Instructions regarding War Diaries and Intelligence Summaries are contained in F. S. Regs., Part II. and the Staff Manual respectively. Title Pages will be prepared in manuscript.

Place	Date	Hour	Summary of Events and Information	Remarks and references to Appendices
HQ N.7 SEC CATS	FEB. 24		The bad condition of the roads. 2/Lt. W. BIDWELL and 2.C.O. PARSONS joined the Bn. Company parades of 2 hrs duration were held in the morning. A lecture to specialist. In the afternoon football was played under company arrangements. A draft of 24 other ranks, composed very largely of Corporals, joined the Bn. for duty. There was a Church Parade in the morning. Football matches were played on	
"	25		Company ground in the afternoon.	
"	26		Company Training proper was commenced. Hours of parade being from 8.30 a.m. till 12.45 p.m. Instruction was given in Musketry, Bombing, Bayonet fighting and in Deploying into Artillery formation. The reorganization of the Bn. in accordance with G.H.Q. letter O.B. 1919 was carried out. by this the Bn. Bombing Section was broken up, and each Platoon became a separate fighting unit consisting of all arms, and made up of 2 Rifle sections, a Lewis Gun Section, a Bombing Section and two R.Kranen sections. 2/Lt. C.H.G. THOMAS joined the Bn. for duty.	
"	27		There was a Battalion Route March in the morning through BERTHEN and BOETCHEPE, and on the return a practice open warfare attack was carried out. In the afternoon platoon football matches were played.	

2449 Wt. W14957/M90 750,000 1/16 J.B.C. & A. Forms/C.2118/12.

Army Form C. 2118.

WAR DIARY
or
INTELLIGENCE SUMMARY

(Erase heading not required.)

Place	Date	Hour	Summary of Events and Information	Remarks and references to Appendices
MONT DES CATS	28		The training of Companies and Specialists was continued throughout the morning. Instruction was given in Musketry, Bayonet fighting and Anti-Gas. Divisional Orders contained a notice of the award of the Military Medal the the under-mentioned being 8700 Cpl. UTLEY, F. 11418 L/C. PAUL, G. 3302 Pte TOOMEY, E, all of "C" Company; two Snipers 13134 Pte BLYTH, F.T. and 29024 Pte BURROUGHS, W. and one Signaller 7156 Pte SHERWOOD, C. These were all for conspicuous gallantry in connection with the raid of 9th July 17 A.E of PLOEGSTEERT WOOD.	

J.S.J. Irvie, Major.
Commdg. 1st Wiltshire Regt.

Army Form C. 2118.

WAR DIARY
or
INTELLIGENCE SUMMARY
(Erase heading not required.)

1st Wiltshire Regt.

Vol 32

Place	Date	Hour	Summary of Events and Information	Remarks and references to Appendices
MONT DES CATS	MARCH 1st 1917	1-16	During this period the Battalion remained in the MONT DES CATS area and the training of Companies and Specialists was carried out daily. The usual routine & programme included Physical Training, Bayonet fighting, Bomb throwing and Musketry. Regular firing parties were held upon improved rifle ranges in the slopes of MONT DES CATS hill. Battalion Route Marches took up two mornings in the week, and on the 9th a long Brigade march was held. Company schemes were carried out upon a Brigade training area. Sel of NERTHEN and the attack in open warfare was practised. In the afternoons inter Platoon Football was played, but it was impossible owing to lack of opportunity to complete the competition. In a Rugger match against the 9th R. L. N. Lancs Regt. on the 4th the Battalion was defeated.	
"			On the 4th a draft of 8 other ranks joined the Battalion. On leaving the Brigade rest hutment area the 1st D HAZEBROUCK, the Battalion marching to SERCUS South West of HAZEBROUCK.	

Army Form C. 2118.

WAR DIARY
or
INTELLIGENCE SUMMARY
(Erase heading not required.)

Place	Date	Hour	Summary of Events and Information	Remarks and references to Appendices
SERCUS	12-18		During this period the Bn remained at SERCUS and training was continued when the same lines as at MONT DES CATS. On the 13th. the whole of A Company proceeded to the Divisional Musketry School near HETERON for a week's musketry training. On the 15th and 17th route marches were held by the Brigade and the RENETCURE, WARDRECQUES and BLARINGHEM. On the afternoon of the 18th the Battalion gave NAYED the 5th Loyal N Lanes Regt at RUGBY in which 2 PUSHED near SERCUS Bn was defeated. Four officers joined the Battalion for duty on the 13th - Capt G.B. RUSSELL D.S.O. Lt D.M. JEANS, Lt W.D. ROWE and 2/Lt C.H. ATKINSON, the Lieut. having from but stat'd in France.	
PRADELLES	19		Orders for a move into the BORRE area were received during the night of the 18th/19th.98 and on the 19th the Bn proceeded to that area via HAZEBROUCK. The Battalion was allotted billets at PRADELLES.	
	20		Usual inspection parades were held by Companies and specialist and foot Bn Refresher practices were carried out. 2/Lt D.P. HANNAH, a Warrant Officer and two other ranks joined the Battalion for duty.	

Army Form C. 2118.

WAR DIARY
or
INTELLIGENCE SUMMARY
(Erase heading not required.)

Instructions regarding War Diaries and Intelligence Summaries are contained in F. S. Regs., Part II. and the Staff Manual respectively. Title Pages will be prepared in manuscript.

Place	Date	Hour	Summary of Events and Information	Remarks and references to Appendices
OUTTERSTEENE	21		The Brigade moved into the OUTTERSTEENE area, the Battalion being allotted billets East of the village.	
	22		The Companies held independent parades of three hour duration, the programme of work including Physical Training, Bayonet fighting and Box Respirator Drill.	
MOOTE ROOM	23		The Battalion moved into the MOOTE ROOM area S.W. of BAILLEUL. The move was completed by midday and the remainder of the day was spent in preparing grounds for parades, football etc.	
"	24		The Companies held parades upon their own grounds during the morning, the usual programme being followed. The Tunnel Attack and the "Shakes" formation were practised.	
"	25		Church Parade was held in the morning. The service being taken by the Attd. A.P. Chaplain General of the 2nd Army. In the afternoon the Semi-finals of the Inter-platoon football were played : C Company defeated the Scout Company and A Company defeated D Company.	
"	26		Owing to rain little could be done in the way of outdoor parades and Lectures were given in the barns. A new Lewis Gun Class was formed, consisting of 2	

2449 Wt. W14957/M90 750,000 1/16 J.B.C. & A. Forms/C.2118/12.

WAR DIARY
or
INTELLIGENCE SUMMARY

Army Form C. 2118.

Place	Date	Hour	Summary of Events and Information	Remarks and references to Appendices
MOOTE ROOM	26		Officers and 2 men per Company. This Class was held throughout the week. An inter-Company Both-Country run which should have taken place in the afternoon had to be postponed owing to the bad condition of the ground. Three Officers joined the Battalion for duty: 2/Lt. W.R. HOLMES, 7/Lt. C.H. WHITE and 7/Lt. A.H. PARSONS.	
"	27th		Baths at PONT DE NIEPPE were allotted to almost the whole Battalion. The first party left at 7.30 a.m. and parties of 50 proceeded to PONT DE NIEPPE throughout the morning and afternoon. Only the Lewis Gun Class and a small Bombing Class were held.	
"	28th		B Company proceeded to ST MARIE CAPPEL near CASSEL for a six days' Musketry Course. The other three Companies held parades upon their own grounds, the usual programme being followed. Remainder of the inter-Platoon football was played; A Company defeated C Company. No 10 Platoon by 1 goal to nil. The winning team of the R.B.C. 7th Inf. Bge. On the same afternoon too other ranks of D Company were required for work under the Ordnance Officer of the New Zealand Division at PAPOT	

Place	Date	Hour	Summary of Events and Information	Remarks and references to Appendices
MOOTE ROOM	28th		Near NIEPPE, South of the BAILLEUL - ARMENTIERES road. The party was required for unloading ammunition and was kept at DEPOT for the remainder of the month.	
"	29		The Brigade Training Area was placed at the disposal of the Battalion, but owing to the bad weather no use was made of it, and training was carried out by A and C Companies to sub-Companies assembled in the vicinity of billets.	
	30th		A scheme for the attack of the village of STEENTJE was carried out in the morning by A and C Companies. 2 platoons of A Company defended the village, and C Company formed the attacking force. The snipers and scouts were divided between the two sides.	
"	31st		Practically the whole of A Company was required for working parties in the neighbourhood of BAILLEUL. C Company, the snipers and scouts, and a few of D Company carried out a practice of the French attack on the Brigade Training Area near BAILLEUL.	

A.W.Wilson Lt Col
Comdg 1/5 R.W. Kents Rgt
30.3.17

Army Form C. 2118.

WAR DIARY
or
INTELLIGENCE SUMMARY
(Erase heading not required.)

Jan 1st Battn Rec'd
33

Place	Date	Hour	Summary of Events and Information	Remarks and references to Appendices
STEENTJE	APRIL 1		Church Parade was held in the morning but the greater part of the Bn was employed upon working parties in the neighbourhood of BAILLEUL and DRANOUTRE. 1 Officer & 24 men TERR. Coast Reinforcement. 9 Other ranks joined the Bn for duty. This draft included 1 on Corporals.	
"	2 - 4		During these three days the Battalion continued to furnish working parties, and only a small number of each company were available for training. The Lewis gun class was continued. This consisted of 9 officers and other ranks. Its purpose was to specialize and supply trained and moving for Lewis guns. New non commissioned officers in the Bn were also instructed. On 4th the Brigade moved to a new area. The Battalion Brigade was to be billeted between in the night 5/6th to relieve an Australian Brigade.	
	5, 6		TOURNET Secto. B Company was brought back to the battalion in reserve from St. Marie CAPPEL. Since the company had been through a March by Orders. Regulated Scout, ground and snipers proceeded in advance of the Battalion to locate portable guns and snipers in advance of the Battalion to locate suitable positions for making by daylight. The remainder of the Battalion left STEENTJE by company parties between 6pm and 11pm and via STEENWERCK - NIEPPE to billets in DE SEECH FERME.	

WAR DIARY or INTELLIGENCE SUMMARY

Army Form C. 2118.

Place	Date	Hour	Summary of Events and Information	Remarks and references to Appendices
TREMODEZ LE TOURET	5.5		At about 3 a.m. and not complete until 6 a.m. This had the effect of In D Company Col. BAYES F.C. Rennell Rodd took over the whole of the LE TOURET Posn from the River Lys to to N. of GAP Z, South of FORTYSEVEN ROAD. The 8th L.N. Lancs. Regt. was the Bn. in Support and 3rd O/Cheshires Regt. the Bn. in Brigade Reserve. Bn. 3/4 Worcestershire Regt. was about ¼ Reinforcement. 3 men [?] MARIE COPSE. The remainder of the 1/5 S.W.B. to stand to to S.R. Reinforcements of 3 men joined the Bn. for duty in the L.F.	
	5–10		During the period the Battalion remained in the line and spent its own individual intensive wire and safety [?] displayed by stations [?] enemy's own left, apparently and displayed by stations [?] Left half of the Battalion [?] compelled [?] with the approach of advancing [?] to enemy's front line it was subjected more than [?] to enemy's fire [?] at least holding his own [?] C and D Company and [?] furthest on the right of the Bn to advance limits time though it a front was still most if [?] in which of though it was position intended [?] to [?] line was occupied. Lieutenant DAVIS was not [?] to a low to further getting through and forming an identification	

Army Form C. 2118.

WAR DIARY
or
INTELLIGENCE SUMMARY

(Erase heading not required.)

Instructions regarding War Diaries and Intelligence Summaries are contained in F. S. Regs, Part II. and the Staff Manual respectively. Title Pages will be prepared in manuscript.

Place	Date	Hour	Summary of Events and Information	Remarks and references to Appendices
TRENCHES LE TOUQUET	6-10		2nd Lts R. Tate and Two Canadian's viz C. Company due to 2 Lt's who proceed Sergt. Wm. Dyke, C. and Sisfr Pte. Musgrove, C. Reinforcement joined 2/Lt H.W.B. Burkett with 50 men joined the Bn for duty on 6th PR. On the night of the 10th the Bn was relieved by the 8th L.N. Lancs Regt and proceeded to Pont de Nieppe as Bn in Brigade Reserve. To relieve Rest found the Bn in Bde Support to Canadians drawn a number short.	
PONT DE NIEPPE	- 12		During this period to Bn to Bde Res. were used on Brigade Reserve at Pont de Nieppe Moveload to Grande Paul by Bn Bn were every provided working parties under R.E. supervision. Two conferences were organised daily for Coll. Tring & M.O. of 2 Bret Stept 36 A.M. (Major) 3-8 and Capt Long-staff was registered for work upon heavy gun positions near Le Rossignol. Our parties worked in toads of Bue L usual to south. Moreover PC Reinforcement joined the Bn as follows: On 12th. 30 other ranks or B.R. 1 man on 19th. 2 other ranks. These were a few Canadians to working parties 2/Lt B.A. 3 men recruited 10490 Pte. Riffin, C. (Died 25 B.R.) 25799 Pte. Shepard, F. and 23020 Pte. Wallis, E.	

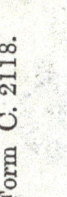

WAR DIARY or INTELLIGENCE SUMMARY

Army Form C. 2118.

Place	Date	Hour	Summary of Events and Information	Remarks and references to Appendices
NEUVE EGLISE	19		The Battalion moved to BULFORD CAMP S. of NEUVE EGLISE. The remainder of the Brigade moved into the NEUTRAL AREA.	
	20-27		Throughout the period practically the whole Battalion was required for working parties East of and in NEUVE EGLISE and at RAVOT & S. of BAILLEUL – NIEPPE Rd. Two Companies were employed from time to time on the partial use of dug outs & unloading material to used on the Rd. highly and for use of or & track railway near NEUVE EGLISE. In the evenings parades were held for training officers and N.C.O's. Musketry instruction was given and several lightning sketches were utilised. A Ref. Scheme was carried out. Two Officers joined the Battalion on 31st. 2/Lt E H GURGE (about 1/2" CLARKE). There were two Casualties to working parties. Wounded 22235 L.C. HALL W. died on 24/9/19 Pte CARTER T. & S.E.3 Fighting Sough Battalion on 29R – 2/Lts. 42 Other Ranks etc. No Bombs, Lewis Gunners & Signallers. Gas Helmets inspected and Box respirators arriving 10 stores. June 21 1917.	

Army Form C. 2118.

WAR DIARY
or
INTELLIGENCE SUMMARY
(Erase heading not required.)

Place	Date	Hour	Summary of Events and Information	Remarks and references to Appendices
MERRIS	30		The Brigade as the result of orders received at a short notice moved up to MERRIS also to the Battalion who of proceeding to an area N. of STRAZEELE between STRAZEELE and CAESTRE.	
			31.4.17	

W. Matthews Lt Col.
Commdg 1st Bn. Wiltshire Regiment.

Army Form C. 2118.

WAR DIARY
or
INTELLIGENCE SUMMARY
(Erase heading not required.)

1 Wilts Regt' JL 34

Place	Date	Hour	Summary of Events and Information	Remarks and references to Appendices
STRAZEELE	MAY 1st		The greater part of the day was taken up with Refitting at the Battles near OUTTER- STEENE. Kit inspections were held and Company arrangement.	
"	2nd		There were Company parades during the morning on ground in the neighbourhood of Billets. Bayonet fighting, rifle exercises, platoon and company drill were carried out and for a few minutes at hand practice for recruits were made. Lt. J.F. TERRY was appointed Adjutant of the Battalion in place of Capt. GOODHART. (June 2/6) N.C.Os. were detailed to be Officers in 2nd Appointment taking effect from April 27th.	
"	3rd		During the 1st half of the morning Company Training was carried out as on the preceding day. There was Battalion Drill for the last hour of the morning. Two Rifle Bombing Sections were given instruction in the employment of the No. 2s Rifle Grenade, and two Lewis Gun teams were practised in firing from the hip. The Brigade began its move to the 2nd Army Reserves Area, N.W. of MISQUES.	
PERCUS	4th		So the 1/4 th Battalion marched to PERCUS, S.W. of HAZEBROUCK.	
EQUERDES	5th		On the 5th the Brigade completed its move and the Battalion was Billeted in EQUERDES, S.W. of MISQUES.	
"	6th		Church Parade was held in the morning. The day was spent settling down into Billets.	

WAR DIARY or INTELLIGENCE SUMMARY

Army Form C. 2118.

Place	Date	Hour	Summary of Events and Information	Remarks and references to Appendices
HAVERNAS	7th-12th		Throughout the week Platoon and Company Training was carried out on the Bns. Training area near OVERMET; one day was entirely devoted to Rifle and Lewis gun firing practice upon the TIRQUES range. The morning's work included Musketry Training, the training of Bombing and Rifle Bombing Sections, the practice of the Attack at first by Platoons, then by Companies - introducing movement in "Snake" formation and Extended Order, great attention being paid to the part played by the different sections, Lewis Gunners, Rifle Bombers etc. The training of Signallers was carried out independently throughout the week, particular attention being given to instruction in "Visual".	
	13th-17th		Another day's Rifle and Lewis gun firing practice was carried out on a TIRQUES range on the 13th. On the 14th, 15th, 16th & 17th D.R. Battalion and Brigade Training was carried out. This included a Brigade Assembly by night (marching by Coys) a night bivouac and the practice of the Battalion and Brigade Attack. The ground was previously marked out to resemble as closely as possible the actual ground that had been allotted to the Brigade in view of future operations north-east of NUYERGHEM. The farthest objectives and the task of the Battalion and to make this it was necessary to pass through	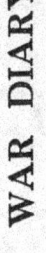

Army Form C. 2118.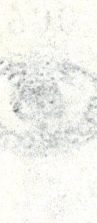

WAR DIARY
or
INTELLIGENCE SUMMARY
(Erase heading not required.)

Instructions regarding War Diaries and Intelligence Summaries are contained in F.S. Regs., Part II. and the Staff Manual respectively. Title Pages will be prepared in manuscript.

Place	Date	Hour	Summary of Events and Information	Remarks and references to Appendices
SERCUS STRAZEELE	18th 19th		Two Battalions of the 3rd Worcestershire Regt. and the 9th L.N. Lancashire Regt. were reported for the capture of the enemy's front and immediate Sup. front lines, and though the 9th Cheshire Regt. whose task was to capture the enemy's second line. Photograph of A taken were taken on the 18th. On the 15th B. Battalion 18 others ranks joined the Battalion. The Battalion moved to SERCUS. On the 19th moved to HAZEBROUCK.	
RAVELSBERG	20th 21-24		The Battalion moved to billets N. of STRAZEELE. The Battalion moved into bivouac in RAVELSBERG HILL E. of RAILWAY. The Battalion remained in RAVELSBERG HILL in tents and bivouacs. On the 21st and 22nd Working Parties (150 other ranks in strength) had to be provided for unloading and carrying Ammunition near NEUVE EGLISE. Except for these parties the men were all off to rest. On the 26th 25 Reinforcements, 5 other ranks joined the Battalion.	
WULVERGHEM TRENCHES	25th 25th - 28th		The Battalion relieved the 9th L.N. Lancs. Regt. (74th Bde.) in the WULVERGHEM sector on the morning of the 25th. The Relief being completed by 5 a.m. During this period the Battalion garrisoned the front line, two Companies in the line, two Companies for Support. All Companies provided Large Parties for work or repairs to the front line trenches in the northern	

WAR DIARY or INTELLIGENCE SUMMARY

Army Form C. 2118.

half of the Battalion Sector. Patrols were sent out each night to ascertain the enemy's method of holding his front line, as everything pointed to his leaving it practically unoccupied throughout the day, and it was observed that each night the greater part of his Very lights were fired from his support and reserve lines.

Throughout the day and night the artillery of 65th Corps was active; a great deal of registration was carried out, several new Batteries moved in. The enemy's shelling of the back areas (generally at about 9 p.m.) resulted in the blowing up of several ammunition dumps in the neighbourhood of NEUVE EGLISE – WULVERGHEM Rd.

There were the following casualties from hostile shell fire:

Killed: 26718   L/C. HARDING, R.   Wounded.
          20269   Pte. STEPHENSON, F.   Missing, reported later.
          29805   "   STEPHENS, C.   Wounded and Missing
          29853   "   BAILLACHE, J.   } Wounded, still at duty.
          9126   "   SEVIOUR, W.   }
          23825   "   WITTS, G.

Other casualties were incurred by patrols on the nights of the 28/29th.

26575   Pte. RICHARDSON, R.P.   25/5/17
23575   "   STAPLES, W.M.   27/5/17
23367   "   COLLARD, F.G.   28/5/17

WAR DIARY
or
INTELLIGENCE SUMMARY

Army Form C. 2118.

Place	Date	Hour	Summary of Events and Information	Remarks and references to Appendices
	29		The Battalion was relieved on the 29th by the 8th E.N. Lancs Regt. The Battalion on either flank were Right, 2nd Bn. Staffs Regt. Left, a Bn. of the Royal Irish Rifles in the 36th Div. On relief the Bn. became the Bn. in Brigade Support, 2 Companies and HQ moving into Bivouacs N.W. of NEUVE EGLISE, while 2 Companies remained in support to the 8th E.N. Lancs Regt in a support line DURHAM TRENCH. The two Companies in Bivouacs were employed to furnish parties to work in the forward area under R.E. Supervision. Rare parties were out by the greater part of the day. 16 other ranks reinforcements joined the Bn.	
	30		Two large parties were provided by the Bn. on the night 30/31st. One party of 200 was employed with other Battalions of the Brigade digging a new fire trench in the Nows land to the MULKERGHEM REDT. The second party was responsible for the wiring of it. The work was carried out successfully, the casualties were sustained subsequently owing to a heavy hostile artillery barrage upon the support trenches who stood 2 Companies had moved after work. The Casualties upon the 30th and 31st were Killed: 10641 Pte BULL, D 22898 " THURWOOD, J.R. 32513 " HAND, J	

Army Form C. 2118.

WAR DIARY
or
INTELLIGENCE SUMMARY
(Erase heading not required.)

Instructions regarding War Diaries and Intelligence Summaries are contained in F. S. Regs., Part II. and the Staff Manual respectively. Title Pages will be prepared in manuscript.

Place	Date	Hour	Summary of Events and Information	Remarks and references to Appendices
	30 cont		Killed: 33179 Pte. SILENCE, A.T.W. 31105 " VALENTINE, F.W. Wounded: Capt. G.B. RUSSELL, D.S.O. 9196 Lt. HUNTLEY, A 33123 Cpl. GODFREY, C 26172 Sgt. PEARCE, H. 11782 Pte. HELM, T.R. 9132 " TOWLSON, E.C. 16259 " STONE A.V. 24130 " CHAPPELLE 3/112 " COOK, S. 24164 " LUGG, R. 21431 " HARRIS, H. 26823 " WATTERS, C 29828 " KING E Died of wounds 6940 L/Cpl. ELLEY F. R. died 20540 Cpl. PICKERING, V.G.A 25690 Pte. COX, E 10103 " WALLIS C 31st On the 30th the "B" Team of the Battalion (6 officers and 117 other ranks left for MORBECQUES	

WAR DIARY
or
INTELLIGENCE SUMMARY

Army Form C. 2118.

Place	Date	Hour	Summary of Events and Information	Remarks and references to Appendices
	31		A and B Companys took the place of C and D Companies in support to the 5th L.N. Lancs Regt. and C and D Companies bivouacked near NEUVE EGLISE.	
			The following were mentioned in despatches following during the month in A.R.O. 7 READER. LT J.R. TAYLER. LT H. WEBBER. 2/LT W.E. ROSE.	
			3 C.D.	

W Williams Lt Colonel
Commanding 5th Welsh Regt.

WAR DIARY or INTELLIGENCE SUMMARY

Vol 3 — 1st Bn. Wiltshire Regt.

Army Form C. 2118.

(Erase heading not required.)

Place	Date	Hour	Summary of Events and Information	Remarks and references to Appendices
	JUNE 1 and 2		During these two days the Battalion continued to furnish Brigade Support at WULVERGHEM in Partial Support to the Battalion in the front line. 6th. S.W. Lancs Regt: The remainder of the Bn. was encamped near NEWE EGLISE. Often of the Other were engaged on fatigue days and practically the whole of the Bn. When not called upon, Casualties on the 1st were — Wounded, 1 other rank. Wounded still at duty, 2 other ranks.	
RAVELSBERG HILL	3		On the morning of the 3rd, the Battalion was relieved to by the 8th BORDER REGT. and went into a Camp on the RAVELSBERG HILL near BAILLEUL In the evening a raid was attempted by a party from two Companies upon the enemy's line opposite the WULVERGHEM Redt. This was unsuccessful, and no identification was obtained. There were the following Casualties: Wounded, 7 other ranks. Wounded, still at duty, 2 other ranks.	
	4 — 6		During this period the Battalion remained at RAVELSBERG CAMP, and except for being called upon to supply two small working parties, the men were able to rest. On the 4th, reinforcement of 10 other ranks, joined the Battalion. In the afternoon of the 5th, a party of 50 other ranks from 'C' and 'D' Companies under Mrs BROWN, D.F and LUDFORD W.E. carried out a raid upon the enemy's defence opposite the WULVERGHEM Redt. and penetrated to his 2 trench. Owing to his first system of trenches unfortunately most of the enemy were encountered, and the trenches were found to be quite unoccupied. Casualties were	

Army Form C. 2118.

WAR DIARY
or
INTELLIGENCE SUMMARY
(Erase heading not required.)

Instructions regarding War Diaries and Intelligence Summaries are contained in F.S. Regs., Part II. and the Staff Manual respectively. Title Pages will be prepared in manuscript.

Place	Date	Hour	Summary of Events and Information	Remarks and references to Appendices
	6		caused by enfilading fire from the flanks and by one or two of our own shells falling short. The numbers were, killed 1 other rank. Wounded 8 other ranks. Wounded still at duty 3, and missing 2 other ranks. The notification was received that the attack on the MESSINES RIDGE pro day was to 7th. The whole of the 6th was spent in making all necessary preparations	
WULVERGHEM TRENCHES	7		On the night 6/7th the Battalion moved into assembly trenches in the WULVERGHEM sector. The attempts being completed by midnight. It was carried out with few casualties. Zero hour for the attack was 3.10 a.m. and at that moment several mines were exploded and an intense barrage commenced. The Battalion, in the lead of the Brigade to move forward and debouched from its assembly trench at 3.40 a.m. and moved forward in artillery formation. In spite of the fact that it was not yet light and in spite of the smoke and dust obliterating all landmarks with the exception of L'ENFER WOOD, the men kept excellent direction. After the STEENBECQUE had been crossed the Barrage pending on the left bore away to the left slightly, and it was necessary to keep in touch with them. This however was soon corrected, and the Battalion now that it had passed through the other Battalions continued its ad-	

2449 Wt. W14957/M90 750,000 1/16 J.B.C. & A. Forms/C.2118/12.

Army Form C. 2118.

WAR DIARY or INTELLIGENCE SUMMARY
(Erase heading not required.)

Place	Date	Hour	Summary of Events and Information	Remarks and references to Appendices
			vance in accordance with the Barrage time table. At 3am + two minutes the Battalion charged its first objective OCTOBER TRENCH. Our resistance was swamm- ered in strong trench Assault that were thoroughly dealt with and in each case the garrison were either killed or taken prisoners. The attack on 4 HUNS' FARM and OCTOBER SUPPORT, the Battalion's second objective, was delayed for some time on account of the standing artillery barrage not lifting at the correct time, and at this juncture several casualties oc- curred. Eventually this Objective fell and prisoners and two machine guns were taken. A gap was however left in existence which threatened this Left flank and a hostile machine gun was active in LUMM'S FM. and was causing casualties. An immediate attack was made upon this strong point and the garrison of 40 was killed or captured. Although the Battalion had now reached its final objective the advance was continued, the enemy retreated by the fact that the Division's Left flank was still exposed. A number of the enemy who had congregated in a farm now called WILTS FM. (O.26.d.85.90 in France. Sheet 28 S.W.) were killed or captured and 2 more machine guns were taken. Previous to this a line of posts had been formed East of the road that turned through O.26.d.	

Army Form C. 2118.

WAR DIARY
or
INTELLIGENCE SUMMARY
(Erase heading not required.)

Instructions regarding War Diaries and Intelligence Summaries are contained in F. S. Regs., Part II. and the Staff Manual respectively. Title Pages will be prepared in manuscript.

Place	Date	Hour	Summary of Events and Information	Remarks and references to Appendices
	7th		At 4 P.M. 2nd 8 to morning the 75th Brigade passed through the Battalion, and all men of this Battalion S. of OCTOBER SUPPORT were withdrawn, as that on the evening of the 7th the disposition of the Bn. was :— 2 Companies in OCTOBER TRENCH and 2 in OCTOBER SUPPORT. to the former were attached entirely destroyed by an our shell-fire a fresh trench was dug about 30 yards in advance of it.	
	8th		The work of consolidation was continued on the 8th and much digging was done and wire was put out. At night the 2 Companies in OCTOBER TRENCH moved forward into OCTOBER RESERVE, the trench S. of OCTOBER SUPPORT.	
	9th		Orders were received on the 9th that the Bn. was to take over the Red Line from the 52nd Bn. Australian Imperial Force after dark. This line was ODIOUS TRENCH running from O.27.a 9.1 to O.33.c.5.4 (Bernet Sheet 36 S.W.), and in addition the advanced posts between ODIOUS TRENCH and ODIOUS SUPPORT were to be taken over. It was impossible to reconnoitre the line by day, there being no communication trenches, and all approaches were under observation from the enemy. The Battalion moved up after dusk	

WAR DIARY or INTELLIGENCE SUMMARY

Army Form C. 2118.

But at the Australian guides lost the parties arriving the relief was not complete until 3 a.m. The Left Company got into touch with a INDIAN Regiment of the 11th Division, and its right company with 2 officers and 38 men of an Australian Battalion. One Company was Reg't in support in the neighbourhood of Bn. Bns. H.Qrs. at 0.28 c 2.8.

During the 8th and 11th the Battalion remained in this position. By day his snipers were active, and at night his machine guns. His Stokens was directed chiefly against Bn Support company and in the vicinity of Bn. H.Q. at 0.27 c 3.9. Not many casualties were caused. On the night of the 11/12th the Bn. was relieved by the 6th York and Lancs Regt. relief being complete by 1.30 a.m.

The Battalion bivouacked near, MULVERGHEM by the NEUVE EGLISE Rd. and rested in the 12th. Roll calls were held and checks taken of after serves in equipment and arms. The Brigade received complimentary messages from Army Corps and Divisional Commanders.

The Battalion's total capture were 148 prisoners and 7 machine guns.
The Casualties for the period 7/4 — 11/4 inclusive were: Killed, 2

WAR DIARY
or
INTELLIGENCE SUMMARY

Army Form C. 2118.

Places	Date	Hour	Summary of Events and Information	Remarks and references to Appendices
			Officers (Lt N.G.B. KING and 2/Lt. P.F.G. JONES), and 19 Others ranks; Wounded, 2 officers (Lt. I.R. TAYLER and 2/Lt. B.W. BIDWELL) and 96 other ranks. Died of wounds 1/1 officer (Lt. C. SAINSBURY, M.C.) and 7 other ranks. Wounded (still at duty), 3 officers (Capt. P.F.T. HAYWARD, M.C. and 2/Lt. G.R. TANNER) and 2 other ranks. Missing 13 other ranks. On the 11th the "B" team, which had been at MORBECQUE, rejoined the Bn. So then each had moved by train from "B" team on the 5th but in view of the shortages in numbers and as a third of casualties returned in the first week of June. The Bn. bivouacked in a field near NEUVE EGLISE upon the western side of the LINDENHOEK RD. During the day the men rested. Only Guards provided for Companies were held in the morning. In the evening the 1st/4th reinforced the Brigade moved up into support to the I.F. Inf. Bn. who garrisoned the Divisional front line. Sent 2 Hughes running from the northern end of own support, along own support, unknown	ffc ffc ffc
	13			
	14, 15			

Place	Date	Hour	Summary of Events and Information	Remarks and references to Appendices
	19		SUPPORT AND UNDULATING SUPPORT by the RIVER DOUVE. The Bn. marched via NEUVE EGLISE. Shells the No 1 of the Brigade took up position South and East of MESSINES.	
	20		During this period the Battalion was called upon to furnish back working & making parties to its strength of No 3 Coy. & then made for digging a communication trench from the MESSINES ridge S.E. of MESSINES to the Road line. These parties were sent from 8 p.m. to 4 a.m. daily. Considerable hostile shelling was encountered and the following casualties were caused. 15th 1 O.R. wounded. 18th 2 O.R. wounded. 19th 2 O.R. wounded. 20th 8 O.R. wounded and 4 O.R. killed. In spite of the shelling the work was carried out to the entire satisfaction of the R.E. During the day the men rested undercover and what proved taking place in the afternoon.	J.C.
NEUVE EGLISE	21		Notice was received that the Battalion would be relieved by the 5th Australian Inf Battalion and preparations were made for the relief. The working parties went out on the night 21/22.	J.C.

WAR DIARY
or
INTELLIGENCE SUMMARY

(Erase heading not required.)

Army Form C. 2118.

Place	Date	Hour	Summary of Events and Information	Remarks and references to Appendices
RAVENSBERG HILL	22		The Battalion was relieved by the 34th Australian Inf. Battalion at 9.30 a.m. and moved by Companies to the trenches on the RAVENSBERG HILL occupied on June 5th. Short Company parades were carried out during the afternoon. Orders were received for the Battalion to move to the evening of the 23rd.	
	22/23		SWARTENBROUCK and on Short parades took place in the morning, the remainder of the day being spent and preparations for the march. The Battalion moved off at 2.30 p.m. and marched by BAILLEUL-STRAZEELE-LA MOTTE to LILLERS at LE PARC arriving at 3 a.m.	
LE PARC	24/25		During the day the men rested and at ... of fourteen men was sent to the HAZEBROUCK area. The Battalion moved to Lillers half a mile W. of ST VENANT marching through MERVILLE-LEBART ST VENANT arriving in billets at 3 a.m.	
ST VENANT	25/26		After resting during this day the Battalion moved off at 9 p.m. and marched by LILLERS-AURIONVILLA-NORRETTE-ST NEDONCHELLES arriving in billets & LEEN... In spite of very heavy rain & darkness the men came in excellent spirits	

WAR DIARY or INTELLIGENCE SUMMARY

Army Form C. 2118.

Place	Date	Hour	Summary of Events and Information	Remarks and references to Appendices
NEDONCHELLE	26/27		apart never fell out. After writing during the day the Battalion marched off at 12 p.m. and arrived at DEULLE via AIRE - LUMBRES - FRUGES-DELETTE arriving in billets at 3 a.m. Throughout the 4 days the marching was fortunately good, not a single man fell out on any march.	
DELETTE	27		The day was devoted to fixing up billets, bathing places etc, & out fitting.	
	28.		Eighteen men carried out musketry Company arrangements.	
	29		The Battalion commenced training. Conference hold afternoon from 6.15 a.m. and carried out Training in the use of uniform between Company and Battalion Drill. Lectures were given in the evening.	
	30		In the morning the men went bathing. Very bad weather interfered with training.	

5.5.0 gave St agot
C in C 1st Wiltshire Regt.

Army Form C. 2118.

WAR DIARY or INTELLIGENCE SUMMARY
(Erase heading not required.)

1 Wilts Regt Vol 36

Place	Date	Hour	Summary of Events and Information	Remarks and references to Appendices
At DELETTE	July 1st		Church Parade was held in the morning. In the afternoon in the First Round of the Divisional Football Tournament the Battalion defeated the 2nd R.C. Lowe's 71st H. Regt. by 1 goal to nil. Reinforcement of 2 other ranks joined the Bn.	
	2.5		During Recreation the Batta Coy engaged at DELETTE and carried out training in fighting up a communication trench upon a Bombed area & Rifle Bombs. Each Coy were independent parades for Lewis gun Section and a Lewis gun Class was held. In the Evening practice (rifle and lower tank) for the Whole Battalion was carried out into a 400 yard length was organised. In the 4th Battalion at COYECQUES came a Lecture to the Bn. and as it was raining during the morning little else was possible in the way of parades.	
			Divisional Football Tournament won by Brigade against the Yeomanry defeated in 71st R. Dub. Fusiliers 2 goals to 1. Teams.	
			In the afternoon 2/Lt. G. Bainford (front was killed) and an to Tunning. There was an Inter-company Inn Athletic Grand 67 & lee Company.	
			On the 3rd a staff Inst. given to the 4th Royal Irish Rifles under musters to be held	

WAR DIARY or INTELLIGENCE SUMMARY

Army Form C. 2118.

Place	Date	Hour	Summary of Events and Information	Remarks and references to Appendices
	July 6.7		On the 6th the Battalion moved by Bases and train to STEENBECQUE & to HAZEBROUCK. The following day the move was continued partly by train & partly by march from to DOMINION CAMP. E of BOESCHEPE. Lieut Capt. C. REAVON, C.F. joined the Battalion for duty as Chaplain. Lt Major W.C. SQUIRE, D.S.O. proceeded on leave on the 7th Capt G.D. BROWN M.C. assumed command of the Battalion.	
	8		In the day the men rested. A few officers and NCO's reconnoitred routes to YPRES.	
	9		Rest paraded were held in the morning and in the evening the Battalion marched by Companies to YPRES and relieved the 10/CHESHIRE REGT. in the ramparts near the Station. The Casualties on the 9th were. nominal. 2 other ranks	
	10–14		During this period the Battalion remained in the Ramparts in Brigade Support. It was called upon each night to furnish working parties in the forward area and parties for carrying dead rations &c. As a party of the strength of 240 other ranks was required for work under the C.R.E. for 5 days out of the Battalion in YPRES and remained the C.R.E. party (under Lt Lyons at MONTEER CAMP. had G. was E. TURCO DUGARDOT and KRUISTRAAT.	

WAR DIARY
or
INTELLIGENCE SUMMARY

(Erase heading not required.)

Army Form C. 2118.

Place	Date	Hour	Summary of Events and Information	Remarks and references to Appendices
	6-17		The casualties during the fight were very largely due to a form of gas shell used extensively new and here christened "Mustard Gas". This gas attacks the eyes of all and of persons and was very difficult to detect. But for a first symptoms an furious sneezing & watery eyes caused hours later. Vomiting and affectation of the eyes caused. Casualties that have worked at Gas were caused by hostile shelling and to casualties were at Potiyze. Killed 3 other ranks. Wounded 17 and 2/Lt T Wilson and 3 other ranks. Wounded field strength 4 other ranks. 11th: Casualties other ranks Wounded 2 other ranks. 12 H: Wounded (Gas) 22 ☰ other ranks. Wounded 2 other ranks. Wounded NCO & 1 O/Rs (Gas) 4 other ranks. BH: Wounded (Gas) 3 other ranks killed. Reinforcements joined the Battalion to be following date. 11 H: 131 other ranks. 12 H: 4 other ranks. 13 H: 6 other ranks. 14 H: 5 other ranks. The 28th November Bn moved to the transport lines of the Essex Regt Shed.	

WAR DIARY
INTELLIGENCE SUMMARY

(Erase heading not required.)

Army Form C. 2118.

Place	Date	Hour	Summary of Events and Information	Remarks and references to Appendices
	14/6		On the nights of the 14 & 15 often that the Battalion marched up to relieve the CHESHIRE REGT. in the line between a farm opposite the new Zonnebeke BRUGE ROAD and LAKE and the YPRES PILCKEM railway to N.E. of KLEINER ZILLEBEKE on the left. The relieving came their occurred during relief; killed & other ranks, however 2 other ranks.	
	15-19		During this period the Battalion held the large party under the C.R.E. & 1 PIONEER CAMP remained in the line with a company of the 15/CHESHIRE REGT. in close support throughout. We have been very great artillery activity in the first 6 days, & Battalion's Chief task whole in the line was consequently harassed by hostile shellfire continually, Flying on push work. The relief was very... between 11pm and midnight also, with each enemy difficult. The relief of the Battalion by the 16/CHESHIRE REGT. took up the greater part of two days 19th. 20th. and was carried out by detail, fixed went in platoons in phases/a moving at large intervals the Battalion moved back in support support in the Ramparts near the Station. YPRES. The Casualties during this period under review were :-	

WAR DIARY
or
INTELLIGENCE SUMMARY

Army Form C. 2118.

(Erase heading not required.)

Place	Date	Hour	Summary of Events and Information	Remarks and references to Appendices
			17/2. Killed 2 other ranks. Wounded 3/L.t. R.H. STIRLING Army 5 other ranks. Wounded & still at duty 10 other ranks.	
			18/2. Killed 1 other rank. Wounded 6 other ranks. Wounded (P.O.) 10 other ranks. Wounded, still at duty, 3 other ranks.	
			19/2. Killed 1 other rank. Wounded 10 other ranks. Wounded (gas), 1 wounded so still at duty 3/Lt. Brailes, Chelmsford, 2, & suffered still at duty (field ranks) 1, wounded still at duty (gas). Also 3 P. HAMMs	
			8/1. Wounded 2 other ranks	
			20/2. (After arrival in cantonment of Siselip). Wounded 4. N. still at duty, 3	
			During these two days the battalion remained in Brigade & Bn. was called upon to provide working parties as to forward area as required by the 2nd dur div. On the night 21/22. 22nd The battalion was relieved by the 2nd. N. YORKS Reg't of 8th division and marched back to DOMINION CAMP.	
	21, 22		In these two days the Casualties were :— 21/2/17 Wounded 3 other ranks. Wounded (gas) 2 other ranks.	

Place	Date	Hour	Summary of Events and Information	Remarks and references to Appendices
	July 23		About Wounded 7 other ranks. Wounded. Officer on duty (?)	
	24		The men at DOMINION CAMP today put to party at PIONEER CAMP had to do more nights work on the nights of 23rd/24th as the ground was very unprepared many camouflets. On 23rd Artillery 1 Wounded, 2 other ranks missing Officers killed 1. Attacked by fumes to have been killed. On 24th. Died of wounds. 3. In the ... in ... 5th the Battalion moved into a Camp S. of Busseboom as known the Ridge Wood RENINGHELST.	

WAR DIARY
or
INTELLIGENCE SUMMARY

Army Form C. 2118.

Place	Date	Hour	Summary of Events and Information	Remarks and references to Appendices
BRINGHURST	30/7/17 — 31/7/17		During the forenoon the men were all to get a considerable amount of rest. Training was carried out by Companies in the morning. The semi final of the Division inter-battalion Competition was played against the 1/6th Field Ambulance resulting in a win for us. The final played against the 13th CHESHIRE Regt resulted in a draw. Reconnaissance of the forward area tracks and assembly positions was made by all Officers and cadre's issued to Companies in preparation for the attack. Major MACLAINE of LOCHBUIE, 1/5th Hussars, joined the Battalion on the 30th as 2nd in command. On the night of the 30/31.7.17. the Battalion moved to the forward concentration area in the neighbourhood of BELGIUM CHATEAU, moving then until 3 a.m. in the morning of the 31st. Zero hour for the attack was 3.50 and at HALF WAY HOUSE plans 4 the Battalion moved up to the dug out at HALF WAY HOUSE ready to perform to plans followed by the remainder of the Brigade. The Battalion remained in the shelter	

Army Form C. 2118.

WAR DIARY
or
INTELLIGENCE SUMMARY
(Erase heading not required.)

Instructions regarding War Diaries and Intelligence Summaries are contained in F. S. Regs., Part II and the Staff Manual respectively. Title Pages will be prepared in manuscript.

Place	Date	Hour	Summary of Events and Information	Remarks and references to Appendices
			During the night of the 31/1. A number of parts were a fresh enemy the enemy to account in digging out field guns which had been blown up by shells which fire.	

S. E. O. Gythe
LT. COLONEL
COMDG. 1st Bn. WILTSHIRE REGT.

2449 Wt. W14957/M90 750,000 1/16 J.B.C. & A. Forms/C.2118/12.

WAR DIARY or INTELLIGENCE SUMMARY

Army Form C. 2118.

1st Wiltshire Regt. Vol 3

Place	Date	Hour	Summary of Events and Information	Remarks and references to Appendices
(Shut Hooge)	1.8.17		The Battalion on this date was in the HALF WAY HOUSE dugout. At noon orders were received to relieve the 1st Sherwood Foresters on the WESTHOEK Ridge. The Battalion moved off by half platoons and on arriving in the neighbourhood of the BELLEWAARDE Lake such heavy hostile shelling was encountered as to render further movement impossible. The men were put in such cover as was available and remained there until 5 p.m. when the shelling was less intense. The relief was then proceeded with by very small parties. The position on the ridge was somewhat obscure and we took one from men of the 1/SHERWOOD FORESTERS, 3/WEST YORKSHIRE R.B. and 2/LINCOLNS. The relief was finally completed at about 10 p.m. a line being taken up West of the village of WESTHOEK, 3 Companies being in the front line from J.7.b.2.3. to J.7.b.8.8. with A. Coy. in support. C. Coy were on the left, B. in the centre and D. on the right. The casualties during this day were 5 killed and 26 wounded.	
	2.8.17		During the night off ½ rations were brought up by the regimental pack pony convoy to a point immediately North of Mt BELLEWARDE Lake.	

Army Form C. 2118.

WAR DIARY
or
INTELLIGENCE SUMMARY
(Erase heading not required.)

Place	Date	Hour	Summary of Events and Information	Remarks and references to Appendices
			beyond extent it was impossible to proceed. During the whole time in the line Companies were obliged to send back carrying parties to the dump and owing to the heavy rain and the marshy nature of the ground in the valley between the WEST HOEK and BELLEWARDE Ridges this was most exhausting and arduous work. The trenches were improved and deepened and the support line dug. During the day messages were received on several occasions from the Company on the left to the effect that our own shells and droppings short and late in the afternoon from our night barrage as well. This was also reported by the units on the flanks. The 10th CHESHIRES on the left and the 8th LOYAL NORTH LANCASHIRES on the right. Hostile shelling was confined to the BELLEWARDE Ridge and CHATEAU WOOD area; the front line and the valley were hardly shelled at all. The enemy exposed himself a great deal during the morning and it is thought that a relief must have been carried out. Our snipers were very active and some obtained complete superiority. Forty nine	

2449 Wt. W14957/Mg0 750,000 1/16 J.B.C. & A. Forms/C.2118/12.

WAR DIARY
or
INTELLIGENCE SUMMARY

Army Form C. 2118.

Place	Date	Hour	Summary of Events and Information	Remarks and references to Appendices
	3.8.17		hits were reported during the day. Our casualties were 3 officers and 119 OR wounded. During the night of 2/3 each Company in the line sent out patrols with a view to ascertaining the enemy's dispositions and strength. A patrol of "B" Coy located the enemy and of a force 50 to 70 in front of our line and occupied it. During the day the enemy shelled the valley intermittently and about 8 p.m. commenced to shell the BELLEWAARDE Ridge heavily and continued until dawn. Our casualties were 1 killed and 6 wounded.	
	4.8.17		At 3.50 a.m. the enemy put down a heavy barrage on the front line of the Battalion on the right and on our support lines. The S.O.S. signal was sent up on our immediate right and was flashed back by lamp from the support Company on WESTHOEK Ridge. It was repeated at Battalion H.Q. on the BELLEWAARDE Ridge. The artillery was very slow in replying. No attack was actually made against our sector. During the day we were much troubled by short shooting on the part of our artillery, reports being received from all Companies in the line	

WAR DIARY
or
INTELLIGENCE SUMMARY
(Erase heading not required.)

Army Form C. 2118.

Place	Date	Hour	Summary of Events and Information	Remarks and references to Appendices
			During the night we established posts on either side of the road formed by our previous advance and the Right Company sent a patrol to a point where a hostile machine gun was believed to be in position. This had been withdrawn and a new trench was dug from J.7.8.50.30 to J.7.4.85.35 (Sheet HOOGE 1/10,000) straightening out our line at this point. Our casualties were 2 killed and 11 wounded.	
	5.8.17		During the night of the 4/5 the left Company advanced their line establishing posts immediately W. of the WESTHOEK-FREZENBERG Road. During this morning orders were received for the relief of the 7th Brigade by the 74th Brigade. The relief was arranged as it was carried out by portions of this Battalion. Eventually the right half sector relieved by the 2nd R.I.R. and the left half sector by the 9th Royal N. Lancashire Regt. relief being complete about midnight. While the last company was still between the BELLEWAARDE ridge and the CHATEAU WOOD the enemy commenced to shell very heavily using large numbers of mustard gas shells and also some phosphorus shells. No casualties were caused and with the exception of a few of H.Q. the Battalion was able to make its way back to the	

WAR DIARY
or
INTELLIGENCE SUMMARY
(Erase heading not required.)

Army Form C. 2118.

Place	Date	Hour	Summary of Events and Information	Remarks and references to Appendices
			transport when a hot meal was in readiness. Our casualties were 1 Officer and 3 O.R. killed and 1 Officer and 3 O.R. wounded. 2/Lt NWOOD was killed by a shell in the support trench and 2/Lt G. FILOR MC was wounded by a fragment of shell on the MENIN Road	
	6.8.17		After a meal at the transport lines the Companies marched their way to HALIFAX Camp on the OUDERDOM - VLAMERTINGHE Road. Baths and a clean change were provided for all men arriving the afternoon. The men were billeted in huts.	
	7.8.17		This day was devoted to inspections and reorganizing. There were few Aidens and Purret performances for the men in the afternoon.	
	8.8.17		During the day Companies drew Box Respirators to replace them old ones which were practically all unworkable owing to their having been wet beyond the period of 40 hours which is their life. Warning orders were received for the Battalion to be prepared to move at half an hours notice to the RAMPARTS of YPRES and from there to the HALF WAY HOUSE dugout.	
	9.8.17		Orders were received for the Battalion to proceed to the RAMPARTS of YPRES and then return to the 11th CHESHIRE Regt	

WAR DIARY
or
INTELLIGENCE SUMMARY
(Erase heading not required.)

Army Form C. 2118.

Place	Date	Hour	Summary of Events and Information	Remarks and references to Appendices
	10.8.17		This relief was completed by 5 a.m. Early in the morning a warning order was received to the effect that the Brigade was being relieved by the 8th Division and would be taken to STEENVOORDE by lorries. At 8.a.m. a warning order was received to be prepared to move at short notice to the HALF WAY HOUSE dugout, followed half an hour later by the order to carry out this move. This was completed by 12 noon. On arrival at HALF WAY HOUSE the Battalion came under the orders of the G.O.C. 74th Brigade. Orders were received from the 7th Brigade to the effect that the Battalion would be relieved by the 2nd LINCOLNS. In the mean time almost the entire Battalion was out carrying rations to the Battalions in the line. At	
	11.8.17		about 2 a.m. orders were received by the 74th Brigade for the Battalion to move up and strengthen the line, putting two companies in close support on the WESTHOEK Ridge and two companies and H.Q. on the BELLEWAARDE Ridge. All men remaining in the HALFWAY HOUSE	

dug out were collected and taken to the MENIN Rd. The 2nd LINCOLNS
arriving as the last were left. The carrying parties were met
on the MENIN Rd. as they returned and Companies made their way
independently to the positions allotted to them, A & B being on the
WESTHOEK and C & D on the BELLEWAARDE Ridge.
At 12.30 a.m. orders were received to move the two Companies and
Headquarters from the Bellewaarde Ridge to a position on the WESTHOEK
Ridge in order to be in a position to held up any attack from
our right flank. One Company was sent over in small parties
but the Battalion Commander in the front line at once sent back
a message to the effect that he was not in any need of support,
This was reported to Brigade who agreed to the two Companies being
kept on the BELLEWAARDE Ridge. The Battalion Commander in the
line sent back the Company who had gone up.
During the night the 74th Brigade was relieved by the 75th.
At 10 p.m. orders were received to send up 1 Company in support
from the BELLEWAARDE Ridge to the WESTHOEK Ridge. This was done

WAR DIARY
or
INTELLIGENCE SUMMARY
(Erase heading not required.)

Army Form C. 2118.

Place	Date	Hour	Summary of Events and Information	Remarks and references to Appendices
	12.8.17		but the O.C. 2nd SOUTH LANCASHIRE Regt. who had relieved the Battalion of the 7th Brigade in the line refused to help them up then as no cover was available and he was not in need of extra support. This was reported to Brigade who finally agreed to the original dispositions of 2 Companies on WEJTHOEK and 2 on BELLEWAARDE Ridge. During the day relief orders were received. The 2 Companies on the WESTHOEK Ridge were to be relieved by a company of the 3rd LONDON Regt. and the 2 Companies on the BELLEWAARDE Ridge by 2 Companies of the 7th MIDDLESEX Regt. Guides were sent back to the BIRR X Roads. The relief by the 1st MIDDLESEX was completed by 9 p.m. but owing to extreme darkness and difficult nature of the country the company of the 3rd LONDON Regt. did not finish relieving until 3 a.m.	
	13.8.17		On relief the Companies marched through YPRES to VLAMERTINGHE and were taken by busses to the STEENVOORDE area. The men were billeted in barns. The remainder of the day was devoted to rest and general cleaning up. The casualties during this tour were as follows:- 10th. 5 oh. wounded. 11th. 8 oh. killed 17 oh. wounded.	

WAR DIARY
or
INTELLIGENCE SUMMARY

Army Form C. 2118.

Place	Date	Hour	Summary of Events and Information	Remarks and references to Appendices
	14.8.17	12 m.	8 killed 17 O.R. wounded.	
RWELD near STEENVORDE	15.8 -18.8		During this day the Companies carried out completions of kit, rifles, Box respirators etc. Otherwise the men were always to rest. During this period the Battalion remained in billets at RWELD, carrying out training in the mornings. This training included Steady Drill. Physical Training and Bayonet fighting, Musketry, instruction in gas drills and drill etc. The Battalion was reinforced a drake as follows :- 13.8. 33 other ranks: 14.8. 50 other ranks: 17.8. 39 other ranks. The following awards of the Military Medal were notified in routine orders of the I.C.M. 73817 Sgt. SADLER. (S.D) COLEMAN 28823 L/C. POSTANS 13473 Pte. GAINSBOROUGH.	
	19.8.		The Battalion proceeded by much route to DOMINION CAMP near arma BUSSEBOOM in two and half which the Battalion was to bivouac was not marked out. this evening the men remained at in a field throughout the day in the pouring a V8 Century service was held	

WAR DIARY
or
INTELLIGENCE SUMMARY

Army Form C. 2118.

Instructions regarding War Diaries and Intelligence Summaries are contained in F. S. Regs., Part II. and the Staff Manual respectively. Title Pages will be prepared in manuscript.

(Erase heading not required.)

Place	Date	Hour	Summary of Events and Information	Remarks and references to Appendices
DOMINION CAMP AREA	20th –22nd		The Battalion remained in the area till the morning of the 23rd and was unable to continue its training in the mornings. Owing to the absence of suitable ground no attack schemes could be practised and training was confined to close order drill. Daily Physical Training and Bayonet fighting. In the afternoon of the 21st the Battalion was inspected (by Companies) by the B. G. C. 7th Infy Bde. General GRIFFIN D.S.O. 3 Casualties were caused to the Battalion by bombs dropped in the neighbourhood of the Camp by enemy aeroplanes on the night of the 20th November viz. Q.R. MILLINGS and 2 Other ranks.	
STEENVOORDE	23rd –29th		The Battalion marched to the STEENVOORDE area on the morning of the 23rd to billets W. of the STEENVOORDE – MEREZELE RD. East of STEENVOORDE. Here until the 29th inclusive the Battalion was manoeuvred for further training. Pan was worked upon firing and Lewis gun practice upon Battalion rifle range. Close order drill, Physical training and bayonet fighting attack drill and the practice of the reduction of strong points. Less band throwing for the recent draft.	

2449 Wt. W14957/Mgo 750,000 1/16 J.B.C. & A. Forms/C.2118/12.

Place	Date	Hour	Summary of Events and Information	Remarks and references to Appendices
	30 & 31		On the afternoon of the 30th the Batt'n entrained from STEENVOORDE area to ASYLUM, YPRES from where they marched to front line, CLAPHAM JUNCTION sector, via SANCTUARY WOOD, relieving the 8th Yorks and Lancs. B team was left in the Steenvoorde area under Capt. Grigell. On the march up to the line the Batt'n sustained the foll'g: Casualties; 2 killed, 6 wounded, 1 wounded still at duty and one shell shock. Capt. Turner O.C. "C" Co. was badly wounded by an enemy sniper on the 31st. The disposition in the line was A Co. on the right, B in the centre, C on the left, D & HQ Menin road and D in support.	Signature [illeg.] Major for Lt. Col. Comm'g 8./Wilts

Army Form C. 2118.

WAR DIARY
or
INTELLIGENCE SUMMARY

(Erase heading not required.)

1/1 Wiltshire Regt Vol 38

Place	Date	Hour	Summary of Events and Information	Remarks and references to Appendices
TRENCHES E of YPRES	SEPT. 1, 2		During these two days the Battalion continued to hold the line at the northern edge of INVERNESS COPSE. There was little shelling of the front line, but the back areas SANCTUARY WOOD, MENIN RD. &c. received intermittent attention. Our artillery was considerably more active upon the forward and rear systems of the enemy's defences. Throughout the 3rd the relief of the Battalion by the 2nd LEINSTER REGT. was carried out in small parties. No casualty was sustained by either Battalion. The relief to Battalion was the road in Brigade Reserve, and occupied dugouts along the southern and western edges of ZILLEBEKE LAKE. The were the following casualties on Sept. 1st. Capt. H.F.B. TURNER, Disd of Wounds. Killed, 3 men. Wounded, 8 other ranks. On Sept. 2nd. Wounded, Rev. Capt. A. M. ROBINSON, C.F. attached to this Battalion, and 1 man. On Sept. 3rd. Killed, 1 man. Wounded, 1 man.	
	3			
	4, 5		During these two days the Battalion remained in Brig. Reserve at ZILLEBEKE LAKE. On the morning of the 4th the vicinity of the dugouts was	

Army Form C. 2118.

WAR DIARY
or
INTELLIGENCE SUMMARY

(Erase heading not required.)

Instructions regarding War Diaries and Intelligence Summaries are contained in F. S. Regs., Part II. and the Staff Manual respectively. Title Pages will be prepared in manuscript.

Place	Date	Hour	Summary of Events and Information	Remarks and references to Appendices
	8th		shelled by 6" Hows. and there were three casualties, 2 killed and 1 wounded. Subsequently the enemy's artillery was quiet. On the evening of the 8th the Battalion was relieved by the 8th S. LANCS REGT. and went back to VANOOST CAMP near DICKEBUSCH, where it remained until the morning of the 9th.	
	9th		On the 5th and 7th short Company parades were held in the mornings, for Bayonet fighting, Bombing, Arm Drill &c. On the morning of the 8th the Bn. was relieved by the 8th LONDON REGT. and marched to a Camp 2 miles N. of A REELE. The Battalion rested at the Camp during the day, and only a non-commissioned Service was held	
	10th		On the morning of the 10th the Battalion began its move to the 1st Corps area in the Fifth Army, to which the Division was being transferred. The first stage was to a Camp just South of CAESTRE.	
	11th		From CAESTRE the Battalion marched to TANNAY via HAZEBROUCK and THIENNES STEEN BECQUE. The last stage was accomplished on the following day when the	

WAR DIARY or INTELLIGENCE SUMMARY

Army Form C. 2118.

Place	Date	Hour	Summary of Events and Information	Remarks and references to Appendices
LOZINGHEM	13th – 30th		Battalion marched to LOZINGHEM via AIRE, LILLERS, ST. HILAIRE and BURBURE arriving at LOZINGHEM during the month. The Battalion remained at LOZINGHEM up to training, the hour of parade being 7 a.m. to 7.30 a.m. and again to 12.30 p.m. In the afternoon inter-platoon and inter-company football was played. The best in the mornings included a large amount of Musketry. Battalion Ranges were made, and in addition two other ranges, one near BURBURE and one near ALLOUAGNE were allotted to the Battalion in turn. A Divisional Musketry Competition was held on the 26th preceded by a Brigade Competition. The Battalion obtained 39 places in the first 100 shots of the Brigade and the Battalion's team of 11 won both the Brigade and Divisional "Falling Target" Competition. The morning's work included also Physical Training, Bayonet Fighting, Drill and the Handling of Arms. Ceremonial, Dummy Box-Respirator, — (the Bombing officer held classes of rifle grenadiers and gave instruction in the firing of the No. 23 Rifle Grenade and the Mills Piper No. 22.)	

Particular attention was paid to instruction in Bombing, more especially in firing Rifle Grenades, owing to the the importance attached to this on the front held by the Bn. Coy. A new of operations on that front street fighting was practised at two sorts of ruined houses upon the LIÈRES — AUCHY AU BOIS Road: These mornings were devoted to this training.

The attacks of a more open nature were continually practised upon the Brigade Training Area West of LOZINGHEM, and in particular the reduction of strong points by platoons with the special object of demonstrating to the men the cooperation of a platoon's weapons and the importance of covering fire.

The training of Signallers and Scouts was carried on in 07/8hr daily, and a Lewis Gun Class was held throughout this period.

The afternoons and evenings were largely devoted to organized recreation, inter-platoon and inter-Company football matches and practising for the 105th Field Company R.E. Sports and the Divisional Sports which took place on the 22nd and 26th respectively. In the latter the Battalion was to follow ing places:—

WAR DIARY
or
INTELLIGENCE SUMMARY

Army Form C. 2118.

Place	Date	Hour	Summary of Events and Information	Remarks and references to Appendices
	1st		Place Pillow fighting.	
	2nd		Officers' Relay Race. Relay Obstacle Race Mess Cart turnout. Driving Competition.	
	3rd			
	8th		In the Divisional Tug of War Competition the Battalion after defeating the S. Lancs Regt. to Divnl. R.E. and the 13th CHESHIRE REGT. were defeated in the semi-final by the R.A.M.C.	
	9th		Reinforcement joined the Battalion to take as follows :- O.M. and Hon. Lieut. G. ELLISON, Rev. Capt. J.S. BARSTOW, and 3 other ranks.	
	15th		4 other ranks.	
	16th		One Man.	
	17th		Three men.	
	19th		Capt. G.R. RUSSELL, D.S.O. rejoined; was wounded on May 31st. 1917.	
	20th		One Man.	
	23rd		Three men.	
	25th		11 men.	
	27th		4 men	
	28th		Three Officers : 2/Lts. E.T. BURRY, J.G. KING and G.T. MORLEY.	

WAR DIARY or INTELLIGENCE SUMMARY

Army Form C. 2118.

The following promotion was approved on the 22nd :-

2/17. J. READER to the Acting Captain.

The strength of the Battalion at the conclusion of the month was :-

Total Strength. 42 Officers, 911 Other Ranks.
Actually with Bn. 29 "   714   "   "
Detached from Bn. 13 "   197   "   "

E.S.G...... Lt Colonel
(Command of 1st Bn. The Wiltshire Regt.)

Army Form C. 2118.

WAR DIARY
or
INTELLIGENCE SUMMARY
(Erase heading not required.)

1st Bn Wiltshire Regt
Vol 39

Place	Date	Hour	Summary of Events and Information	Remarks and references to Appendices
LOZINGHEM	OCT. 1-3		The Battalion remained at LOZINGHEM, near LILLERS, until 4th inst. On Oct. 1st, 2nd and 3rd the usual training parades were held, and on the evening of the 3rd notification was received that the Brigade would be moving on the following day to the BETHUNE area. On the evening of the 3rd 11 general transport drivers were held. Reinforcements at follow joined the Battalion at this time:- On 1st, for duty as Chaplain, CAPT. D.A. POLHILL. C.F. On 2nd, 10 other ranks all with two exceptions, casuals.	
BETHUNE	4		On the 4th the Battalion marched to BETHUNE and was billeted in the ECOLE DES JEUNES FILLES, where it remained until the evening of the following day when it relieved the 2nd. S. STAFFS REGT. in Brigade Support in the GIVENCHY sector. During the 5th, reconnaissances of the forward area and the approaches were made by officers and N.C.O.'s, and in the evening the Brigade relieved the 6th. Infantry Brigade. Two Battalions went into the line, 1st R. CHESHIRE REGT. on right in trenches east of GIVENCHY and LE	

Army Form C. 2118.

WAR DIARY
or
INTELLIGENCE SUMMARY

(Erase heading not required.)

Instructions regarding War Diaries and Intelligence Summaries are contained in F.S. Regs., Part II. and the Staff Manual respectively. Title Pages will be prepared in manuscript.

Place	Date	Hour	Summary of Events and Information	Remarks and references to Appendices
GIVENCHY Sector	5-10		PLANTIN, 3rd WORCESTERSHIRE REGT. on Left occupying line from A 3 a 8.6. to QUINQUE RUE (Sheets LA BASSÉE 36 C.N.W.1 and RICHEBOURG 36 S.W.3). The Battalion moved into Brigade Support, Bn. H.Q. and two Companies at WINDY CORNER, 1 Company garrisoning GIVENCHY KEEP and the remaining Company occupying Old British line S. of QUINQUE RUE to its junction with WILLOW ROAD. On the 6th a draft of 6 other ranks joined the Battalion. Throughout this period the Battalion remained in Brigade Support. Working parties were furnished by the two Companies at WINDY CORNER for the 218th Tunnelling Company, R.E. with reference to the mining in progress in this sector. The Company in the Old British line worked upon it own trenches and strong points, Shelters and was responsible for the maintenance of BARNTON RD. C.T. and FIFE RD. C.T. The Keep Company worked upon the defences of the Keep. Officers and N.C.O's thoroughly reconnoitred the line the Battalion was	

WAR DIARY
or
INTELLIGENCE SUMMARY

(Erase heading not required.)

Army Form C. 2118.

Place	Date	Hour	Summary of Events and Information	Remarks and references to Appendices
			To take over from the 10th CHESHIRE REGT. and also the approaches to the line from support positions, particularly our land route. Both guides were very poor during this period. Officers and other ranks joined the Battalion for duty in drafts as follows:- On 7th. for duty as Second in Command, in place of Major G.D. BROWN, M.C. attending Commanding Officers' Course at ALDERSHOT, Major C.L. KLEIN, D.O. CENTER HUSSARS attd. 3/ WORCESTERSHIRE REGT. On 8th. four Officers. 2/Lts. W.E.H. KENNEDY, D.A. OWEN, A.V.S. GRANT, F.L.A. GOARD. On 9th. 2 men. 11th. On the afternoon of this date the Battalion relieved the 10/CHESHIRE REGT. in the line. The relief was effected without casualty. On the right was the 2nd. S. LANCS. REGT. of 7th. Brigade, and on the left the 8th. L. N. LANCS REGT. The Battalion's line extended from WOLFE ROAD (A 9 d) to northern end of WARWICK SOUTH ISLAND (A 3 a 8.6) Three Companies held the front line and one was in support in GUNNERS SIDING. THE AVENUE and UPPER CUT.	

WAR DIARY
or
INTELLIGENCE SUMMARY

Army Form C. 2118.

Place	Date	Hour	Summary of Events and Information	Remarks and references to Appendices
	1/1-16		During this time the Battalion remained in the line. The enemy's attitude throughout was very quiet, and his line appeared to be held lightly, particularly at night; his artillery was not active except in the neighbourhood of GIVENCHY CHURCH which was shelled almost daily with 77 mm. and 5.9" shells. Enemy's trench mortars only fired occasionally, chiefly upon the right Company's sector, and the grenade fire of these fell in rear of the front line. Apart from this, Platoons were formed for purposes of work in the line, any here & men and all available men of companies were employed upon the maintenance of front, support and communication trenches. The work was particularly urgent as on the approach of wet weather portions of the trenches began to collapse. To combat this a large amount of revetting was taken in hand, and the work continued throughout the Battalion's tour. In addition the trenches were kept well drained. The regimental snipers had few targets, but some hits were claimed (more conclusive than usual). Hostile snipers were observed by these observers, but our artillery generally was superior to enemy's. Hostile fire was opened by the Stokes mortars in the Battn's sector on several occasions and were answered, but our artillery generally was M.W.Tw.S	

WAR DIARY
or
INTELLIGENCE SUMMARY

Army Form C. 2118.

Place	Date	Hour	Summary of Events and Information	Remarks and references to Appendices
	17		Officers' patrols were out each night and raided & in taking a few of the enemy's posts and machine guns, but no identification was obtained.	
			The following officers joined for duty:-	
			On 11th. 2nd Lt./Actg. Chaplain, Capt. W.B. CHURCH. C.F. in place of Capt.	
Pol Hill.				
			On 12th. 2/Lt. J.T. RIDDLE, and on 15th. 2/Lt. A.T. FROST.	
			On the 13th. during the absence on leave of G.O.C. 7th. Inf. Bde. Lt.Col. J.S. OGILVIE. D.S.O. assumed command of the Brigade, and Major R.E.W. RAN 1/c the Battalion.	
			On the afternoon of the 17th the Battalion was relieved by the 16th. CHES. HIRE REGT., and went back into Brigade Reserve at GORRE. Barely casualties during the tour were 3 other ranks wounded :-	
GORRE			16.A. Pte. SHARPE, H.	
			17.A. Pte. SHORT H. and a/c MATHISS, T.W.	

Army Form C. 2118.

WAR DIARY
or
INTELLIGENCE SUMMARY
(Erase heading not required.)

Instructions regarding War Diaries and Intelligence Summaries are contained in F.S. Regs., Part II. and the Staff Manual respectively. Title Pages will be prepared in manuscript.

Place	Date	Hour	Summary of Events and Information	Remarks and references to Appendices
SORRE	18-22		During this period the Battalion remained in Brigade Reserve at SORRE CHATEAU. 1 Company was required daily for providing working parties for the 106th. Coy. R.E. for the Town Commandant, and for cleaning up the Chateau billets and their vicinity. For the other three Companies training parades were possible. Short ranges were available for rifle firing and Lewis gun practice. Bombing ground was used for gong instruction in throwing of rifle grenades. On the 21st. a Church of England Parish service was held. In the afternoon the Battalion's "Second Eleven" defeated the 130th Fd. Coy. R.E. at Soccer by 6 goals to nil. In the evening of the 22nd. a Battalion concert was held.	
TRENCHES	23		On the afternoon of the 23rd. the Battalion relieved the 10th Cheshire Regt. in the line. There were no casualties during relief.	
	24 -29		During this period the Battalion remained in the line. There was only slight activity on the part of the artillery and trench mortars on either side, except on the night of the 24/25th when a hostile raid (uncarried) was made upon the Battalion on the right flank, the 2/6 S. LANCASHIRE REGT. This took place at 4 a.m. and 2	

WAR DIARY or INTELLIGENCE SUMMARY

Army Form C. 2118.

Instructions regarding War Diaries and Intelligence Summaries are contained in F. S. Regs., Part II and the Staff Manual respectively. Title Pages will be prepared in manuscript.

(Erase heading not required.)

Place	Date	Hour	Summary of Events and Information	Remarks and references to Appendices
			Barrage of shells and trench mortars was put down on the right Company's sector. Trench mortar fire was also directed on the left Company front. In no case were any casualties sustained by the shelling. Patrols were sent out by the front line Companies each night, strongest in sight than previously and with a more offensive object, that of securing an identification. No weaker, however, attended these efforts. The brightness of the moon largely hampering activity in the selected area. Two particularly fine patrols were carried out by the left Company, led by 2/Lt. F.S.C. PARSONS, M.C. On one occasion one of the patrol was located by the enemy's wire: he was carried back towards him, several hundred yards away, by that officer. On the night of 27/28th. an entry into the enemy's trench was effected north of the farm in A.3.d. (Sheet 1A BAISIEUX 36 c N.W. 1): one of the enemy was killed but the body could not be brought away. The patrol returned safely, although the alarm was at once given and the patrol was fired on from a machine gun post.	

WAR DIARY
or
INTELLIGENCE SUMMARY

(Erase heading not required.)

Army Form C. 2118.

Place	Date	Hour	Summary of Events and Information	Remarks and references to Appendices
			Work upon the maintenance and drainage of front line, support and communication trenches, upon the construction of dugouts, revetting of front line etc. continued throughout the tour. At night wire was put out in front of each Company and in the gap existing between the Battalion and the Bn. on its right, so as to form a defensive flank on the southern side of Givenchy Hill. The casualties during the tour were: 22nd. Accidentally wounded, 1 other rank. 23rd. Wounded, 5 other ranks: one of these died on 25th. 25th. Wounded, still at duty, 2. 26th. Wounded, 2; 1 of these died on 27th; 1 wounded still at duty, 1. 27th. Wounded, Capt. J. Rekser and 2 other ranks, the latter fatally wounded, 1. 28th. Killed, 1 O.R. On the 29th the Battalion was relieved by 10th Cheshire Regt. and went into Brigade Support: the Company previously garrisoned the Keeps of Givenchy Hill.	
	29			

WAR DIARY
or
INTELLIGENCE SUMMARY
(Erase heading not required.)

Army Form C. 2118.

Place	Date	Hour	Summary of Events and Information	Remarks and references to Appendices
	30, 31		One Company occupied the OLD BRITISH LINE, S. of QUINQUE RUE and for tactical purposes was in support to the Battalion in the LILY sub-sector of the Brigade. 3 of the remaining two Companies and Bn. Hq. were in billet in the vicinity of WINDY CORNER, S. of LE PLANTIN. During these two days the Battalion was in Brigade support, furnishing parties from all companies, except the Keeps Company, for work under R.E. supervision. These parties were provided for the 130th Field Coy. and for the 25th Tunnelling Company, R.E. Returned parties worked in the support and communication trenches in the Brigade sector on trench repairs, the erection of elephant shelters, the construction of M.G. emplacements &c.	
		12.00	Reinforcement arrived as follows:— On 24th, 3 other ranks: On 27th 50 other ranks: on 30th, 3 Officers, (Lt. E.G. WHITE, 2/Lt. F.G. PITT, 2/Lt. A. JENKINS), and 130 other ranks. The Battalion's fighting strength on this date was 40 Officers, 776 other ranks.	

C.L. Stew, Major
Comm'g 1st Wiltshire Regt.

War Diary or Intelligence Summary

Army Form C. 2118

1st Bn; Wiltshire Regt.

Place	Date	Hour	Summary of Events and Information	Remarks and references to Appendices
Regt HQ 1A BN OSES 35c N.W.1 (1/10000)	Nov. 1-3		During these three days the Battalion was in Brigade Support, one company furnished to keep on Guinchy Hill, one company occupied to C.T's Bates & Co & Posen Willow Rd and Quinque Rue, two companies and Bn. HQ were in the vicinity Windy Corner. The Battalion was called upon to furnish the usual working parties to the 254th, 254th Tunnelling Company R.E. for work in connection with the Guinchy Hill mines, and to the 130th Field Company R.E. for maintenance work upon the communication and other trenches in this sector and in rear of the front line. Three parties worked tonight to Grenades part of the day.	
	4		9.30 a.m. 2nd Lt. Overman was wounded, No. 6257 Pte. Hunt, G. The Battalion relieved the 1st Cheshire Regt in the Guinchy subsection. There were no casualties during relief.	
	5-10		Throughout this period the Battalion remained in to line. The attitude of the enemy was very quiet, evidently two casualties are sustained during the tour. On the night B, C/Lt. Kohlewhy our new pioneer were invited...	

WAR DIARY or INTELLIGENCE SUMMARY

Army Form C. 2118.

Place	Date	Hour	Summary of Events and Information	Remarks and references to Appendices

Sniping was directed upon communication trenches, roads and saps worn to man. About every day the Divisional artillery carried out retaliatory operations. Guns in co-operation with medium Trench Mortars along the Battalion front. Whilst mortars were usually employed in retaliation for hostile fire and fire upon many front and support lines. The registered snipers were often more rigid than usual particularly in the S.W. B.P. and the rifle covered his own Observations. The enemy on the other hand seems little interested in his subject. His artillery retaliation however was generally directed upon the vicinity of Givenchy Church, crop road and New Rose Trench in the left company's sect. Some also shelled 77 mm. and 4.2 shells.

Patrols parties sent nightly along the whole Battalion front, mainly with the object of ascertaining the extent of the gaps made in the enemy's wire. No hostile patrols were encountered.

On the 10th the Battalion was relieved by the 10th Cheshire Regt. and went into Brigade Reserve at GORRE. The only casualties

10th

WAR DIARY or INTELLIGENCE SUMMARY

Army Form C. 2118.

Place	Date	Hour	Summary of Events and Information	Remarks and references to Appendices
GORRE	11-16		(ambulance) being the two mules. 2/L. S.H. WHITE wounded (by a shrapnel) & Sgt. Luis & 7 moneybts the following day. Sgts. E & 93, 1 other rank was wounded but remained at duty. During this period the Battalion remained at GORRE in Brigade Reserve. On the 11th a C.O.'s & O.C. Coy's hands, reconnaissance was held. On the 5 other days working parties were provided for the 184th Coy R.E. chiefly on entrance posts. One party was employed to complete & repair dug-outs in Burbure-Gorre Road Sec. New Lewis units Company arrangements for supplies to platoons of this availed for. Making up deficiencies in trench war outfits from tools and Mess-platoon organization of A Company was carried into effect, so the present strength of the Battalion admits of it. There was had to send some away from Le QUESNOY to bring further out of two trench scarpel in the wood adjoining GORRE CHATEAU offence. Little training was possible. One Company or so WR was the log a road near Hinges & 1 Company or so WR near BETHUNE and BEURY.	

WAR DIARY
or
INTELLIGENCE SUMMARY

Army Form C. 2118.

Place	Date	Hour	Summary of Events and Information	Remarks and references to Appendices

Trenches 16

Owing to information obtained from prisoners of the 400th but Regt. to the effect that the enemy were preparing to make an attack on Trenches on the Givenchy Hill during the following few nights special precautions were taken to meet an attack but nothing happened. The Chester Regt. and the 15th R. Welsh D/the 14th A Company of this Battalion had to serve up as a party between PICCADILLY and a party between CALEDONIAN RD. and PICCADILLY with a patrol between. Nothing untoward happened owing to night of 14/15th and on the afternoon of 15th the Company was relieved by D Company and returned to GORRE.

On the evening of the 15th R. Company held a concert on the morning of the 15th Capt. E.M. GINGELL 7 of the Battalion took up an appointment as Major on Headquarters of 8th Div. Shortwood

FORESTERS.
During the six days at GORRE. for the front line since January 1915 a Battalion Officers' Head were in force.

On the 15th the Battalion returned to the Cheshire Regt. to the line.
No casualties were sustained during relief.

WAR DIARY or INTELLIGENCE SUMMARY

Army Form C. 2118.

(Erase heading not required.)

Place	Date	Hour	Summary of Events and Information	Remarks and references to Appendices
	17-22		During this period the Battalion remained in the line. As a hostile raid or attack on a grand scale was still suspected, special vigilance was maintained, and several flare lines for cordoning any hostile operation. Hostile artillery, however, remained to the greater part of its time inactive, and the enemy's attempts to register his trench mortars and our artillery carried out necessary operation on the 17, 18 and 19th, and several night patrols went out of 17, 18 Bn. I/Wilts as to patrol in the enemy's wire. On the 20th in the afternoon a bombardment of the enemy's wire front and support trenches and subjects French mortar positions was carried out on the GIVENCHY RIDGE front lasting to 4.5 Hows. and Trench mortars of 9in, bore. The stokes mortars fired 4.8 mm and they continued to fire hard, and, in addition, two Trench mortars and stokes in reply were made by the enemy during the shoot, but at 4pm retaliatory fire was carried onto the enemy, lasting for 20 minutes. 150 5.9; and 300 shells of smaller calibre fell in A9d, A9c, A9a, A3c, the vicinity of WINDY CORNER and HERTS REDOUBT (A 8 & 7 3). This battalion	

WAR DIARY or INTELLIGENCE SUMMARY

Army Form C. 2118.

Place	Date	Hour	Summary of Events and Information	Remarks and references to Appendices
	22		Sustained only one casualty — Pte. B. CANNINGS of C Company wounded. Patrolling was carried on each night, our activity in this direction was rather restricted owing to the extreme brightness of the moon, and our working and burial parties were made to enter hostile zone in A.9.b. and b.3 to enemy's wire beyond trenching. On the early morning of the 19th, a party of "C" Coy's bombing approached say 6 and threw two baths. They were met with bomb and rifle fire and retired. On support was officers moving forward during the first half of the tour and remained but were strained. There being abnormal movement in support, and more tired during those days. Other casualties in officers & other ranks were on 20th. were :— R.A. Killed 5985 Pte. CROOK, T.S. Wounded: 22755 Pte. WHITE, J. (died the following day), 217640 Pte. CARPENTER, W.J. HENLEY, H. On the afternoon of the 22nd the Battalion was relieved by the 16th R. Crobies Regt. and went into Brigade Support.	

WAR DIARY
or
INTELLIGENCE SUMMARY
(Erase heading not required.)

Army Form C. 2118.

Place	Date	Hour	Summary of Events and Information	Remarks and references to Appendices
	26-27		On this date 8 officers left the Battalion for duty with the 2nd DEVONS. They were Lt. E.G. WHITE, 2/Lts. S.A. BUCK, C.H. ATKINSON, A.F. FROST, A. JENKIN, W.E. LUDFORD. During this period the Battalion remained in Brigade Support. Reinforcements were received whilst previously in front line bringing the fit & fives strength up to war R.A.R. On the 23rd, 24th, 25th, & 26th the Battalion found working parties for the 109th Tunnelling and 130th Field Companies R.E. The work is to Brigade H.Q. area. During this absence two enemy aeroplanes were taken.	
	27/1		The Brigade was relieved by the 127th Inf. Brigade, the Battalion being relieved by the 7th MANCHESTER REGT. The relief was carried out in the afternoon without casualty. After relief the Battalion proceeded to billets at VENDIN-LES-BETHUNE west of BETHUNE. This was reached at 8p.m.	
	28/1		The Battalion marched to BURBURE, south of ALLIERS via CHOCQUES and ALLOUAGNE, arriving in billets at 11.30 a.m.	
	29/1		The Battalion completed its move into the First Army Training area by marching to DIEVAL. Their was no train travelling as this held is 20th and JAFETTE	

WAR DIARY
or
INTELLIGENCE SUMMARY

Army Form C. 2118.

Place	Date	Hour	Summary of Events and Information	Remarks and references to Appendices
	30		Bn. marched by 3 km. [illegible] taken was: ECQUEDECQUES — LESPRESSES — AUCHY AU BOIS — LIGNY-LEZ-AIRE — ST. CUHEM — ERQUIN ST. JULIEN (Reg. Hd.) HAZEBROUCK (A). The day was spent in [illegible] operations with Company ?? of the battalion were met and to the fixing up of training areas for ??? The adjutant T. Killick Reinforcements throughout the month [illegible] as follows:— 1st. 2 other ranks 2nd. 3 " 3rd. 1 " 5th. 1 " 7th. 2 " 10th. 2 " 13th. 2 " 188. 9 other ranks and on the 6th Lt. H.T. SARGEANT. The fighting strength of the Battalion at the end of the month was 29 officers, 727 other ranks. 30/11/17. 55 [illegible] H. Glover Commanding 1st Bn. The Wiltshire Regiment	

WAR DIARY or INTELLIGENCE SUMMARY

Army Form C. 2118.

Place	Date	Hour	Summary of Events and Information	Remarks and references to Appendices
SELETTE	DEC. 1st		Company training was carried out during the morning. After parade in the vicinity of the village, and in the afternoon a 1/2 Platoon ½ Coy played held football matches. In the evening warning was received that the Brigade would move the following day into the Third Army.	
(Rep. Strt. HAZEBROUCK 5A				
LENS 11)	2nd 3rd		Leaving SELETTE at 10.20 a.m. the Battalion marched to LISBOURG via BOMY having SELETTE at 10.20 a.m. the Battalion marched to LISBOURG via BOMY BEAUMETZ-LEZ-AIRE and LAIRES. In this village the Battalion remained for one day, the 3rd, resting.	
LISBOURG	4th		Leaving LISBOURG at 5.30 a.m. the Battalion marched to WAVRANS via EQUIRRE, BERGUENEUSE, ANVIN, MONCHY CAYEUX and SAUTRECOURT. At WAVRANS the Battalion entrained at about 10 a.m. for MIRAUMONT which was reached at about 6 p.m. after a journey through ETAPLES and AMIENS. The Battalion after detraining marched to COURCELLES-LE-COMTE to an encampment 5 M. of the village, via ACHIET LE PETIT and ACHIET LE GRAND. This was reached at 10 p.m. and here the Battalion remained until the following afternoon, when orders were received for a move to BERTRES.	

WAR DIARY
or
INTELLIGENCE SUMMARY

Army Form C. 2118.

Place	Date	Hour	Summary of Events and Information	Remarks and references to Appendices
BARASTRE	5TH.		Leaving COURCELLES LE COMTE at 2A.M. the Battalion marched to BARASTRE via ACHIET LE GRAND, BIHUCOURT, BIEFVILLERS, BAPAUME, BANCOURT and HAPLINCOURT and were billeted in huts between HAPLINCOURT and BARASTRE. The destination was reached after four and a half hours marching.	
"	6TH.		Short parade was held in the morning for inspection of rifles and box respirators. In the afternoon the Battalion defeated the 6th. CHESHIRE REGT. at "Soccer" by 3 goals to 1.	
"	7TH.		Throughout the first week of December the weather was very cold. A medium day Company parades were held in the morning in the vicinity of the Camp. Squad drill, bayonet fighting and gas mask drill. In the afternoon the Battalion defeated the 4th. S. STAFFS REGT. at "Soccer" by 4 goals to nil.	
"	8TH.		The morning was received that the Battalion might have to proceed to the neighbourhood of HAPLINCOURT WOOD at short notice. Only short parades were held by the Companies in the morning. In the afternoon inter Company football was played.	

WAR DIARY or INTELLIGENCE SUMMARY

Army Form C. 2118.

Place	Date	Hour	Summary of Events and Information	Remarks and references to Appendices
	9		It was notified at midday that the Brigade would be relieving the 9th Inf. Bde. that Division the following day in the sector between LAGNICOURT and QUÉANT. At 2 p.m. the Battalion left BARASTRE and proceeded to the line as LEBUCQUIÈRE and MORCHIES. the first party that being the trenches shortly after that. The Battalion took over the front line from S.13.d.1.1 (French Map. Sh. 57. N.E. 1/20000) to the junction of the front line with the Sunken road running from LAGNICOURT to QUÉANT in C.18.f. Two Companies manned the front line and two were accommodated in the Sufford Lane immediately East of LAGNICOURT. BRADFORD RESERVE and SKIPTON RESERVE Bn. Hd.Qrs. and the Q.M. & Light Support Company occupied dug-outs in the Sunken road S.E. of LAGNICOURT, C.24.d. The front line was held by a system of posts, there being four posts in each Company sector in with the one Lewis Gun. The unit relieved was the 13th. Kings LIVERPOOLS. No casualties were sustained during relief.	

WAR DIARY
or
INTELLIGENCE SUMMARY

Army Form C. 2118.

Place	Date	Hour	Summary of Events and Information	Remarks and references to Appendices
TRENCHES East of BAPAUME	16/9		The enemy's attack was quiet throughout the day, and there was but slight reply to our heavy artillery, which was active during morning and afternoon. It is early morning of the 11th, enemy was learned that the Third Army was expecting a hostile attempt to regain part of the late HINDENBURG line. On the morning of the 11th Artillery patrol was sent out to ascertain if there were any indications of hostile assembly and concentration, and by 6 a.m. these had been stabilised well in advance of our line upon the Battalion front. Said of the strength – 1 N.C.O., 12 men and a Lewis Gun. There was no Hostile action, but the enemy was a gun quiet at dawn. There was no hostile action throughout the day. Heavy artillery shelled QUÉANT, and registration was also carried out. Hostile shelling with 4.2" was directed upon the vicinity of BRADFORD RESERVE between 10 a.m. and 12 noon and between 1 p.m. and 2.30 p.m.	
	12		The day passed without incident on the Battalion front. There was considerable aerial activity on the part throughout the day, and low flying	

WAR DIARY
or
INTELLIGENCE SUMMARY
(Erase heading not required.)

Army Form C. 2118.

Place	Date	Hour	Summary of Events and Information	Remarks and references to Appendices
TRENCHES East of LIGNY-COURT	12 & 13-15		Tomorrow was extraordinarily over the lines. The Battalion remained in the line until to-night. During this two days there was no incident of importance. There was no infantry enterprise by the enemy, and the artillery replied but weakly to our continuous shelling of his front areas. No target presented itself to our snipers, and attention was mainly devoted to active patrolling during the early part of the night. Several attempts were made to obtain an identification at MAGPIE NEST (D.13.b.6.) but the hostile wire proved too strong. On such occasions the enemy's sentries were plainly seen. No hostile patrols were encountered. In the matter of work, chief attention was paid to wiring: the wire in front of the front line was strengthened, and in addition new was put out so as to form a flank defence to each post, or northern and southern sides. In the front line elephant shelters were constructed, and the trench deepened and fire-stepped in places where it was necessary. On the night of the 14/15th, a new support line was dug 150 yards in	

Army Form C. 2118.

WAR DIARY
or
INTELLIGENCE SUMMARY

(*Erase heading not required.*)

Place	Date	Hour	Summary of Events and Information	Remarks and references to Appendices
	15th		was of the front line, north of HARROGATE AVENUE. (C.18.d). On the evening of the 15th at dusk the Battalion was relieved by the 4th S. STAFF: REGT. and after relief moved back into Brigade Reserve at VAUX-VRAUCOURT. No casualties were sustained during relief.	

Army Form C. 2118.

WAR DIARY
or
INTELLIGENCE SUMMARY

(Erase heading not required.)

Place	Date	Hour	Summary of Events and Information	Remarks and references to Appendices
VAUX	16 to 2		During this period the Battalion was in Brigade Reserve at VAUX. Two Companies nightly carried on the work of digging a support line behind RAGNICOURT. The remaining two Companies were employed during the morning and afternoon in road mending under R.E. supervision, on the VAUX – NOREUIL and VAUX–RAGNICOURT roads. Excellent work was accomplished by the "Lewis Platoon" in opening up & always constructing bombproof dugouts; room for 100 men was provided during the Battalion's stay in VAUX. Except for a few shells on the night of the 16th and 20th the enemy was quiet.	

WAR DIARY
or
INTELLIGENCE SUMMARY

Army Form C. 2118.

Place	Date	Hour	Summary of Events and Information	Remarks and references to Appendices
VAULX	21		On this day the Battalion was relieved at 2 p.m. by the 2nd SOUTH LANCASHIRE Regt. and marched back to No. 6. Camp, FAUREUIL H.16.b. (5)*. The men being billeted in huts. The 7th Brigade after relief became the Brigade in Divisional Reserve.	
FAUREUIL	22		This day was devoted to inspections and rest.	
	23		On the night of the 23/24 the Battalion furnished 400 men for burying cable. The Battalion was allotted approximately 1800 yards to dig and the work was to be done by two shifts, the first to dig to a depth of 5 feet and the second to dig down to 4'6" and fill in after the cable was laid. On the first night some 400 yards were completed, in spite of considerable difficulty in digging through two roads which had to be crossed. The parties were taken to and from their work by the light railway.	

Army Form C. 2118.

WAR DIARY
or
INTELLIGENCE SUMMARY

(Erase heading not required.)

Instructions regarding War Diaries and Intelligence Summaries are contained in F. S. Regs., Part II. and the Staff Manual respectively. Title Pages will be prepared in manuscript.

Place	Date	Hour	Summary of Events and Information	Remarks and references to Appendices
FAVREUIL	24		The Battalion celebrated Christmas Day on this date. The men had an excellent dinner and in the afternoon and evening the Divisional Pierrots gave fine performances.	
	25		During the night of the 25/26, another 500 yards of cable were buried.	
	26		During the night of the 26/27, some particularly fine digging was accomplished, about 500 yards of cable being buried.	
	27		The task allotted to the Battalion was completed during the night of the 27/28, being one of the best performances in digging ever done by the Battalion.	
	28		The men rested during the morning; the afternoon was devoted to games and a whist Drive.	
	29		A few small working parties were found by the Battalion. The remainder of the men were employed in digging trenches for cover against aeroplane bombs and in building parapets round the huts.	

Army Form C. 2118.

WAR DIARY
or
INTELLIGENCE SUMMARY

(Erase heading not required.)

Instructions regarding War Diaries and Intelligence Summaries are contained in F. S. Regs., Part II. and the Staff Manual respectively. Title Pages will be prepared in manuscript.

Place	Date	Hour	Summary of Events and Information	Remarks and references to Appendices
FAVREUIL	30		Two Companies were employed on various R.E. working parties. There was a parade service for the remainder of the Battalion.	
	31		During the morning all Companies were employed in digging shelter trenches. In the afternoon inter company football matches were played. The following Reinforcements were received during the month 2.12.17. 4 O.R.s 10.12.17 2 O.R.s 12.12.17 3 O.R.s 25.12.17 2 O.R.s. Lt. E.A.H. McNIVEN joined the Battalion on the 11.12.17. Casualties during the month. Killed 10.12.17 15.12.17 1 Wounded 16.12.17	

C.L.T.Shepley
for. LT. COLONEL.
COMDG: 1st Bn. WILTSHIRE REGT.

WAR DIARY or INTELLIGENCE SUMMARY

Army Form C. 2118.

1st Wiltshire Regt.

Place	Date	Hour	Summary of Events and Information	Remarks and references to Appendices
Hohenzollern Sector	2.1.16		In the evening of the 2nd inst. the Battalion relieved the 2nd Battn. Lancashire Regt. (Lt. Col. Maxwell) in the right subsector of the Hohenzollern sector. The relief was effected without a casualty. The left subsector was held by the 8th Royal North Lancashire Regt. (Lt. Col. Cardwell D.S.O.). Throughout the tour that evening the enemy's attitude was generally quiet. His principal activity being directed against the right of Hohenzollern. His relief was rather restricted owing to the weather, which was very cold frosty also a good deal of snow fell. On January 5th the enemy was reported having rather had fights (coughs?) on our left south west of Mercatel. His men were apparently effectively dealt with by our artillery as his attack fell in No Man's Land. During this tour the Battalion only sustained two casualties, both wounded and removed for duty. The new C.T. Bond Avenue was completed in two hours and dugouts for Coy HQ were started by the 1st Battalion taken over under Lt. 2/Lt. Curry.	
Hohenzollern	7.1.16		The work of protecting the huts with sniping pillboxes trenches was carried on	

to Camp near Farbus.

Army Form C. 2118.

WAR DIARY
or
INTELLIGENCE SUMMARY
(Erase heading not required.)

Instructions regarding War Diaries and Intelligence Summaries are contained in F.S. Regs., Part II. and the Staff Manual respectively. Title Pages will be prepared in manuscript.

Place	Date	Hour	Summary of Events and Information	Remarks and references to Appendices
LAGNICOURT SECTOR (Ref Sheet PRONVILLE Scale 1/10000)	Jan. 8th		In the evening the Battalion was relieved by the 4th S. STAFFS REGT. and upon relief became the Battalion in Brigade Support. No casualties were sustained during relief. The dispositions in Brigade Support were:— Bn. H.Q. & 2 & 3 & 5 & 6. 90 1 Company in SKIPTON RESERVE under the command of O.C. Right Front Line Battalion for tactical working purposes. 2 Companies in Support and billeted upon the LAGNICOURT — NOREUIL Road, one of these the most northerly Company in Support, upon the road just south of NOREUIL had under the command of the O.C. Left Front Line Battalion for tactical and working purposes. During this period the Battalion remained in Brigade Support and was called upon to provide daily parties for work in the Brigade Sector under R.E. supervision. One Company was daily employed with the 252th Tunnelling Company R.E. carrying away spoil from a Bn. H.Q. Dugout which was being made at C.17.d.90.60.	
	9-14			

2449 Wt W14957/M90 750,000 1/16 J.B.C. & A. Forms/C.2118/12.

WAR DIARY or INTELLIGENCE SUMMARY

Army Form C. 2118.

Place	Date	Hour	Summary of Events and Information	Remarks and references to Appendices
FAVREUIL	15/-20		Other parties & in number were procured at dusk daily for carrying R.E. material from LAGNICOURT DUMP to forward dumps. Another party was engaged upon the erection of a Cook house in EDINBURGH SUPPORT. While the Battalion's Pioneer Platoon were employed upon sinking shafts to a new Company Headquarters the men buffoned[?] time in the night front line Battalion into the platoon remainers in the line to continue this work when the Battalion was relieved by the 2nd. S. LANCS. REGT. on the evening of the 14th. The relief was effected without a casualty, and upon relief became the Brigade Divisional Reserve. The Battalion was billeted in No. 5 Camp south of FAVREUIL.

The Battalion remained in the camp until the morning of the 18th. They were honest[?] any parades during this time as the Battalion was carried with to find two Reinf parties & shovel[?] work day upon fuse days. The 17th & 18th. On the 19th, 233 and all to the Battalion marched upon the MORY - HOTCHIES reserve line with three companies continued the Digging of trench the front Company moved up to the Digging to trench the front Company | |

FAVREUIL

WAR DIARY
or
INTELLIGENCE SUMMARY

Army Form C. 2118.

Place	Date	Hour	Summary of Events and Information	Remarks and references to Appendices
FAUQUISSART	15-2-15 (continued)		Parties were furnished for work at the Camps & to the 25th D.A.C. & to N.S. Coy. A.S.C. Officers of the unit not [so] employed were occupied [training] and [instructing] other Battalions and [grades] of [Reservists] & [parties] [furnishing] [some] music for the band of [Infantry] of [XIII] [Army?] [Corps] & for the 20th S.L. Hut. On the night of the 20th/21st [parties] [from] the Brigade were [employed to move] of the HIRONDELLE VALLEY. The Battalion was responsible for [removal] [charge] of [trenches] [near] to No. 4pm's [land] preparatory to being [taken] [over] [and handed over] by the 15th CHESHIRE REGT. to which the [Commander] were [to report] [going] [into] [march] from the [front] [trench] had remained on duty. [Patrol] [had returned] to Camp by 11.30 p.m. that [day]. In [days] before which training was possible, [parties] were [instructed] [thoroughly] [in] [duty] [expected] [resulting] [from] [trench] [routine]. [Beyond] [lightest] [armament] [etc.] Local [Companies] too were [given] the [opportunity] [for] [such] [work] & [class] for the [instruction] of N.C.O's (4 per Company) was [formed] and held.	

WAR DIARY
or
INTELLIGENCE SUMMARY

Army Form C. 2118.

Place	Date	Hour	Summary of Events and Information	Remarks and references to Appendices
			daily during the period under review. Lecture were given upon N.C.O.s duties &c. Communication drill and the firing of trail to air and squad drill were practised. It were being used the Supervision of 2/Lt ST MORLEY, M.H. On the reports	
			of the Brigade Boxing Matches were held inter Company and inter platoon arrangement. On the 25th Divisional Theatre by the Corps and it is hoped a pleasing (there was printed and held during the morning and afternoon and to give them of 2/Lt J.F. RIDDLE This was attended by those whose names for each Company	
LATIGNICOURT TRENCHES	26		On the morning of the 26th the Battalion relieved the 2nd 3 Lowland Regt in the Line, in the right subsector of the LATIGNICOURT sect. The relief had effected by 8 p.m. L/C LAMB REST was reported was taken ill to the 8th L/C LAMB REST	
	27-31		was sent that a casualty. No Enemy's activity until the end of the month. No enemy attempt The Battalion remained in line until the end of the month. The enemy artillery was quite particularly up to the 27th When the enemy's undoubted known to enforce. activity, when he was to know and shown Men were Carry Trench Mortars assault activity in the front of fire area, and all night shelling in vicinity of TRAPAUHE and TARGIVE rail trunks There were very little hostile shelling	

WAR DIARY or INTELLIGENCE SUMMARY

Army Form C. 2118.

Place	Date	Hour	Summary of Events and Information	Remarks and references to Appendices
Reserve in MONCHIET SECTOR	27-3-?		7 The Battalion's work had been [chiefly] upon the MONCHIET WIRE ENTRENCHMENT and the FURNESS [set?] of Posts and are not high upon to the Battalion front held so as no direction encountered any of the enemy. Throughout the tour work was largely confined to the clearing of trenches and the making of them in many places in fact the dry weather enabled me to prepare and in his way preventions were taken to prevent the sides of the trenches slipping in again as had happened during the wet weather in the middle of the month. No Co. (less one of the 1st of 2nd STAFF POST) was attached to the Battalion for working and worked further. This Company provided parties for work upon the Coffered in Course of [erection] to the W.E. of the two front line Companies and in addition was responsible for the clearing of EDINBURGH AVE. and this term of the trench was now put out in front of the new outposts of the Left front line Company towards all available labour was devoted to trench maintenance.	

Army Form C. 2118.

WAR DIARY
or
INTELLIGENCE SUMMARY
(Erase heading not required.)

Instructions regarding War Diaries and Intelligence Summaries are contained in F.S. Regs., Part II. and the Staff Manual respectively. Title Pages will be prepared in manuscript.

Place	Date	Hour	Summary of Events and Information	Remarks and references to Appendices
	31/1/18		During the month reinforcements joined the Battalion on dates as follows:— 1st. 2 officers. 2/th. T.W. GUNNING and L.C.K. WYATT and 2 men. 17th. 21 other ranks. 19th. 15 men for work parties to replace R.A.M.C personnel 20th 2 men 29th 4 signallers. The fighting strength of the Battalion at the end of the month was 23 officers and 630 other ranks. One one change in the Command of the Battalion as follows:— On 24th Lt Col OGILVIE D.S.O. took over Command of the Brigade owing to absence of Brig Gen EPSTEIN on leave. From 24th until 25th Capt HAYWARD M.C. commanded the Battalion. From 26th inclus. until the end of the month Major G.D. BROWN M.C. Commanded. Signing to Battalion on 25th and for H.S. STAFF DUTY. [signatures] Major C for Lt Col. The Wiltshire Regiment	

Army Form C. 2118.

1 Wilts Regt Vol 4 ?

WAR DIARY
or
INTELLIGENCE SUMMARY

(Erase heading not required.)

Place	Date	Hour	Summary of Events and Information	Remarks and references to Appendices
ENGLECOURT DE TORY	FEB 1/17 1918		The Battalion was relieved by a Company 8th Bn of N. Staffordshire Regt and marched and took over Reserve at FEUY-BANCOURT. Relief was reported complete at 11.15pm. Carriers and rations parties for front line troops found by the Battn which was a close Bn. Working parties on defences throughout the day. 16 OR's to Bart RC who were holding Nests morning & evening party to the front line at B.9./d.9.	
AMX	2nd		The Battalion remained in Reserve Billets at FEUY. Reveille at 10.30am. The day only spent in cleaning up the previous position. The unit to be brought into condition & fit for a Sudden advance and movement on the PAPIX - LAGNICOURT RD. Lectures and night operations to be thought of to the other units in ½ A.M. Arrangements for working to its relief. Each Coy of the Bn to work on Bodily front line Bn in B. Com. B.9 ON-NINE POST. This morning I visited the front lines & was much pleased with [...] work. 27 & 28 Bn's improving their posts and their Lewis and Rifle to defend to other lines on [...] Battles Brigade. No other has led to relieve the deficit in Brigade Reports a movement of the Bn. to relieve the deficit as another of the R.A. Kitchen while supported by [...] & Hilton and Squad on to LAGNICOURT & moved from the Bn.	

2449 Wt. W14957/M90 750,000 1/16 J.B.C. & A. Forms/C.2118/12

Army Form C. 2118.

WAR DIARY
or
INTELLIGENCE SUMMARY
(Erase heading not required.)

Place	Date	Hour	Summary of Events and Information	Remarks and references to Appendices
LONGUEVAL SECTOR Pt. Neuf Wood Farm and ARONVILLE Trench Reld. (4 coys)	FEBY.		Army front held by the 8th Division being 3 under the command of A.C. 12th CHESHIRE REGT. (Left front held by the bn.) the 7th cheshire Regt. (Right front was (left front line battalion) the right and working parties therefrom to (Centre) was IN SKIPTON RESERVE (0.24.d), under the commands of O.C. 4th S. STAFFORDS. REGT. (Right front line battalion) Bn. Headquarters were situated at 0.23.d.70.95. While in Brigade dugout the Bn. has been called upon to furnish parties daily using the travelling (infantry) tramline a fatigue at C.1.3.a. 45.45. & a mining party from the R.A.M.C. of 50 N.C.O.'s and men to look after & hand over 80 to hand over-land parties for clearing and covering in trenches and running tramway Parts on the night 7/8 chiefly for clearing and communication trenches and running tramway Parts on the night 9/10 20. full. and on the night 8/9 M/SGT FOXON 20, 12 men, 30, & 45 of the 73 men on the night 4/10, BOLTON AVENUE, RIPON ALLEY and KNIGHTLEY and the front line on C. 12 a/c 9a. During the daily working of Bn. inhabiting and being worked AS hands and suffered Casualties of 14 O.R. 10th CHESHIRE REGT, and 1 officer & 3 OR. 1st 12th CHESHIRE 5 R. 190. A draft of the 10th CHESHIRE REGT and 1 officer & 3 OR. 1st 12th CHESHIRE 5 R. has be actually been several hundred men strong was sent up in full on the 7th and 8th this draft was handed over to C. B. OC. on arrival to the 8.th CHESHIRE REGT. No were in DONZELUR and BOLTON AVENUE. These parties were employed for pulling and a cleaning & rebuild. and tryng to keep sundry to build trenches.	

WAR DIARY
or
INTELLIGENCE SUMMARY

(Erase heading not required.)

Army Form C. 2118.

Place	Date	Hour	Summary of Events and Information	Remarks and references to Appendices
TRY REUSE	9		Rate at BAPAUME was altered from the Battalion Headqrs the morning and the men were on parade till 9.30am ran to Boleong 4. H.M. R. RUPERT had of LORDS MANSON (?) which is placed at Map 67.P24.9.8 observation was proceeded to be placed on a few men had four of say R Flarers amount we manoevered Bill Sgt Cpl D Gallo (?) Lt Sgt Q Ward H H 1 St (Q C F Terry) H.H. Staff attended to the Battalion and said I said(?) for the country district of Westthorpe question in the 1st Regt and August 1917 The Brigade was inspected by the R.A. Infantry Brigade on 1st Monday NS Conf was seen by Major S. ACHIET LE GRAND (9 g P field Room) - the Battalion His Majesty ad 1.3am Sq B in R Bn KINGS OWN SHROPSHIRE LIGHT INFANTRY (NC) In the Camp saw the HIET LE GRAND and wandered in Camp 2 mens and started to march with two of Hom POIRALL(?) SE	
ACHIET LE GRAND	11		Then 11.30am and 1pm. The Bn Companies with Lt Sgts Sp Pfc Mc	

WAR DIARY
or
INTELLIGENCE SUMMARY

Army Form C. 2118.

Place	Date	Hour	Summary of Events and Information	Remarks and references to Appendices
AUGUST LE GRAND	11.12		Had a great turn of having up a Sort of Sand to within 30 ft. of the works was continued on the following day & the whole Battalion relying on this in the morning fire 9 A.M. until Breakfast was improving trenches. On the night of Lewis gun class were formed and continued to be useful in the following. Lectures were issued to half offices to in the Infantry of the C.S.M.R. The was afforded but also to the higher officers in place of Col. H.M.R. Burnett. In the afternoon a half hour musketry handling was held. Sub- Company drill and platoon matters were practiced but were not found to be successful. The squad is the platoon lay in the vicinity of the Camp.	
	13th 14th		Parades for all companies were held in the morning from 9.15 a.m. until 11 o'clock for Squad Drill, Bayonet fighting, Handling of arms etc and for Physical training. Handshaking & arms etc and for Marching towards and aircraft issued work upon the construction of the hut was continued, and anti-aircraft issued gun positions were dug upon the hills north of the Camp. Twenty-eight positions were dug for the use of the 6th. CHESHIRE REGT. and the Battalion, and at	

Army Form C. 2118.

WAR DIARY or INTELLIGENCE SUMMARY

(Erase heading not required.)

Instructions regarding War Diaries and Intelligence Summaries are contained in F. S. Regs., Part II. and the Staff Manual respectively. Title Pages will be prepared in manuscript.

Place	Date	Hour	Summary of Events and Information	Remarks and references to Appendices
	15/4		Soon as the night became moonlight four from the Battalion were mounted and the remainder remained on 1 at three battalion until the Moon set. Two working parties were requisitioned from the Battalion. A Power Platoon and the Signallers worked upon a new site for the Regimental transport lines. B Company provided a party of 50 other ranks for entrenching an assembly trench for the Brigade's use at G.3.5.2.3. Other Companies found parties for strengthening beyond Drills. Beyond fighting to unload wagons and then continued work upon the fortification of the huts.	
	16/4		The Power Platoon again worked upon the site for the transport lines. All Companies found upon the usual lines until 11am and then (excl. 30) paraded to complete the fortification of the huts. Instruction in the use of the Lyle Pattern band was given to two Companies by the Brigade Officer. Parades (except where useful in the morning) for C. of F. for Roman Catholics and NonConformists. There were no parades for training.	
	17/4		The Whole Battalion was given both at ACHIET LE PETIT and B??? HAM and 1/p.k all at the Rev Respirators by the Battalion were posted by the D???.	

WAR DIARY or INTELLIGENCE SUMMARY

Army Form C. 2118.

Place	Date	Hour	Summary of Events and Information	Remarks and references to Appendices
	19		Gas Officer; all men were passed through a gas Chamber. Two Classes were held in the morning, the Lewis Gun, and a N.C.O's Bayonet fighting class. Otherwise Tactics was in training. A and B Companies fired Grouping and Application Practices upon a 185 yards Rifle Range near ACHIET LE PETIT. (G7 2d 6.9). This firing was carried out in fighting kit. C and D Companies Practised Company attack in the valley S.E of LOGEAST WOOD. Rough G 3 a and 4. A Stretcher Bearers Class was formed under the Medical Officer for the purpose of supplying the 2nd Battalion 1 to 32 per Battalion. This was quite ready in one week. A Company provided 40 men for bombproofing the huts of the 108d. Fd Cy. R.E. Camp. There were trench parades to this Companies. The attack being again practised by C and D Companies in the valley S.E of LOGEAST WOOD. Major T.G. WYNNE. D.S.O. left Board in Command to the 11/4 attached O.R. L.N. LANCASHIRE REGT. was posted to this Battalion and in the morning of the 21st. assumed Command in place of Major G.D. BROWN. M.C.	
	20A			
	21st		The attack was practised upon the same ground as previously by A and B Companies.	

Place	Date	Hour	Summary of Events and Information	Remarks and references to Appendices
ACHIET LE GRAND	22		There was a route march for C Company in fighting kit, and the rifle range was allotted to D Company.	
	23		C and D Companies branched the attack. There was a route march for B Company and the rifle range was allotted to the Lewis gun section and H A Company. A Practise of Shoumls was found with Box Respirators on. In the afternoon in the semifinal of the interplatoon football Competition No 3 Platoon defeated No 2 Platoon. No 1 drew with No 14. There being no score on either side. The attack was practised by A and B Companies, the assault of the interplatoon foot[ball] Competition was continued and No 1 defeated No 14. This left Nos 1 and 3 Platoons left of A Company in the final. Parades were held for Morning funned and Roman Catholic, and a Voluntary C. of E. Service.	
	24		In the afternoon No 3 Platoon defeated No. 1 in the final of the Football Competition	
	25		Owing to the weather in training parades were possible between warm given in the huts.	

WAR DIARY
or
INTELLIGENCE SUMMARY

(Erase heading not required.)

Army Form C. 2118.

Instructions regarding War Diaries and Intelligence Summaries are contained in F.S. Regs., Part II and the Staff Manual respectively. Title Pages will be prepared in manuscript.

Place	Date	Hour	Summary of Events and Information	Remarks and references to Appendices
	26.8		D Company provided a party for work at Divl Headquarters in ACHIET LE PETIT for the remain- der of the day. Company there was a route march. The rifle range was allotted to C Com- pany and the Battalion's Pioneer Platoon. A and B Companies practised the attack in the valley east of LOGEAST WOOD. In the afternoon a Stokes mortar demonstration was held by the 7th T.M. Battery, attended by all Battalion of the Brigade.	
	27.8		Baths at ACHIET LE PETIT were allotted to the Battalion throughout the day. Returns H.Q. and 1 Coy. Battalion attack practice was held in the valley east of LOGEAST WOOD the capture of these objectives was practised and the establishment of an outpost line in advance of the last objective. The Divisional Roving Competition opened in the afternoon. Two Competitors from the Battalion were to fire in. Pte. WHATLEY, Stretcher Representative of the DSA. Field Coy. R.E. and L/C. MILLS for just a tyr. C and D Companies practised Company attacks and the relation of setting points.	
	28.8		A Company party upon the range from ACHIET LE PETIT and from B Company three was a route march in Hutting Kit to RIHOCOURT. In the afternoon in inter-Company football A Company defeated D Company by	

WAR DIARY
or
INTELLIGENCE SUMMARY.

Army Form C. 2118.

Place	Date	Hour	Summary of Events and Information	Remarks and references to Appendices
			6 O.R.s to hd: [illegible] R. and C Companies held pushed Off. Crosby rear.	
			During the month reinforcement joined the Battalion a takes as follows:-	
			2nd Lt. 1 Other rank	
			Q.M. Lt. C.F. JEFFERIES	
			1st. 42 Other ranks	
			22nd 1 Other rank	
			25th 3 Other ranks	
			Casualties were:-	
			1st. Wounded 2/Lt. E.R.C. PARSONS, M.C.	
			1st " Lt. ARNOLD, Q.A. Crajaut	
			Total strength of the Battalion at the Close of the month was 20 officers 854 other ranks.	

J Byrne
LT. COLONEL:
COMDG: 1st Bn. WILTSHIRE REGT.

ORDERLY ROOM
RECD
28 FEB. 1918
1st BATTN. WILTSHIRE REGT.

25th Division.
7th Infantry Brigade.

WAR DIARY

1st BATTALION

WILTSHIRE REGIMENT

MARCH 1918

1009

Army Form C. 2118.

WAR DIARY
or
INTELLIGENCE SUMMARY.
(Erase heading not required.)

1st Bn. Wiltshire Regt

Place	Date	Hour	Summary of Events and Information	Remarks and references to Appendices
ACHIET LE GRAND	1918 MARCH 1st		The Battalion remained at RITZ CAMP upon the LOGEAST WOOD – ACHIET LE GRAND Road at G.9 & G.8 (Sheet 57 c N.W. scale 1/20000) On March 1st two Companies in the morning practised attacks in the valley east of LOGEAST WOOD : one Company used the ranges at G.9.d. & G.9. for firing 9 pounders : the fourth Company marched in fighting kit to BIHUCOURT.	
"	2nd		In the afternoon in continuance of the inter Company football competition there was a match between B and C Companies. This resulted in a draw. Lt. Col. S.S. OGILVIE D.S.O. upon returning from leave, resumed command of the Battalion. The Battalion which was practised in the valley east of LOGEAST WOOD, three operations having been previously flagged out. Immediately after the attack as the weather was slightly cold Company inter munches were held. No football was played in the afternoon	
"	3rd		Church services were held in the morning for all denominations. The semi-finals and finals of the Divisional Boxing Competition were fought in the afternoon Pt. WATLEY of this Battalion defeated his opponent in the welter weights.	

WAR DIARY
or
INTELLIGENCE SUMMARY
(Erase heading not required.)

Army Form C. 2118.

Place	Date	Hour	Summary of Events and Information	Remarks and references to Appendices
	4th -10th		The Battalion remained at the Camp near ACHIET LE GRAND during the week 4th - 10th and training continued upon the usual lines each day. Rapid loading practice and steady drill were included in each morning's programme also the 4th two new Lewis guns were issued which were then allotted to Companies, two per Company bringing the MCOs and men who have been selected to Companies for their Gun. The MCOs and men who have been selected to Companies continued their instruction daily in the use of the Lewis gun. Class consisted of the specially trained Lewis Gunners of the Battalion. The morning too, of the rifle grenade section continued throughout the week to Nos. 23 and 24 Grenades being chiefly employed. The Companies trained at PELICAN - B Company field upon the range near ACHIET LE PETIT. There was a route march for C Company to BIHUCOURT. Two were for the first half of the morning of Musketry instruction, Physical Training and Respired fighting. During the latter part of the morning these two Companies marched to a field upon ground east of LOGEAST WOOD. Similar training was carried out the following day, with the exception of Snipers.	

2353 Wt. W2544/1454 700,000 5/15 D.D. & L. A.D.S.S./Forms/C. 2118.

Army Form C. 2118.

WAR DIARY or INTELLIGENCE SUMMARY.

(Erase heading not required.)

Place	Date	Hour	Summary of Events and Information	Remarks and references to Appendices
	6		On the F.A. Company fired upon the ACHIET LE PETIT range. There was a note issued for Company until 11.30 a.m. A and B Companies carried out rapid loading practice, bayonet fighting, and rifle grenade firing, and C and D Companies were by which practice the swinging practice. Main Turn out of the Battalion and the First line Transport was held.	
	7		The Non Gunners of the Companies were given firing practice at short range. In the latter part of the morning C and D Companies practiced the shoot for the field ammunition was used and wire rifle grenades were fired, live firing with the ground available in the valley south of LOGEAST WOOD. In the evening there was night-firing practice by Very lights for the Battalion at the IV. Corps range off the ACHIET LE PETIT — MIRAUMONT road. In the afternoon in the front of the inter-Company football A Company defeated C Company by 2 goals to nil.	
	8		In the first part of the morning an hour's training was carried out with Box Respirators on. During the latter part of the morning a demonstration of Lewis Gun defence was held and all Companies practiced the attack.	

WAR DIARY
or
INTELLIGENCE SUMMARY.
(Erase heading not required.)

Army Form C. 2118.

Place	Date	Hour	Summary of Events and Information	Remarks and references to Appendices
	8th cont.		In the afternoon D Company played A Company, 1st CHESHIRE REGT. at football. Pte L was stopped. The preparation for Battalion Sports which were to be held on the 9th October had also been run off. Another practice was run off at the first Band Practice was held at 5 p.m. as the pioneer one had been unsatisfactory.	
	9th		The Lewis Gunners of the Battalion were taken to the II Corps Ranges on to MIRAUMONT - ACHIET LE PETIT ROAD and there carried out firing practice during the morning. The Companies marched upon the road and were seen to Camp. In the afternoon any recruit Battalion Sports were held. Parade Services for all Denominations were held in the morning.	
	10th 11th		Training was carried out each morning throughout the week 11th - 16th inclusive. Particular attention being paid to the musketry training of the Companies firing practices upon the range near ACHIET LE PETIT and upon the short ranges in the valley east of LOGEAST WOOD was carried out daily by two Companies, except on the 12th. - This day allotted to the Battalion for bathing at ACHIET LE PETIT. The Lewis Gun Team, mornings were devoted to Platoon and Company attack exercises: all ranks, in particular were trained to act upon surprise orders, and officers were an occasion.	

WAR DIARY or INTELLIGENCE SUMMARY

Army Form C. 2118.

Place	Date	Hour	Summary of Events and Information	Remarks and references to Appendices
	7th		Modernisation, in order to develop the initiative of the N.C.O.s. & Lewis Gunners of the Battalion were during the week taken in syllabus by the Lewis Gun Officer men elected to form the Lewis Gun carrying parties of the Companies were daily given practice in the use of its Lewis line. The systematic training of the Signallers and Snipers was proceeded with throughout the week. Recreational training, football and boxing, occupied the afternoon. On Thursday 14th the Battalion played the 15th CHESHIRE REGT. at "Soccer" football and drew. Parade services were held in the morning and during the course of the day all ranks & officers of the Battalion were inspected by the Brigade Gas Officer. The afternoon all officers reconnoitred the scene of the Brigade attack practice which was to take place the following day.	
	18th		A Brigade Attack Practice was carried out during the morning from an imaginary assembly line just East of LOGEAST WOOD against the objective, the final objective being the railway two hundred yards from ACHIET LE GRAND & COURCELLES. The Brigade started upon a three Battalion front all four Companies of each Battalion were in the front line upon a Platoon frontage, and has been	

2353 Wt. W2544/1454 700,000 5/15 D.D.&L. A.D.S.S./Forms/C. 2118.

WAR DIARY
or
INTELLIGENCE SUMMARY.

Place	Date	Hour	Summary of Events and Information	Remarks and references to Appendices
	19th		Promptly organized into three platoons. The leading platoon capturing the first objective. The 2nd platoon taking the second objective. The enemy having through the first and taking the second objective. The creeping barrage moved at the rate of 100 yards in 3 minutes but rested for a longer time on each objective. After the capture of the final objective posts were pushed out in front, but of that without during this & the following day training was carried out on the usual lines.	
	21st		On the morning of this day at 4.40 a.m the German offensive commenced & at 5.a.m the enemy commenced shelling the station & mainly of ACHIET-LE-GRAND with high velocity shells (large calibre one of which hitted in the camp wounding three officers (Lt Holmes, Lt King + Lt Riddle) and caused casualties to 4 warrant officers, 6 Sergeants + 7 other ranks. At 11.30 a.m the Battalion moved to the area N.W of FREMICOURT and the same evening proceeded to the Army line occupying the central position in the Brigade on a line running from the E of BEUGNATRE and FREMICOURT	SSO

Army Form C. 2118.

WAR DIARY
or
INTELLIGENCE SUMMARY.
(Erase heading not required.)

Place	Date	Hour	Summary of Events and Information	Remarks and references to Appendices
	22nd		Weather fine but cold at night. The enemy made strong attacks upon the Corps line (VAUX – MORCHIES line) in front of the Brigade sector & by the evening had carried the line by assault. The Battalion spent the day in consolidating the position & getting up stores, rations, S.A.A. etc. The Battalion each gave fort hires & the utmost value in this connection. There was some shelling of the Battalion front and a few casualties were caused. The evening of the 22nd – 23rd was quiet.	
	23rd		In the morning the enemy after a heavy bombardment for about 3 hours twice attacked the Battalion front but was in each case repulsed sustaining very heavy casualties. In the attacks the Battalion Lewis gunners did great execution amongst many lakes of the enemy. The Battalion suffered considerable casualties from shell fire including Capt Thirkes D.S.O. R.A.M.C. Capt Hayward M.O. & Lt Rainy. The night of the 23rd–24th was somewhat lively owing to the enemy continuously trying to creep up & cut the wire.	

E.S.O.

Place	Date	Hour	Summary of Events and Information	Remarks and references to Appendices
	24		In the morning the enemy shelled the whole of the Battalion trench system, fire seems directed by hostile aeroplanes, the absence of our planes was noticeable. Our guns retaliated but unfortunately there was a considerable amount of short shooting causing several casualties. In the afternoon there was an intense bombardment by the enemy and about 4.1. The enemy assaulted. fighting was in progress but the attack had for all practical purposes failed on the Battalion front, when the C.O. received a verbal message on the telephone to retire at once. This was passed on to the Companies but at the same time the two Battalions on the right flank broke & came back leaving the Companies in the front system in the air. They attempted to come back as ordered but were practically exterminated by machine gun fire that right the Battalion reassembled at ACHIET-LE-PETIT numbering about 3 officers and 5th other ranks. The casualties suffered in the fighting of that date amounted to 413.	

WAR DIARY or INTELLIGENCE SUMMARY

Army Form C. 2118.

(Erase heading not required.)

Place	Date	Hour	Summary of Events and Information	Remarks and references to Appendices
	25th		In the morning the Bn. was ordered with its reg't. Sec Brigade to dig in and occupy a line North and West of Ackister-Grand. In the afternoon the enemy shelled the position somewhat severely but caused no casualties. In the evening 4th Brigade on our flank withdrew but no orders were received from 7th Inf Bde. Lt. Col. T.G. Gilchrist CO. who was in command of our Brigade such other Brigade officers as he could distribute to establish liaison. The 4th Brigade stopped straight Manchay - arriving - commenced to entrench on G. and.	
	26th		The Bn. was ordered to take up a line of positions in Government Wood to meet a threatened attack from the East, the attack did not develop and Stat.- morning the Bn. received instructions to return to billets which were reached about mid-night. The Brigade was relieved at the front by the — Covering detachment.	
	27.		About midday the Bn. was ordered forward to Puchrillers where the night was passed in Government Wood billets, accompanied by Engineers.	

[signature]

WAR DIARY
or
INTELLIGENCE SUMMARY.
(Erase heading not required.)

Army Form C. 2118.

Place	Date	Hour	Summary of Events and Information	Remarks and references to Appendices
	27 & 28		Capt. H. Webber took over the duties of Adjutant. At 9.a.m. on this day the Brigade marched to the CANAPLES area the Batt. being billeted at MONTRELET and staying there that night and the following day & night where the time was spent in reorganising the Battalion. The Battalion was divided into 4 No 1. No 2. Company of 2 platoons each called "A", "B", "C", "D". Platoons under the command of Lt Thomas & Capt Want respectively.	
	30		On this day the Battalion marched to DOULLENS + entrained there at 10.p.m.	
	31st		The Battalion arrived at GODAEWERSVELDE and detrained there at 11.a.m. afterwards proceeding in motor lorries to NEUVE EGLISE where they spent the night, the weather still remained fine.	

S.S. Jerring
Capt
1st Bn. 34 Wilshire Regt

25th Division.

7th Infantry Brigade.

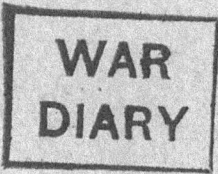

1st BATTALION

THE WILTSHIRE REGIMENT.

APRIL 1 9 1 8.

983

Army Form C. 2118.

WAR DIARY
or
INTELLIGENCE SUMMARY.
(Erase heading not required.)

1st Bn. Wiltshire Regt.

Place	Date	Hour	Summary of Events and Information	Remarks and references to Appendices
NEUVE EGLISE	1st April		On this day the Battalion marched from NEUVE EGLISE and relieved 2nd Australian Division in the DOUVE Sector N.E. of PLOEGSTEERT WOOD. The relief was carried out expeditiously & no casualties incurred.	H.C.C.
Trenches DOUVE SECTOR, N.E. PLOEGSTEERT WOOD.	2nd		Fairly quiet day with a certain amount of shelling of the DOUVE. Situation to the Battn. "B" & "C" Companies hold bomb-left & right sectors of front line. "A" Coy in close support on a line of strong points. "D" Coy in reserve with Battn. H.Q.	H.C.C.
do.	3rd		On this day the enemy were active with trench mortars on the front line system and the support line & Battn H.Q. were equally so. Considerable damage was done to the parapet & trenches [illegible] [illegible] the Town valley and a work was ordinarily & [illegible] for health.	H.C.C.
			Casualties O.R. 1 killed 3 wounded 1 missing.	
do.	4		This day was still quiet & in the evening the Battn mustered to be relieved & [illegible] [illegible] CATACOMBS at HYDE PARK CORNER were reached at 1 [illegible]	H.C.C.

Army Form C. 2118.

WAR DIARY
or
INTELLIGENCE SUMMARY.
(Erase heading not required.)

Place	Date	Hour	Summary of Events and Information	Remarks and references to Appendices
	APRIL 4 (cont)		The relief was without incident except to the fact that the Batt. was finally relieved until 4 a.m. owing to an enormously dark night.	App.a
CATACOMBS	5.		Casualties, O.R. 5 wounded.	
W. & PLOEGSTEERT WOOD			The day passed quietly - the men had an opportunity of having rest. Several [illegible] horses was made on the strong points along the [illegible]. Lieut. H.B. BURKETT returning from his [illegible] for one of the [illegible] [illegible].	App.c
			Capt. H. WEBBER [illegible] to be transferred in our coy. [illegible] G.M. Jeffries was cancelled.	
			Casualties. O.R. 1 wounded.	
do.	6.		Enemy did not do much had bursts of a few machine guns were mostly various objects.	App.c
do.	7.		[illegible] down [illegible] company 7 Bn [illegible] company arrived [illegible] on at 7 pm & went forward [illegible] the [illegible] Bn [illegible] men and [illegible] scenes.	App.c

WAR DIARY
INTELLIGENCE SUMMARY

Place	Date	Hour	Summary of Events and Information	Remarks and references to Appendices
Trenches N of RIVER LYS	APRIL 8th		Yes day was comparatively quiet on our front but the [illegible] posts/trenches to the R of us were heavily shelled by the enemy and the attack on the right was driven back inflicting heavy casualties on the enemy. One of the enemy's aeroplanes was brought down in flames by A L/S Gun mounted on the right flank of the Bn. Anna + infantry 2 wounded. (SEE APPENDIX) PLOEGSTEERT SECTOR	W.C
do.	9th		Quiet day. The dispositions of the Battalion were as follows 'A' Coy in front line, 'D' Coy in close support, 'C' Coy in support at IRON GATE, 'B' Coy in reserve in PLOEGSTEERT WOOD. Casualties. O.R. 1 wounded.	W.G
do.	10.		After an extremely heavy bombardment the enemy attacked at 3.30 a.m. & 'A' penetrated the line on both flanks of the Battn with result that the Battalion was cut off. After resisting the hostile attacks for more than 1 hour, 'D' Coy. retired to ZAMBUK POST & the Battalion took up the line of ZAMBUK POST & ULTIMO CRATER which was held for the remainder of the day. Casualties Officers: Major F.G. Wynne. D.S.O. Lt. F. Naylor killed. Lt. G.S.S. Ogilvie D.S.O. 2nd Lt. S.J. Parker. M.C. D.C.M. Capt. F. Smith (Horning). O.R. 13 killed 90 wounded 75 missing.	W.C

Army Form C. 2118.

WAR DIARY
or
INTELLIGENCE SUMMARY
(Erase heading not required.)

Instructions regarding War Diaries and Intelligence Summaries are contained in F.S. Regs., Part II. and the Staff Manual respectively. Title pages will be prepared in manuscript.

Place	Date	Hour	Summary of Events and Information	Remarks and references to Appendices
	APRIL			
Trenches E. of PLOEGSTEERT WOOD.	11		Hostile artillery bombarded the Battalion's position during the whole day. Owing to the enemy enfilading the CATACOMBS & PLOEGSTEERT WOOD the battalion was forced to withdraw to vicinity of RAVELSBERG. Casualties O.R. 1 killed 5 wounded.	K.C.
Trenches around NEUVE EGLISE	12		The battalion took up a position around NEUVE EGLISE. Hostile artillery very active all day. After dark the Battalion marched to BAILLEUL to support the troops fighting to the East of that town but the Battalion was dispatched to hold a position at CRUCIFIX CORNER between NEUVE EGLISE & the RAVELSBERG. Casualties. Officers Lt. R.M. Evans. U.S.A.R.A.M.C. missing O.R. 4 killed 16 wounded 282 Missing.	K.C.
Trenches at CRUCIFIX CORNER near NEUVE EGLISE	13		Owing to the enemy having approached his line very near to that of the Bn. a counter attack was decided upon in which the Battalion took part, driving the enemy back to his original position. Hostile artillery very active all day. Casualties. Officers Capt. R. Cecil, K.H.B. Burkett killed. Capt. G.K. Wait. M.C. wounded. O.R. 8 wounded	K.C.
do	14		Hostile artillery heavily bombarded our positions. No infantry action	K.C.

Army Form C. 2118.

WAR DIARY
or
~~INTELLIGENCE SUMMARY~~

(Erase heading not required.)

Instructions regarding War Diaries and Intelligence
Summaries are contained in F. S. Regs., Part II.
and the Staff Manual respectively. Title pages
will be prepared in manuscript.

Place	Date	Hour	Summary of Events and Information	Remarks and references to Appendices
Trenches at CRUCIFIX CORNER Near NEUVE ÉGLISE.	APRIL 15.		Hostile artillery again very active at dawn. During the morning the Battalion was relieved & marched back to LOCRE CHATEAU on the BAILLEUL ROAD.	M.C.

Army Form C. 2118.

WAR DIARY
or
INTELLIGENCE SUMMARY.
(Erase heading not required.)

Place	Date	Hour	Summary of Events and Information	Remarks and references to Appendices
	APRIL			
LOCRE CHATEAU.	16.		At midday Batt. moved to the vicinity of MONT NOIR when it was in reserve to the French. The same evening the Batt. moved to the Cafe Line near WOLFHOEK still in reserve	H.C.C
Trenches near WOLFHOEK.	17		This day was spent at WOLFHOEK the Batt. was very heavily shelled for during the whole afternoon but only one casualty was occasioned. Casualties. O.R. 1 killed 3 wounded 1 missing.	H.C.C
do.	18.		The Batt. moved from WOLFHOEK to the old Cafs School Camp near BOESCHEPE where it stayed until 3 p.m. At 3 p.m Batt moved to the left Reinforcement Camp near STEENACKER where it stayed the rest of the day & night	H.C.C
STEENACKER.	19.		This day spent at STEENACKER when no work was required of the Batt. Two Companies were formed consisting of five platoons each A B C & D platoons with the intention of moulding the Batt into the only	H.C.C

WAR DIARY
INTELLIGENCE SUMMARY

Army Form C. 2118.

Place	Date	Hour	Summary of Events and Information	Remarks and references to Appendices
STEENACKER19 (Cont'd).	APRIL		Officers who survived the severe ordeal were as follows: Lieut. Col. I/4th N.S.C. PRIESTLEY, LIEUT H B BROWN, M.C. & CAPT H WEBBER who acted as A.M. & T.O. together with three other officers. From the base a few days previously came there Lieut the Batt strength of the Batt. Knows the length from the 13th to this date the Standard was (approx) under the command MAJOR BLEW. It will & and works took about daylight in the area with the regiments of the Stratton without Suffering any loss either in horses or personal. It is also noteworthy that rations when S.A.A. & supplies of all kinds were more issued to reach the fighting line till dark shorters & suddenly in fact contribution to the little that is in one bade defence in the Batt front. Difficulties were increased by each shift wandering all over a great many shellfully [illegible] to be accounted for the dead & wounded effected & no stores fallen into the abandoned to the enemy	

Army Form C. 2118.

WAR DIARY
or
INTELLIGENCE SUMMARY.
(Erase heading not required.)

Instructions regarding War Diaries and Intelligence Summaries are contained in F. S. Regs., Part II. and the Staff Manual respectively. Title pages will be prepared in manuscript.

Place	Date	Hour	Summary of Events and Information	Remarks and references to Appendices
STEENACKER	20		The Batt. still remained at STEENACKER & the inhabitants continued by installments a draft of 150 O.R. which had arrived on the 15th	It. C
do.	21		At 7.a.m. another large Batt. move't. of 1000 O.R. (Out as A.B. 27) and the transfer med. of 400 OR. being given later in the day.	It. C
JOCK CAMP. N.4. POPERINGHE.	22		Batt. in rest at JOCK CAMP. MAJOR A.G. CADE D.S.O. 11Cy arrived to take over command of the Batt.	It. C
do.	23		Batt. in rest at JOCK CAMP. A party sent to help 330 men arrived on this day during the day. The Batt. strength is Officers 21 Other Ranks 7.0 O.R. will the 3 mis officers returning from U.K. on furlough gaining	It. C

2353 Wt. W2544/1454 700,000 5/15 D. D. & L. A.D.S.S./Forms/C. 2118.

WAR DIARY or INTELLIGENCE SUMMARY

Army Form C. 2118.

Place	Date	Hour	Summary of Events and Information	Remarks and references to Appendices
TOCK CAMP N. of POPERINGHE.	APRIL 24.		Batt. in rest at TOCK CAMP. Battalion again reorganised on the 4 Company basis. CAPT G PRIESTLEY assumed duties Adjutant. The following became Company Commanders. A Coy LIEUT H.G. BROWN. B Coy 2/LT P. RATHONE. C Coy 2/LT F.E. TURNBULL. D Coy 2/LT B. BURTON. CAPT H. WEBBER remained T.O. & relieving QM., QMS BALST returning RSM in succession to LT B PARKER who was killed and was buried at PLOEGSTEERT.	K.e.2
do.	25.		Batt in rest at TOCK CAMP. The Battalion marched off at 1.30 p.m. to a concentration point in vicinity of OUDERDOM. Orders were received that a counter attack was to be made by 25th Division in village of KEMMEL in conjunction with the French who were to attack MT. KEMMEL. The 7th. Brigade on right, 74th Brigade on left. 75th Bde in reserve. The 1th. S. Stafford Regt & 10th Cheshire Regt were in front line, 11st Wiltshire Regt in immediate support of 7th. Bde. Casualties other O.R. wounded	K.c.

WAR DIARY
INTELLIGENCE SUMMARY

Army Form C. 2118.

Place	Date	Hour	Summary of Events and Information	Remarks and references to Appendices
Vicinity of OUDERDOM	APRIL 26		At 12.30 a.m. the Battalion moved off & marched via RENINGHELST & LA CLYTTE. Forming up for the attack 200x S. of LA CLYTTE. At 3.30 a.m. the advance commenced, little opposition was given by the enemy who were completely surprised. At 3.30 a.m. 200 prisoners had been taken and 3.45 a.m. KEMMEL village was in our hands. During the French, on the right being unable to advance at 6.0 a.m. the 7th. Brigade with orders to its right made position S. of LA CLYTTE. The 74th. Brigade relieved the 7th. Brigade, after dusk the Battalion moving to trenches 1000x N. of LA CLYTTE, the relief being complete by 11.30 p.m. Quiet night. Casualties Officers. Major CADE. D.S.O. M.C. killed 2nd Lt. C. Buxton wounded 2nd Lt. G.E. Walker wounded. 2nd Lt. W.E. Pritchard missing. O.R. 5 killed 39 wounded 7 missing.	H.C.C
Trenches 1000x N. of LA CLYTTE	27		During the morning the 7th. Brigade was relieved by the 75th. Brigade, the Battalion being relieved by the 8th. Border Regt. The Battalion moved to shelter trenches S.E. of RENINGHELST. MAJOR. H.C. CANNON. H.C. "The Queen's" Regt. having been appointed 2nd in command took over command of the Battalion. Quiet night. Lt. Casualties O.R. 1 wounded	H.C.C

WAR DIARY
~~INTELLIGENCE SUMMARY~~
(Erase heading not required.)

Army Form C. 2118.

Place	Date	Hour	Summary of Events and Information	Remarks and references to Appendices
Trenches N.E. of RENINGHELST	APRIL 28.		Quiet day. Vicinity of the Battalion shelled during the evening. Routes to forward area reconnoitred with a view to supporting the forward Brigade. At 8.0 p.m. the Trench were attacked around SCHERPENBERG. The Battalion was bombarded with gas shell. Casualties.	early H.S. H.S.C.
do.	29.		Heavy bombardment commenced 3.0 a.m. The Battalion again shelled with gas. At 12 noon orders were received to the effect that the enemy had broken through on the right that the Brigade were to dig a defensive flank. W. of the RENINGHELST - LA CLYTTE road. Information was received that the French on the right were in their original line. The Battalion moved to a valley 1000 x forward to a trench line was reconnoitred & be dug at dusk. Touch was gained with the 146 & 156. French regiments. Orders were received to return to original positions which manoeuvre was complete by 8.0 p.m. The Battalion was placed under the command of the 39 French Division. Quiet night. Casualties.	H.S.C.

Army Form C. 2118.

WAR DIARY
INTELLIGENCE SUMMARY.
(Erase heading not required.)

Place	Date	Hour	Summary of Events and Information	Remarks and references to Appendices
Trenches S. of the B.E.	APRIL 30.		At 1:15 a.m. orders were received to concentrate the Batt⁵. S. of DE STEER CABT. to be ready to support an attack to be made by 15th French Regt. at 2:00 a.m. The Batt⁵. Appendix I moved off at 1:45 a.m. Int: orders were received cancelling the operation so that the Batt⁵. returned to its former position. Quiet day until battle gas shelling in the evening. Orders were again received to support the French at Mt. SCHERPENBERG. The Battalion was in position by 7.30 p.m. The Lt. Col. Commdg the 15/6 French Regt. gave orders for the Batt⁵. to be concentrated 1000ˣ N. of DE STEER CABT. to which position it had moved two reconnoitered in small shelter trenches by 8.05 p.m. the Zero hour of the French attack. At 12 m.n. orders were received from the French to move back to the former position N.E. of RENINGHELST, which move was complete by 11.05 p.m. The French attack was successful. Casualties Nil.	HEC

Mathews
Lt. Col.
Commdg 1st. Battⁿ. The Wiltshire Regt.

Ordre pour le B^{tg} de la 7e Brigade W

Le 30 Avril 1918 – 23^h

Le B^{tg} de la 7e Brigade W fera rejoindre sa
Division –

Le Lt Colonel Col^t le Rég^t le remercie du
Concours si bienveillant prêté au Rég^t

Le Lt Colonel Col^t le Rég^t

Louis

20e C.A
—
39e Division
—
146e Reg^t d'Inf^ie

WAR DIARY OR INTELLIGENCE SUMMARY

Army Form C. 2118.

Instructions regarding War Diaries and Intelligence Summaries are contained in F.S. Regs., Part II. and the Staff Manual respectively. Title pages will be prepared in manuscript.

(Erase heading not required.)

Place	Date	Hour	Summary of Events and Information	Remarks and references to Appendices
	MAY			
Trenches N.E. RENINGHELST	1		Quiet day with a certain amount of hostile shelling in vicinity of Battⁿ H.Q. After dusk the 7th. Brigade relieved the 75th Brigade in front line S. of LA CLYTTE. The 8th. Border Reg^t relieved the 1st. Wiltshire Reg^t, the relief being complete by 8.30pm. The Battⁿ then took up the positions in Brigade Reserve vacated by the 8th. Border Reg^t in a trench 1000" N. of LA CLYTTE, the Companies being accompd B.A.C.D from the right. Quiet night. Casualties. 1O.R. wounded	H.C.C
Brigade Reserve Trenches 1000" N. of LA CLYTTE	2		Hostile artillery active at dawn. Postions reconnoitred with a view to possible counter attack. Quiet day with enemy shelling again active at dusk. Casualties NIL	H.C.C
Do.	3		Enemy shelling active at dawn. Quiet day. Officers of 1st Batt. 15 Regiment 5 French Division arrived during the afternoon to reconnoitre the positions prior to relief. The Battⁿ was relieved by 3 Companies of the French, the relief being complete by 12.30 a.m. 4th. Hay. Casualties 1 O.R. wounded	H.C.C

WAR DIARY
INTELLIGENCE SUMMARY

(Erase heading not required.)

Army Form C. 2118.

Place	Date	Hour	Summary of Events and Information	Remarks and references to Appendices
	MAY			
Trenches E. of HOOGRAAF. CAPT.	4.		After relief the Batt⁴ marched to Shelter trenches E. of HOOGRAAF. CAPT. arriving there 2.30.a.m. At 8.30 a.m. the Batt⁴⁵, with the remainder of the 7th Brigade marched via ABEELE + bivouacked in a field N. of STEENVOORDE, arriving at 1.0 p.m. Lieut. Col. FURZE D.S.O. M.C. took over the command of the Batt⁴⁵. Remainder of the day spent in resting.	H.C.C
W. of RENINGHELST				
Bivouac. N. of STEENVOORDE	5.		The Brigade resumed its march (the Batt⁴ starting at 9.20a.m.), via STEEN-VOORDE, WORMHOUDT + ESQUELBECQ was billeted in farms N. of BISSEZEELE arriving at 4.0 p.m.	H.C.C
Billets N. of BISSEZEELE.	6.		Day spent in resting, cleaning up + bathing.	H.C.C
do.	7.		Training commenced	H.C.C
do.	8.		Training Continued. Advance party left for new area of 9th Corps 6th French Army.	H.C.C
do.	9.		The Battalion marched to REXPOEDE for entrainment + commenced its journey at 10.30 a.m travelling via ABBEVILLE + PONTOISE, finally detraining at 8 pm 10th inst. at SAVIGNY + then marched to	H.C.C

WAR DIARY

INTELLIGENCE SUMMARY

Army Form C. 2118.

Place	Date	Hour	Summary of Events and Information	Remarks and references to Appendices
	MAY.			
	9 (Cont'd)		ARCIS-LE-PONSART where it was accommodated in huts S. of the village.	Itc.c
ARCIS-LE- PONSART.	11.		Day spent in cleaning up, training commenced. G.O.C. 25. Division inspected & addressed the Brigade during the afternoon.	Itc.c
do.	13 to 22		Training Continued	Itc.C
do.	23		The Battalion moved at 7.0.p.m. marched via SAVIGNY & TONCHERY to PROUILLY, arriving at 12 m.n., where it was accommodated in huts W. of the village	Itc.C
PROUILLY	24		Training Continued	Itc.C
	25		Training Continued	LRq
	26		Church Parade - At 7.30 P.M. orders received to be ready to move by 8 P.M. 9.15 P.M. Battalion moves to position beyond BOUVANCOURT & in front of OUYENCOURT.	LRq
	27th		1 AM Enemy starts a heavy Gas Bombardment which lasts until 5 A.M. when	LRq

WAR DIARY or INTELLIGENCE SUMMARY

Army Form C. 2118.

Place	Date	Hour	Summary of Events and Information	Remarks and references to Appendices
	27/12		he commenced to attack the forward battalion line held by the 8th Division	
		7.30 AM	Orders received to move forward to cover retirement of front line troops &	₤ Reply
			Capt PRIESTLEY with 3 coys taken up position position forward –	
		10.45 AM	Battalion hqrs moved forward & took line in front of BUSSUS-BUSSEREL.	
		11.30 AM		
		11.30 AM	line held as follows: D – left coy, C, B, A. 1 Platoon of C Coy only under 2/Lt	
		3.30 PM	Paterson in front line remaining 3 Platoons at C Support D – Enemy shelling	
			constantly Bn H.Q. – to gun fire continually sweeping roads & tracks between –	
			& Front line – Supplies of S.A.A. etc were however maintained –	
		4.15 PM	Capts PRIESTLEY & ARNOTT went situation to C.O. at Bn H.Q. Capt PRIESTLEY	
			wounded still remains on duty	
		5.30 PM	Enemy attacked whole company in greatly superior forces the battalion was compelled	
			to retire & shifting up into small parties strongly withdrew fighting rearguard	
			actions. Lieut Furze R.S.O. we was killed – a time Capt Brooke R.A.M.C.	
			Capts Arnott & Priestley left behind to tend wounded & prisoners hereto	
			Serves H. Reid, B Duley were wounded & evacuated – also 2/Lt H Anderson	
			& 2/Lt A M Reid	

WAR DIARY or INTELLIGENCE SUMMARY

Army Form C. 2118.

(Erase heading not required.)

Place	Date	Hour	Summary of Events and Information	Remarks and references to Appendices
			The 7th Inf Bde came under orders of the 8th Division - Odd detachments were	
		26/15	re-organized & sent to the Gp Keep 15th line intact -	
			The detachment continued - the battalion still in detachments, now holding under	RDy
			Major Cameron h.q. - & Capt Parkers h.q. -	
			A line was brought maintained by BRANSCOURT - a high ground S.W. of 1st	
			village, the enemy holding Linge and considerable pinches in the left flank.	
			Huning FISMES	
		24/15	The enemy began attacks on the line showing increased & very high spirited M.G.	RDy
			ROSNAY - TRESLON - FAVEROL - LHERY - The XIXth Div came to support the Corps	
			Another detachment from "B" Teams under Capt Green were sent up & held a portion	
			E of FAVEROL to balance who Capt Parkers detachment fell back to —	
		30/15	The enemy again continued his advance to the S.W. but only completed as to	RDy
			active to SERCY.	
		30/15	The Transport crossed the MARNE & except a party under Capt Jones	RDy
			which went up to rejoin the 1st Division, the Wiltshires started to return	
			via —	
		3/15	The 149/15 B.W. Transport via Servan Courtisols near (EUVRIGNY, S of the Marne to BEAUNAY, & Montmort Capt Green	

1st. BN. WILTSHIRE REGT.

Army Form C. 2118.

WAR DIARY or INTELLIGENCE SUMMARY.

1st Loyal North Lancs Regt

(Erase heading not required.)

Place	Date	Hour	Summary of Events and Information	Remarks and references to Appendices
N.Bank of R.ARDRE E. of SARCY	JUNE 1.		The Battalion was divided into 2 forces, one commanded by Major H.C. CANNON M.C. & the other by Capt. J.G. PARKES M.C. The former remain in position in conjunction with 4th K.S.L.I. & 8th B⁄ⁿ 19th Division. Not rev. ARDRE E. of SARCY. A quiet day owing to locality on left flank, the line fell back 500" in the morning, the enemy taking no action. The latter force was fighting with the 9th Gloucester Regt W. of CHAMBRECY the enemy attacked strongly & the line was forced back into the village of CHAMBRECY. The rear H.Q. & transport remained at BEAUNAY	K.C.
do.	2.		Major Cannon's force experienced a very quiet day, the first with no incident since the battle commenced (May 27). Capt. Parkes' force was ordered to withdraw to valley E. of CHAMBRECY, which movement was carried out unhindered by the enemy.	W.C.
do.	3.		Major Cannon's force again had a very quiet day whilst Capt. Parkes' command took up a position on Eastern slopes of the BOIS D'ECLISSE. Quiet day. Major Cannon's force reported to H.Q. 7th Inf. Brigade at BUBLIN where he remained for the night was spent.	W.C.

Army Form C. 2118.

WAR DIARY
or
INTELLIGENCE SUMMARY.
(Erase heading not required.)

Instructions regarding War Diaries and Intelligence Summaries are contained in F. S. Regs., Part II. and the Staff Manual respectively. Title pages will be prepared in manuscript.

Place	Date	Hour	Summary of Events and Information	Remarks and references to Appendices
	JUNE			
BOIS D'ECLISSE	4.		Both Major Cannis & Capt Parkes forces joined the 1/25 Compsite Battalion in BOIS D'ECLISSE	KCG
E d CHAMUZY			As they formed the 4th Company were in reserve in BOIS DE COUTRON. Quiet day.	
do.	5.		Enemy quiet. NAPPES was shelled heavily during the morning	KCG
do.	6.		At dawn the enemy bombarded heavily with gas & H.E. shell, but all attempts upon the part of his infantry to attack were smothered by our artillery	KCG
			In the night the enemy captured MONT de BLIGNY & BLIGNY village but the situation was restored by counter attacks & the line was completely restored by dusk	
do.	7.		Quiet day. Enemy inactive	KCG
do.	8.		The 3/25 Composite Battalion arrived with 7 officers & 210 O.R. of the regiment & took over the line in BOIS D'ECLISSE was en reserve	KCG
	9.		Quiet day. After dark the 3/25 Batt'n relieved the 5th S.W.B. Regt in front line in BOIS D'ECLISSE, the 4th Co. being in centre of front line	KCG
	10.		Quiet day. Desultory hostile shelling	KCG
	11.		Quiet day. The Batt'n came back to support in BOIS de COUTRON after dark.	KCG

Army Form C. 2118.

WAR DIARY / INTELLIGENCE SUMMARY.
(Erase heading not required.)

Instructions regarding War Diaries and Intelligence Summaries are contained in F. S. Regs., Part II. and the Staff Manual respectively. Title pages will be prepared in manuscript.

Place	Date	Hour	Summary of Events and Information	Remarks and references to Appendices
	JUNE			
BOIS DE	12		Quiet day. Hostile Artillery inactive. After dusk the 2/25 Batt⁰ relieved the 2/25 Batt⁰ at CHANTEREINE FARM. The Wells. Coy being in immediate	K.C
COUTRON			support. Batt⁰ H.Q. at REUVES. Transport at BEAURY	
CHANTEREINE	13		Quiet day	K.C
FARM				
do.	14.		Enemy artillery more active.	K.C.
do.	15.		Enemy quiet. Hostile aeroplane brought down by rifle fire in No Mans Land	K.C
do.	16		Quiet day. Much was done to improve the defences, a great deal of wire being put out after dark	K.C
"	17		Quiet day. After dusk the Batt⁰ was relieved by 1st Bt⁰. 19th Regt of the BRESCIA Bde Italian Army, marched to GERMAND. The new H.Q. moved to PEÂS.	K.C
"	18		The Wells. Coy travelled by train to FÈRE-EN-CHAMPENOISE thence marched to PEÂS where it rejoined the Bn. H.Q. & transport	K.C
PEÂS	19.		Day spent in resting & cleaning up. Major J.V. Bridges D.S.O. Worcestershire Regt took over command of the Regt.	K.C
"	20.		The Battalion together with transport entrained at SÉZANNE at 6.0 p.m.	K.C

Army Form C. 2118.

WAR DIARY
~~INTELLIGENCE SUMMARY.~~
(Erase heading not required.)

Instructions regarding War Diaries and Intelligence Summaries are contained in F. S. Regs., Part II. and the Staff Manual respectively. Title pages will be prepared in manuscript.

Place	Date	Hour	Summary of Events and Information	Remarks and references to Appendices
	JUNE			
MILLE-BOSC	21		The Battalion detrained at LONGRY at about 2 a.m. in marched to MILLE-BOSC where it was accommodated in billets in the village by 5.0 a.m. The Battalion now became a unit of the 110th Brigade of the 21st Division. Commanded by Major General D. Campbell.	W.C.C.
do.	22		Day spent in cleaning up.	W.C.C
do	24		Training Commenced	W.C.C
do.	30.		The Division commenced to move to a new strong area, the majority of the transport left by road at 10.30 a.m.	

W.C. Cannon Major.

Commanding 1st. Wiltshire Regt.

www.ingramcontent.com/pod-product-compliance
Lightning Source LLC
Chambersburg PA
CBHW080830010526
44112CB00015B/2485